Java™ Web Services

Related titles from O'Reilly

Creating Effective JavaHelp™

Database Programming with JDBC and Java™

Developing JavaBeans™

Enterprise JavaBeans™

Java™ 2D Graphics

Java™ & XML

Java™ and XSLT

Java™ Cookbook

Java™ Cryptography

Java™ Distributed Computing

Java™ Enterprise in a Nutshell

Java™ Examples in a Nutshell

Java™ Foundation Classes in a Nutshell

Java™ I/O

Java™ in a Nutshell

Java™ Internationalization

Java™ Message Service

Java™ Network Programming

Java™ Performance Tuning

Java™ Programming with Oracle SQLJ

Java™ Security

JavaServer™ Pages

JavaServer™ Pages Pocket Reference

Java™ Servlet Programming

Java™ Swing

Java™ Threads™

Learning Java™

Java™ RMI

Learning Wireless Java™

J2ME™ in a Nutshell

Java™ and SOAP

Building Java™ Enterprise Applications Volume 1: Architecture

The Java™ Enterprise CD Bookshelf™

Java™ Web Services

David A. Chappell and Tyler Jewell

O'REILLY®

Beijing · Cambridge · Farnham · Köln · Paris · Sebastopol · Taipei · Tokyo

Java™ Web Services
by David A. Chappell and Tyler Jewell

Published by O'Reilly & Associates, Inc., 1005 Gravenstein Highway North, Sebastopol, CA 95472.

O'Reilly & Associates books may be purchased for educational, business, or sales promotional use. Online editions are also available for most titles (*safari.oreilly.com*). For more information contact our corporate/institutional sales department: (800) 998-9938 or *corporate@oreilly.com*.

Editor:	Mike Loukides
Production Editor:	Ann Schirmer
Cover Designer:	Emma Colby
Interior Designer:	Melanie Wang

Printing History:

March 2002:	First Edition.

ISBN: 0-596-00269-6
[M]

[6/03]

Table of Contents

Preface

When XML was first introduced, it was hailed as the cornerstone of a new kind of technology that would permit interoperable businesses. XML provided a generic way to represent structured and typed data. Even though it has taken several years, XML standards have started to evolve and multiply. As part of this evolution, XML has been incorporated into every facet of application and enterprise development. XML is now a part of operating systems, networking protocols, programming languages, databases, application servers, web servers, and so on. XML is used everywhere.

Starting in 1998, XML was incorporated into a number of networking protocols with the intention of providing a standard way for two pieces of software to communicate with each other. The Simple Object Access Protocol (SOAP) and XML-RPC specifications blew the doors wide open on the distributed-computing environment by providing a platform-independent way for software to communicate. Even more astounding, nearly every major software company supported SOAP. The instant success of SOAP created the potential for interoperability at a level that has never been seen before. SOAP became the cornerstone protocol of the web services revolution that is going on today.

After SOAP, the Web Services Description Language (WSDL) and Universal Discovery, Description, Integration (UDDI) specifications were introduced with an equal amount of industry support. Other specifications were rapidly introduced, including ebXML, OASIS technical communities, and a variety of SOAP extensions. Some specifications were met with acclaim and others with disappointment. Either way, the industry has unified around SOAP, WSDL, and UDDI. These core technologies are required to achieve true software interoperability for the future.

It was only a matter of time before developers wanted to use web services technology. Even though web services are language and platform independent, developers still have to develop programs in programming languages. With Java and J2EE being the primary environment for enterprise development, it wasn't long before technology used to integrate web services with the J2EE platform appeared. Java programs need to be able to create, locate, and consume web services.

Many specifications and technologies have been introduced to bridge the gap between Java and web services. This book provides an introduction to both web services and the Java technologies that have been introduced to support web services. It highlights major web services technologies and investigates the current happenings in the Java standardization community. As the web services revolution continues, it will be increasingly important for software developers to understand how web services work and when to use them. Reading this book may be one of the smartest career moves you will ever make.

Who Should Read This Book?

This book explains and demonstrates the fundamentals of web services and the Java technologies built around web services. It provides a straightforward, no-nonsense explanation of the underlying technology, Java classes and interfaces, programming models, and various implementations.

Although this book focuses on the fundamentals, it's no "for Dummy's" book. Readers are expected to have an understanding of Java and XML. Web service APIs are easy to learn, but can be tedious. Before reading this book, you should be fluent in the Java language and have some practical experience developing business solutions. If you are unfamiliar with the Java language, we recommend that you pick up a copy of *Learning Java* by Patrick Neimeyer and Jonathan Knudsen (formerly *Exploring Java*) (O'Reilly). If you need a stronger background in distributed computing, we recommend *Java Distributed Computing* by Jim Farley (O'Reilly). If you need additional information on XML, we recommend *Java and XML* by Brett McLaughlin (O'Reilly) and *XML in a Nutshell* by Elliotte Harold and W. Scott Means (O'Reilly). Other O'Reilly books covering web services include *Programing Web Services with SOAP* by Doug Tidwell, James Snell, and Pavel Kulchenko and *Programming Web Services with XML-RPC* by Simon St. Laurent, Joe Johnston, and Edd Dumbill.

Organization

Here's how the book is structured:

Chapter 1, *Welcome to Web Services*
> This chapter defines web services; provides an overview of SOAP, WSDL, and UDDI; and discusses the different business uses for web services.

Chapter 2, *Inside the Composite Computing Model*
> This chapter introduces the role of service-oriented architecture (SOA) and how application architecture can leverage programs developed using a SOA.

Chapter 3, *SOAP: The Cornerstone of Interoperability*
> This chapter introduces the SOAP protocol and shows how it is layered on top of HTTP. It discusses the SOAP envelope, header, and body, and how SOAP

with attachments works. This chapter introduces the Apache SOAP engine and the Apache SOAP client API that provides a Java interface for sending and receiving SOAP messages.

Chapter 4, *SOAP-RPC, SOAP-Faults, and Misunderstandings*
This chapter continues the SOAP discussion by describing how SOAP deals with method invocations, exception handling, and the mustUnderstand header attribute.

Chapter 5, *Web Services Description Language*
This chapter introduces WSDL and the steps involved in creating a web service description. It provides an overview of the different ways WSDL may be created within a Java program.

Chapter 6, *UDDI: Universal Description, Discovery, and Integration*
This chapter discusses the UDDI initiative and the makeup of a UDDI Business Registry. It introduces the inquiry and publishing API for UDDI and demonstrates how to access a UDDI registry using the Apache SOAP client library, a custom library provided by a vendor, and JAXR. This chapter also discusses higher-level abstraction Java APIs for seamless access to a registry.

Chapter 7, *JAX-RPC and JAXM*
This chapter introduces two relatively new client programming models that are evolving as part of the Java Community Process (JCP). The coding examples from the previous SOAP chapters are examined using these new APIs.

Chapter 8, *J2EE and Web Services*
This chapter discusses how an application server might support web services. It discusses where SOAP, WSDL, and UDDI fit into the J2EE picture. It also introduces the Java Community Process standardization efforts currently underway to get web services integrated tightly with J2EE.

Chapter 9, *Web Services Interoperability*
This chapter combines firsthand experience with collective research gathered from message boards, articles, and various interoperability web sites. It explores low-level issues regarding such things as datatype mapping and header processing, as well as higher-level framework issues such as interoperability with ebXML and MS Biztalk. To provide concrete examples of interoperability problems and solutions, this chapter discusses the SOAPBuilder's Interoperability Labs' effort.

Chapter 10, *Web Services Security*
This chapter discusses how issues such as digital signatures, key management, and encryption present new challenges as a result of using XML and SOAP-based interoperable communications. Current specifications and implementations such as XML-Encryption, XML-Signatures, SOAP-Security, and XKMS are examined.

Software and Versions

This book covers many different technologies and uses a number of different examples provided by different vendors. It uses technology available from Apache, IBM, BEA, Sonic Software, Systinet, Phaos, and Sun. In the examples that come with this book, there is a comprehensive set of README documents that outline where the different pieces of software can be downloaded. The README documents also detail the installation and configuration instructions relevant to you.

Examples developed in this book are available from *www.oreilly.com/catalog/javawebserv*. The examples are organized by chapter.

Given the speed at which this field is developing, one of the best strategies you can take is to look at vendors' examples. In the examples archive for this book, we've decided to include separate directions with a number of examples from Sonic and BEA's products. We will add other vendors as we get permission. If you are a vendor and would like to see your examples included in the archive, please contact us.

Conventions

Italic is used for:

- Filenames and pathnames
- Hostnames, domain names, URLs, and email addresses
- New terms where they are defined

`Constant width` is used for:

- Code examples and fragments
- Class, variable, and method names, and Java keywords used within the text
- SQL commands, table names, and column names
- XML elements and tags

`Constant-width bold` is used for emphasis in some code examples.

The term *JMS provider* is used to refer to a vendor that implements the JMS API to provide connectivity to their enterprise messaging service. The term *JMS client* refers to Java components or applications that use the JMS API and a JMS provider to send and receive messages. *JMS application* refers to any combination of JMS clients that work together to provide a software solution.

Comments and Questions

Please address comments and questions concerning this book to the publisher:

O'Reilly & Associates, Inc.
1005 Gravenstein Highway North
Sebastopol, CA 95472
(800) 998-9938 (in the United States or Canada)
(707) 829-0515 (international or local)
(707) 829-0104 (fax)

There is a web page for this book, which lists errata, examples, or any additional information. You can access this page att:

http://www.oreilly.com/catalog/javawebserv

To comment or ask technical questions about this book, send email to:

bookquestions@oreilly.com

For more information about books, conferences, Resource Centers, and the O'Reilly Network, see the O'Reilly web site at:

http://www.oreilly.com/

Acknowledgments

While only two names are on the cover of this book, the credit for its development and delivery is shared by many individuals. Michael Loukides, our editor, was pivotal to the success of this book. Without his experience, craft, and guidance, this book would not have been possible.

Many expert technical reviewers helped ensure that the material was technically accurate and true to the spirit of the Java Message Service. Of special note are Anne Thomas Manes, Scott Hinkelman, J.P. Morganthal, Rajiv Mordani, and Perry Yin.

David Chappell would like to express sincere gratitude to Sonic Software colleagues Jaime Meritt, Colleen Evans, and Rick Kuzyk for their research, contributions, and feedback throughout the book-writing process—as well as other Sonic coworkers who provided valuable help along the way: Tim Bemis, Giovanni Boschi, Andrew Bramley, Ray Chun, Bill Cullen, David Grigglestone, Mitchell Horowitz, Sonali Kanaujia, Oriana Merlo, Andy Neumann, Mike Theroux, Bill Wood, and Perry Yin.

A special thanks goes to George St. Maurice for organizing the download *zip* file and the *readme* files.

Finally, the most sincere gratitude must be extended to our families. Tyler Jewell thanks his friend and lover, Hillary, for putting up with the aggressive writing timeline, dealing with his writing over the Christmas break, and not getting upset when he had to cancel their sunny vacation to finish the manuscript. David Chappell thanks his wife, Wendy, and their children Dave, Amy, and Chris, for putting up with him during this endeavor.

CHAPTER 1

Welcome to Web Services

The promise of web services is to enable a distributed environment in which any number of applications, or application components, can interoperate seamlessly among and between organizations in a platform-neutral, language-neutral fashion. This interoperation brings heterogeneity to the world of distributed computing once and for all.

This book defines the fundamentals of a web service. It explores the core technologies that enable web services to interoperate with one another. In addition, it describes the distributed computing model that the core web service technologies enable and how it fits into the bigger picture of integration and deployment within the J2EE platform. It also discusses interoperability between the J2EE platform and other platforms such as .NET.

What Are Web Services?

A web service is a piece of business logic, located somewhere on the Internet, that is accessible through standard-based Internet protocols such as HTTP or SMTP. Using a web service could be as simple as logging into a site or as complex as facilitating a multi-organization business negotiation.

Given this definition, several technologies used in recent years could have been classified as web service technology, but were not. These technologies include win32 technologies, J2EE, CORBA, and CGI scripting. The major difference between these technologies and the new breed of technology that are labeled as web services is their standardization. This new breed of technology is based on standardized XML (as opposed to a proprietary binary standard) and supported globally by most major technology firms. XML provides a language-neutral way for representing data, and the global corporate support ensures that every major new software technology will have a web services strategy within the next couple years. When combined, the software integration and interoperability possibilities for software programs leveraging the web services model are staggering.

A web service has special behavioral characteristics:

XML-based

By using XML as the data representation layer for all web services protocols and technologies that are created, these technologies can be interoperable at their core level. As a data transport, XML eliminates any networking, operating system, or platform binding that a protocol has.

Loosely coupled

A consumer of a web service is not tied to that web service directly; the web service interface can change over time without compromising the client's ability to interact with the service. A tightly coupled system implies that the client and server logic are closely tied to one another, implying that if one interface changes, the other must also be updated. Adopting a loosely coupled architecture tends to make software systems more manageable and allows simpler integration between different systems.

Coarse-grained

Object-oriented technologies such as Java expose their services through individual methods. An individual method is too fine an operation to provide any useful capability at a corporate level. Building a Java program from scratch requires the creation of several fine-grained methods that are then composed into a coarse-grained service that is consumed by either a client or another service. Businesses and the interfaces that they expose should be coarse-grained. Web services technology provides a natural way of defining coarse-grained services that access the right amount of business logic.

Ability to be synchronous or asynchronous

Synchronicity refers to the binding of the client to the execution of the service. In synchronous invocations, the client blocks and waits for the service to complete its operation before continuing. Asynchronous operations allow a client to invoke a service and then execute other functions. Asynchronous clients retrieve their result at a later point in time, while synchronous clients receive their result when the service has completed. Asynchronous capability is a key factor in enabling loosely coupled systems.

Supports Remote Procedure Calls (RPCs)

Web services allow clients to invoke procedures, functions, and methods on remote objects using an XML-based protocol. Remote procedures expose input and output parameters that a web service must support. Component development through Enterprise JavaBeans (EJBs) and .NET Components has increasingly become a part of architectures and enterprise deployments over the past couple of years. Both technologies are distributed and accessible through a variety of RPC mechanisms. A web service supports RPC by providing services of its own, equivalent to those of a traditional component, or by translating incoming invocations into an invocation of an EJB or a .NET component.

Supports document exchange

One of the key advantages of XML is its generic way of representing not only data, but also complex documents. These documents can be simple, such as when representing a current address, or they can be complex, representing an entire book or RFQ. Web services support the transparent exchange of documents to facilitate business integration.

The Major Web Services Technologies

Several technologies have been introduced under the web service rubric and many more will be introduced in coming years. In fact, the web service paradigm has grown so quickly that several competing technologies are attempting to provide the same capability. However, the web service vision of seamless worldwide business integration is not be feasible unless the core technologies are supported by every major software company in the world.

Over the past two years, three primary technologies have emerged as worldwide standards that make up the core of today's web services technology. These technologies are:

Simple Object Access Protocol (SOAP)

SOAP provides a standard packaging structure for transporting XML documents over a variety of standard Internet technologies, including SMTP, HTTP, and FTP. It also defines encoding and binding standards for encoding non-XML RPC invocations in XML for transport. SOAP provides a simple structure for doing RPC: document exchange. By having a standard transport mechanism, heterogeneous clients and servers can suddenly become interoperable. .NET clients can invoke EJBs exposed through SOAP, and Java clients can invoke .NET Components exposed through SOAP.

Web Service Description Language (WSDL)

WSDL is an XML technology that describes the interface of a web service in a standardized way. WSDL standardizes how a web service represents the input and output parameters of an invocation externally, the function's structure, the nature of the invocation (in only, in/out, etc.), and the service's protocol binding. WSDL allows disparate clients to automatically understand how to interact with a web service.

Universal Description, Discovery, and Integration (UDDI)

UDDI provides a worldwide registry of web services for advertisement, discovery, and integration purposes. Business analysts and technologists use UDDI to discover available web services by searching for names, identifiers, categories, or the specifications implemented by the web service. UDDI provides a structure for representing businesses, business relationships, web services, specification metadata, and web service access points.

Individually, any one of these technologies is only evolutionary. Each provides a standard for the next step in the advancement of web services, their description, or their discovery. However, one of the big promises of web services is seamless, automatic business integration: a piece of software will discover, access, integrate, and invoke new services from unknown companies dynamically without the need for human intervention. Dynamic integration of this nature requires the combined involvement of SOAP, WSDL, and UDDI to provide a dynamic, standard infrastructure for enabling the dynamic business of tomorrow. Combined, these technologies are revolutionary because they are the first standard technologies to offer the promise of a dynamic business. In the past, technologies provided features equivalent to SOAP, WSDL, and UDDI in other languages, but they weren't supported by every major corporation and did not have a core language as flexible as XML.

Figure 1-1 provides a diagram that demonstrates the relationship between these three technologies.

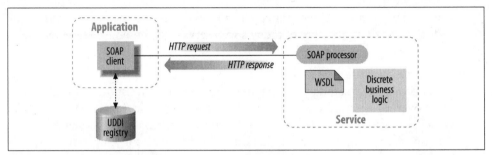

Figure 1-1. Simple web service interaction

The relationship between these pieces (SOAP, WSDL, and UDDI) can be described as follows: an application acting in the role of a web services client needs to locate another application or a piece of business logic located somewhere on the network. The client queries a UDDI registry for the service either by name, category, identifier, or specification supported. Once located, the client obtains information about the location of a WSDL document from the UDDI registry. The WSDL document contains information about how to contact the web service and the format of request messages in XML schema. The client creates a SOAP message in accordance with the XML schema found in the WSDL and sends a request to the host (where the service is).

Service-Oriented Architecture in a Web Services Ecosystem

The web services model lends itself well to a highly distributed, service-oriented architecture (SOA). A web service may communicate with a handful of standalone processes and functions or participate in a complicated, orchestrated business process. A web service can be published, located, and invoked within the enterprise, or anywhere on the Web.

As illustrated in Figure 1-2, a service might be simple and discrete, such as an international currency conversion service. It may also be a whole suite of applications representing an entire business function, such as an auto insurance claims processor. At the mass-consumer market, web services may provide something like a restaurant finder application for a handheld device that knows who and where you are. It could also take the form of an application that participates in an exchange between a business entity and its suppliers.

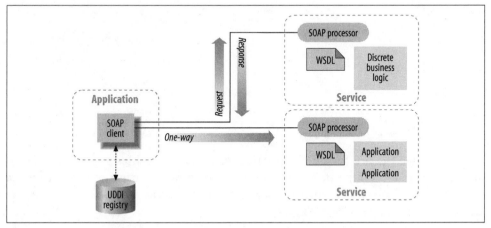

Figure 1-2. Discrete components in a web services architecture

Whether a service is implemented as a fine-grained component performing a discrete operation or as an application suite exposing an entire business function, each can be considered a self-contained, self-describing, modular unit that participates in a larger ecosystem. As illustrated in Figure 1-3, a web service can access and encapsulate other web services to perform its function. For example, a portal such as *www.boston.com* may have a restaurant finder application that is exposed as a web service. The restaurant finder service may in turn access Mapquest as a web service in order to get directions.

Eventually, these small ecosystems can all be combined into a larger, more complicated, orchestrated business macrocosm.

A service-oriented architecture may be intended for use across the public Internet, or built strictly for private use within a single business or among a finite set of established business partners.

Practical Applications for Web Services

Because of the cross-platform interoperability promised by SOAP and web services, we can provide practical business solutions to problems that, until now, have only been a dream of distributed-computing proponents.

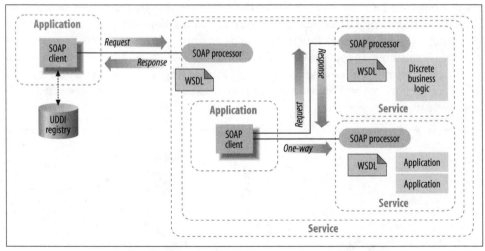

Figure 1-3. Web services within a larger ecosystem

It's easy to see the use for simple, discrete web services such as a currency conversion service that converts dollars to Euros or a natural language translation service that converts English to French. Today, web sites such as *www.xmethods.com* are dedicated to hosting simple web services

This scenario becomes more exciting when we see real companies using web services to automate and streamline their business processes. Let's use the concept of a Business-to-Consumer (B2C) portal. Web-based portals, such as those used by the travel industry, often combine the offerings of multiple companies' products and services and present them with a unified look and feel to the consumer accessing the portal. It's difficult to integrate the backend systems of each business to provide the advertised portal services reliably and quickly.

Web services technology is already being used in the integration between Dollar Rent A Car Systems, Inc. and Southwest Airlines Co. Dollar uses the Microsoft SOAP Toolkit to integrate its online booking system with Southwest Airlines Co.'s site. Dollar's booking system runs on a Sun Solaris server, and Southwest's site runs on a Compaq OpenVMS server. The net result (no pun intended) is that a person booking a flight on Southwest Airline's web site can reserve a car from Dollar without leaving the airline's site. The resulting savings for Dollar are a lower cost per transaction. If the booking is done online through Southwest and other airline sites, the cost per transaction is about $1.00. When booking through traditional travel agent networks, this cost can be up to $5.00 per transaction.

The healthcare industry provides many more scenerios in which web services can be put to use effectively. A doctor carrying a handheld device can access your records, health history, and your preferred pharmacy using a web service. The doctor can also write you an electronic prescription and send it directly to your preferred pharmacy via another web service. If all pharmacies in the world standardized a communication protocol for accepting prescriptions, the doctor could write you a subscription for any pharmacy that you selected. The pharmacy would be able to fulfill the prescription immediately and have it prepared for you when you arrive or couriered to your residence.

This model can be extended further. If the interfaces used between doctors and pharmacies are standardized using web services, a portal broker could act as an intermediary between doctors and pharmacies providing routing information for requests and better meet the needs of individual consumers. For example, a patient may register with an intermediary and specify that he wants to use generic drugs instead of expensive brand names. An intermediary can intercept the pharmaceutical web service request and transform the request into a similar one for the generic drug equivalent. The intermediary exposes web services to doctors and pharmacies (in both directions) and can handle issues such as security, privacy, and nonrepudiation.

Web Services Adoption Factors

Web services are new technologies and require a paradigm shift. The adoption of web services is directly impacted by the adoption of the paradigm of web services development.

A paradigm shift can happen quickly in a large wave, when suddenly the whole world is doing something differently, and no one notices how and when it happened until after the fact. An example of such a shift is the World Wide Web phenomenon that began around 1995. The combination of HTML, HTTP, and the CGI programming model is not the most efficient way to accomplish the services offered by these technologies, yet the CGI model gained widespread grassroots acceptance because it was simple and easy to adopt.

The acceptance of CGI started the wave. To become a lasting paradigm shift, the model of web-based business needed broader acceptance among corporate IT and industry leaders. This acceptance was encouraged by continuing standards development within W3C and IETF and through continuing technology innovations such as ISAPI, NSAPI, Java Servlets, and application servers. Eventually, high-level architectures and infrastructures such as .NET and J2EE were created to hold everything together.

Unlike the initial adoption of the Web, which was driven by grass-roots demand, the adoption of web services will be driven downward by corporations. It's still a paradigm shift, but it's likely to move more slowly. The adoption of the fax machine provides a good analogy. Because fax machines were initially large expensive devices, they were adopted first by large businesses as a way to communicate between their offices. As more companies bought fax machines, they became important for business-to-business communications. Today, fax machines are nearly ubiquitous—

you can fax in your pizza order. We expect to see the same trend in web services. They will be used first for internal business communications before they become part of everyday life. In all cases, though—the rapid adoption of the Web, the slower adoption of the fax machine, and the current adoption of web services—the same factor has enabled the paradigm shift. That factor is a standards communications mechanism. Whether the standard be the phone line and FAX protocols, the TCP/IP stack and HTTP (together with the phone line and modem protocols), or the web service protocols, standards have been, and continue to be, the key factor in enabling the acceptance of new technologies.

Industry Drivers

Many tangible drivers make web services technology attractive, both from a business and a technical perspective. Classic Enterprise Application Integration (EAI) problems require applications to integrate and interoperate. Even within a particular business unit, there exist islands of IT infrastructure. For example, a Customer Relationship Management (CRM) system may have no knowledge of how to communicate with anything outside of its own application suite. It may need to communicate with a third-party Sales Order system so it can know about new customers as soon as they place their first order.

Corporate acquisitions and mergers are also an issue. Entire parallel business application infrastructures have to be synchronized or merged. Business partners such as suppliers and buyers need to collaborate across corporate boundaries.

These EAI and B2B problems exist in abundance and are increasing exponentially. Every new deployed system becomes a legacy system, and any future integration with that system is an EAI or B2B problem. As the growth of integration problems and projects accelerates over the next couple of years, the standards-based approach that web services offer makes adopting web services technology an attractive option for companies that need to cost-effectively accomplish seamless system integration.

Lessons Learned from Recent History

Some industry analysts claim that the web service model is causing a paradigm shift that will change the way distributed computing is done forever. Others say that this model is just a fad that will go away soon. Currently, web services is still very much in the hype phase. Drawing parallels to other new technologies can teach us important lessons.

Other distributed-computing models have had an opportunity to garner universal acceptance and adoption, yet they have not. While these models offer great technical advantages for solving real problems, none have achieved the massive widespread adoption that their proponents had hoped for. This is largely due to their proprietary nature and the inevitable vendor lock-in. Though COM/DCOM had a widespread following, it could not permeate an enterprise because it was limited to

Microsoft platforms. CORBA was controlled by the OMG, a neutral standards body. However, software availability was a problem. There were really only two robust vendor implementations: Iona and Visigenic.

Forcing middleware infrastructure down the throats of other departments and business partners is not easy. Both CORBA and DCOM required that a piece of the vendor-supplied middleware be installed at every node of the system. You can't always force a business partner to install a piece of your software at their site for them to be able to participate in business transactions with your systems. Even within the four walls of an organization, agreeing upon and rolling out an enterprise-wide middleware solution is a huge, concerted effort. CORBA implementations eventually achieved cross-vendor interoperability, but by then it was too late; the wave had already passed.

Crossing corporate boundaries in a secure, reliable fashion is key. If you go back only as far as 1996 to 1997, you would have seen every trade magazine talking about a world of distributed CORBA objects happily floating around on the Internet, discovering one another dynamically and communicating through firewalls. Standards were proposed for firewall communications, and IIOP was going to be adopted by all major firewall vendors as a recognizable protocol. It just never happened—partly due to the aforementioned adoption problems and partly due to widespread adoption and general acceptance of HTTP as a firewall-friendly protocol.

Why Web Services, and Why Now?

What is so different about web services, and why are they poised for success, whereas other preceding technologies have failed to achieve widespread adoption? The answer lies in the challenge that every organization faces today: to create a homogeneous environment while still leveraging its core abilities and existing applications. IT needs a simple, platform-neutral way of communicating between applications.

For starters, XML is ideal for representing data. IT developers have had exposure to XML for a few years and they understand what it's good for. Even though the average IT developer hasn't yet become a walking XML parser, by now most developers understand the concepts behind XML and how it can be used.

Also, the base technologies of SOAP, WSDL, and UDDI are not themselves very exciting; they are just new dressings for the same old distributed-computing model. What draws people to them is the promise of what they enable. Finally, we have a platform-neutral communication protocol that provides interoperability and platform independence. A bidirectional conversation may occur between a Biztalk server and a set of hand-rolled Perl scripts. The Perl scripts may be simultaneously involved in a conversation with a set of applications held together by a J2EE-based application server or a message-oriented middleware (MOM) infrastructure. The minimum requirement is that each participant in the multiparty collaboration knows how to construct and deconstruct SOAP messages and how to send and receive HTTP transmissions.

The heavy involvement of the Microsoft camp and the J2EE camp in web services is good for everyone. It's advantage is not about .NET versus J2EE or .NET versus SunONE; it's about the fact that you no longer have to let that debate or choice get in the way of achieving interoperability across the enterprise. The programming languages and associated infrastructure of each respective camp will continue to coexist and will remain "camps" for a long time.

Low barrier to entry means grass-roots adoption

The widespread adoption of web services can be predicted by drawing parallels to the CGI phenomenon discussed earlier.

Similar conditions exist today. The straightforward approach that SOAP takes— XML messages sent over HTTP—means that anyone can grab Apache SOAP and start exchanging data with the application owned by the guy down the hall. There isn't any overly complex, mysterious alchemy involving a strategic architecture group that takes two years to figure out. A corporate-wide infrastructure adoption shift doesn't need to occur for a company to start working and benefiting from web services; companies can be selective about how and where they adopt these technologies to get the best return on their investment.

Web Services in a J2EE Environment

A common thread found throughout various web services specifications is the regular reference to web services "platforms" and "providers." A *web services platform* is an environment used to host one or more web services. It includes one or more SOAP servers, zero or more UDDI business registries, the security and transaction services used by the web services hosted on it, and other infrastructure provisions. A *web services provider* is generally considered a vendor-supplied piece of middleware infrastructure, such as an ORB, an application server, or a MOM. The provider may fully supply a platform, or it may deliver some base J2EE functionality plus some web service add-ons.

Web services are a new approach for exposing and advertising enterprise services that are hosted on a platform. These platform services still have a variety of enterprise requirements, such as security, transactions, pooling, clustering, and batch processing. Web services do not provide these infrastructure capabilities, but expose the services that do. J2EE and .NET still play an important role in the enterprise as platform definitions: they define the behavior of core capabilities that every software program needs internally. Web services, however, offer a standard way to expose the services deployed onto a platform.

An important question is, "What is being web service enabled?" If the answer is the business systems that run the enterprise, then the role of J2EE in the whole web services picture becomes abundantly clear. The core requirements of a web service enabled ecosystem are the same as they have always been—scalability, reliability, security, etc. Web services provide new ways of wrapping things at the edge of the enterprise, but if you poke your head through the web services hype, the requirements for holding together your core systems don't change that much. The implementation of the web services backbone should still be based on the J2EE architecture. Web services and J2EE come together at multiple points. The use of each J2EE component depends on the application's requirements, just as it did prior to the advent of web services. If the nature of the web service is for lightweight, quick-and-dirty processing, then use a web container and implement the web service directly as a JSP. If the solution requires a distributed component model, then use EJB. If the solution requires a highly distributed, highly reliable, loosely coupled environment, then use JMS. Naturally, any of these combinations is allowed and encouraged, as illustrated in Figure 1-4.

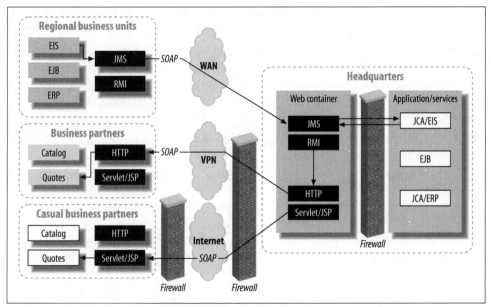

Figure 1-4. SOA based on a J2EE backbone

What This Book Discusses

This is a book on Java and web services. It is for developers who need to develop client- or server-side programs that either use web services or are exposed as web services. Web services are built on XML and have specifications that focus on the XML nature of the technology. These specifications do not discuss how these technologies might be bound to a particular programming language such as Java. As a result, a plethora of industry technologies that facilitate Java/web service integration have been proposed.

This book introduces the basics of SOAP, WSDL, and UDDI, and then discusses some of the different Java technologies available for using each of these platforms within a Java program. The technologies we've chosen range from open source initiatives, such as the Apache project, to big-ticket commercial packages. One reason for touching on so many different packages is that the web services story is still developing; a number of important standards are still in flux, and vendors are providing their own solutions to these problems. Of course, this book looks at the standards efforts designed to consolidate and standardize how Java programs interface with web services. Most notably, this book discusses Java/XML technologies, such as JAXR, JAX-RPC, and JAXM, and how they can be used in a web services environment.

These standards are still works in progress; their status may be clarified by the time we write a second edition. In the meantime, we thought it was important (and even critical) to show you how things look. Just be aware that changes are certain between now and the time when these standards are finalized and actual products are released.

Additionally, for developers who are producing J2EE applications, this book discusses different technologies that are being proposed to web service–enable standard J2EE applications. This book discusses how a web service façade can integrate with a J2EE infrastructure. It also introduces some of the standards efforts proposed for solidifying this work.

This book also discusses the points that developers need to understand to make their web services secure and interoperable with other web services. It provides an in-depth look at web service interoperability across multiple platforms, including the topic of .NET.

CHAPTER 2

Inside the Composite Computing Model

What is the "composite computing model," you ask? The most straightforward definition we've found is:

> An architecture that uses a distributed, discovery-based execution environment to expose and manage a collection of *service-oriented* software assets.

A software asset is nothing more than a piece of business logic; it can be a component, a queue, or a single method that performs a useful function that you decide to expose to the outside world. Like the *client-server* and *n-tier* computing models, the composite computing model represents the architectural principles for governing roles and responsibilities of its constituents. It was designed to solve a specialized group of business problems that have the following requirements:

- Dynamic discovery of the business logic's capabilities
- Separation between the description of the business logic's capabilities and its implementation
- The ability to quickly assemble impromptu computing communities with minimal coordinated planning efforts, installation procedures, or human intervention

The computing industry has been moving towards this model for some time now; much of the last decade has been devoted to defining and refining distributed-computing technologies that allow you to look up components on the fly; discovering a component's interface at runtime; and building applications from components on an ad-hoc basis, often using components in ways that weren't anticipated when they were developed. Listing the steps by which we arrived at the composite computing model is a tangent we won't follow, but remember that Java has played, and continues to play, a very important role in the development of distributed technologies.

In short, the "composite computing model" is the direction in which computing has headed ever since networking became cheap and easy. Instead of trying to build larger applications on ever larger computers, we're trying to assemble smaller components that interact with one another across many computers, and possibly thousands of miles. Instead of building a large, monolithic, proprietary inventory system, for example, we're trying to build services that access inventory databases and can easily be combined as needed. Instead of forcing a customer to call customer service to find out if your plant can deliver 10,000 widgets by Wednesday (and if another plant can deliver 15,000 gadgets by Thursday), you can run an application that knows how to search for vendors that supply widgets and gadgets, figures out how to query each vendor's service interface, and says, "Yes, we can do a production run of 5,000 next week at a cost of $40,000." If you're not working on applications that do this now, you will be soon.

Service-Oriented Architecture

The composite computing model defines a vision for what computing should be. Service-oriented architecture (SOA) represents a way to achieve this vision using the set of technologies that make up the Web Services Technology Stack. This set of technologies currently consists of SOAP, WSDL, and UDDI, though other components may be added in the future.

Like other concepts associated with web services, the SOA seemed to appear almost out of nowhere in September 2000. The originator was IBM and the introduction mechanism was an article by the IBM Web Services Architecture team on the developerWorks web site (*http://www.ibm.com/developerWorks*). Since then, this group has used it as a way to extol the virtues of web services to nontechnical users. The SOA is an instance of a composite computing model, and thus something that can be used to further our understanding of it.

Conceptually, the SOA model is comprised of three roles performing three fundamental interactions. The components of the SOA are our good friends, web services. Each web service is made up of two parts:

Service
> The *implementation* for a web service. A service can be as minuscule as a Java-Script file or as elaborate as a 30-year-old, industrial-strength COBOL application running on a mainframe. The key requirement is that it be on a network-accessible platform, provided by the web service provider.

Service description
> The *interface* for a web service. It is expressed in XML and is governed by one or more standards. This description includes the datatypes, operations, protocol bindings and network location (i.e., the URL, etc.) for the web service's implementation. Additional documents provide categorization and other metadata to facilitate discovery.

Participant Roles

The SOA is based upon the interactions between three roles: a provider, a registry (or broker), and a requestor. These roles are illustrated in Figure 2-1. The interactions between these roles involve publishing information about a service, finding which services are available, and binding to those services.

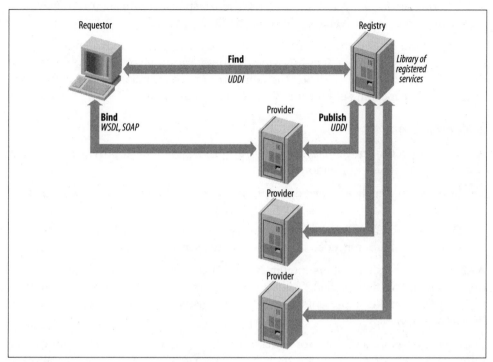

Figure 2-1. The service-oriented architecture

In a typical scenario, a provider hosts the implementation for a service. Providers define service descriptions for services and publish them to a registry. A requestor then uses a registry to find service descriptions for services they are interested in using. With the service description in hand, the requestor binds (i.e., creates a service request for) to a service.

Let's take a closer look at the roles of the SOA.

Provider

In the SOA, a provider is considered the owner of a service. From a composite computing perspective, it is a software asset that others regard as a network-accessible service. In most cases, this software asset is exposed as a web service, which by definition:

- Has an XMLized description
- Has a concrete implementation that encapsulates its behavior

Almost any piece of logic can be exposed as a service in an SOA—from a single component to a full-blown, mainframe-based business process, such as loan processing.

Likewise, how the service is exposed is up to the provider; you can access it through SOAP over HTTP, through a JMS message queue, or via other technologies (such as SMTP); the service may implement a request/response protocol, or it may just receive messages and deliver asynchronous replies.

As is often the case in modern software development, some fundamental ambiguities exist in basic terms such as "provider." Does it mean the organization providing the service, the software itself, or the computer (or computers) on which the software runs? The meaning is almost always clear from the context.

Registry (broker)

A registry, or a broker, manages repositories of information on providers and their software assets. This information includes:

- Business data such as name, description, and contact information ("white pages" data)
- Data describing policies, business processes, and software bindings—in other words, information needed to make use of the service ("green pages" data)

A service broker usually offers intelligent search capabilities and business classification or taxonomy data (called "yellow pages" data). From a composite computing perspective, a broker represents a searchable registry of service descriptions, published by providers.

During the development cycle for a web service, a programmer (or tool) can use the information in registries to create static bindings to services. At runtime, an application can tap into a registry (local or remote) to obtain service descriptions and create dynamic bindings to services.

Registries often sound abstract, but they solve a very concrete problem. They allow you (or, more properly, your software) to ask questions such as, "Who sells widgets?" Once you have an answer to that question, you can ask more questions, such as, "How do I interact with their service to find prices, place orders, etc.?" In short, a registry lets you look up a service and then find its programmatic interface.

Requestor

In the service-oriented architecture, a requestor is a business that discovers and invokes software assets provided by one or more providers. From a composite computing perspective, a requestor is an application that looks for and initiates an interaction with a provider. This role could be played by:

- A person using a web browser
- Computational entities without a user interface, such as another web service

---

Again, there's a lot of ambiguity: is a requestor a person, an organization, or a piece of software? If it's software, is it a browser of some sort, or is it another kind of software? Again, the answer depends on the context.

Participant Interactions

Having defined the roles that participants in web services can play, we'll look in more detail at how they interact. There are three fundamental types of interaction: publishing, service location, and binding.

Publishing

Providers publish information (or metadata) about services to a registry. These providers are usually standards organizations, software vendors, and developers. According to IBM's Web Services Conceptual Architecture document, several different mechanisms are used to publish service descriptions:

Direct

> The service requestor retrieves the service description directly from the service provider, using email, FTP, or a distribution CD. Here, the service provider delivers the service description and simultaneously makes the service available to a requestor. There is no registry as such; the requestor is responsible for locating services and retrieving their descriptions.

HTTP GET request

> This mechanism is currently used at *http://www.xmethods.com*, a public repository of web services that developers can use to test their wares. The service requestor retrieves the service description directly from the service provider by using an HTTP GET request. This model has a registry (the public web repository), though only in a limited sense.

Dynamic discovery

> This mechanism uses local and public registries to store and retrieve service descriptions programmatically. In the web services world, the most frequently used registry is UDDI, though others exist (for example, ebXML R). Contextually, the service provider is an application that uses a specialized set of APIs to publish the service description.

The direct publishing method is a historical artifact and of little interest to us. Publishing with a GET request is more interesting, particularly since *http://www.xmethods.com* has been on the forefront of web services development. However, we see this means of publishing as transitional—a temporary tool to get us from direct publishing to dynamic discovery. (We suspect the developers of XMethods would agree.)

Dynamic discovery (see Figure 2-2) is the most interesting and versatile publishing model. UDDI and other protocols designed to support dynamic discovery are at the center of the web services landscape.

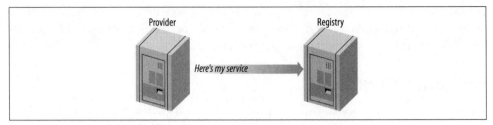

Figure 2-2. Publishing for dynamic discovery

Service location (finding)

Given that registries or brokers publish services, how do you locate services that you wish to use? Requestors find services using a registry or broker. Service location is closely associated with dynamic discovery. In this context, the requestor is an application that uses a specialized set of APIs to query a public or private registry for service descriptions. These queries are formatted in a well-defined, standard XML format and transmitted using an XML messaging format, such as SOAP or XML-RPC. The criteria used to find a service include the quality of service (How quickly can the service respond? How good are its results?), supported protocols (Can my client talk to your service?), and the service taxonomy (What kind of service?). It's easy to imagine other criteria that you could use to locate a service. Figure 2-3 shows the process of service location.

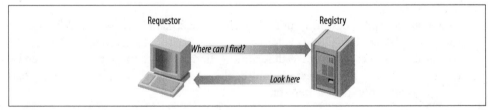

Figure 2-3. Service location

Binding

The binding interaction involves the requestor and provider and, optionally, the registry. In context, binding is what an application does when it uses the service description to create a message to be sent to the service provider. Web service description documents (WSDL documents) specify the network protocols (i.e., HTTP, MIME, SMTP, etc.) that a service supports, the APIs by which the service is accessed, and everything else that a requestor needs to use a service. Figure 2-4 illustrates the binding interaction.

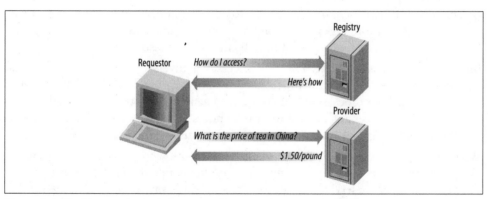

Figure 2-4. Binding to a service

Business Perspectives on the SOA

The participants in an SOA have different objectives, and hence different perspectives on the SOA itself. This section looks at the perspectives of the three main participants in an SOA: the service provider, service requestor, and service broker.

Interestingly, both IBM and Microsoft are setting up business units to function in multiple roles, sometimes simultaneously. For Microsoft, the bCentral initiative will be both a service broker and service provider, MSN will be a service broker, and their desktop products will be service requestors.

Just because these participant roles have been defined with business-to-business interactions in mind, it doesn't mean an SOA can be used only in business technologies. A web service doesn't have to be an e-service or be associated with revenue generation at all. Forward-thinking companies have already predicted that the web services platform will logically evolve into a full-blown, Internet-based "virtual distributed computing environment." In that world, the services supplied by a provider must:

- Perform with high efficiency
- Scale to handle an extremely large volume of requests
- Support versioning and online self-reparation
- Support being part of a workflow
- Be highly available

Service provider

A business that sees itself as performing some degree of an electronic service will most likely identify with the service provider role. Whether that service is defined as processing data or carrying out a specific task, the business entity must believe it is performing mission-critical work for others. Since almost anything can be a service, coming up with an exhaustive list of applicable businesses is difficult. However, we can mention a few straightforward examples:

Independent software vendor. This business owns and maintains software that performs one or more tasks. This software could be made available as an aggregation of services or broken down into distinct service resources.

Business process center. This business accesses a diverse set of applications that perform an entire business process. For example, a bank usually has a business process for loan processing; it may wish to generate additional income by offering its loan processing service to other lenders. The bank could expose its loan processing business process as a web service, thus becoming a service provider.

Web service aggregators. The SOA—and indeed, the whole composite computing paradigm—offers the opportunity for intermediaries to build new services by aggregating other services. In the loan example, it's easy to imagine a service that checks a number of banks to find a good rate and uses another loan processing service to request a loan on the part of a customer. This new service doesn't provide services of its own; it just packages services that are provided by others.

As expected, the service provider views the SOA as a framework for exposing its web services. These services are islands of code designed to solve one aspect of an overall business problem. Here's a short list of what typically goes through the mind of a service provider:

Ensuring availability. A web service is not very useful if it isn't available. Making sure that a web service can accept service requests from a SOAP router is paramount. The web sites that host today's web applications have already figured out how to do this in a load-balanced, scalable way, so ensuring availability should be a piece of cake.

Providing a secure transaction environment. Most businesses already have security in place. However, the SOA presents interesting and nontrivial security problems. An SOA may encompass multiple sites, each with its own way of implementing security. The challenge is to come up with a standards-based mechanism that allows each site in the SOA to propagate a security context, without necessarily having to use the same software. More likely than not, the two main security aspects, authentication and authorization, will end up being web services themselves.

Quality of service. Web services are an innovative and powerful new mechanism for heterogeneous distributed computing, but they still need to follow old "rules of conduct" to gain rapid, widespread acceptance. One of these rules guarantees a certain level of service.

Preventing denial of service (DOS) attacks. DOS attacks are currently the bane of large consumer shopping portals (such as Amazon) and online auction sites (such as eBay). There are mechanisms that deal with these problems, though ultimately the goal is to stay one step ahead of the hackers who try to attack your site. Whenever security is an issue, it's important to run operating-system software that is fundamentally sound and to stay up to date with the latest patches and bug fixes.

Service registry (broker)

A service registry, also called a broker, is a business or software component whose main SOA-related activity involves maintaining service registries and their entries. Service providers customarily pay registration fees to these brokers, who in turn advertise their service offerings. UDDI and ebXML Registries are the main "tools of the trade" for a service broker.

What kind of things would a service broker look for in an SOA? The answer depends on the type of broker. If the broker functions as a gateway, then it is probably interested in finding other service registries (brokers). Gateways serve as a connection point to a network of external service registries. They differ from other service registries in that they are used primarily by the service registries themselves, as opposed to service requestors and providers. This being the case, gateways are primarily interested in finding other brokers and expanding their reach.

Other types of brokers may be concerned with locating and installing documentation for web services. This activity is usually done on behalf of a service requestor. It includes all the work required to obtain, install, version, and configure services before they are made available to clients.

Service requestor

A business that finds some commonality between its own activities and the actions of others who request service will most likely see itself in the service requestor role. Two revenue-generating activities a service requestor might perform are content aggregation and service aggregation. In content aggregation, the business entity interacts with various content providers to process or reproduce such content in the desired presentation format of its customers. A service aggregator interacts with service providers to rebrand, host, or offer a composite of services to its customers. Earlier, we talked about a hypothetical loan service that aggregated several pieces of the loan application and processing puzzle. To its customers, this aggregate service is just another provider; to the banks that provide the loans and the loan processing, this service is a requestor.

A service requestor typically views an SOA as something it uses to access the web services that provide it with the data it gives to its customers. Ideally, these web services allow the business to receive this data in an exact format or structure, thereby eliminating the need for elaborate data integration or mapping. Here's a short list of what is typically on the mind of a service requestor:

Locating the cheapest web services. Cost is one of the chief driving factors for goods and services; a service requestor wants to get the most bang for its buck. We'll see how UDDI can help do this in the next section.

Mechanisms for choosing an alternate service. Networks fail and servers crash with distressing regularity. A service requestor has no control over the availability of a web service, unless it is also the service's provider. Currently, no web services platform detects when a service is unavailable and automatically fails over to another service. For the time being, the service requestor must figure out how to choose an alternate web service when the desired service is unavailable. In the future, the web services platform should be able to take care of this requirement, or at least be sufficiently extensible to allow the requestor to work out its own solution.

Subscribing to a secure environment. Web services will undoubtedly become an incubator for serious hackers and mischievous adolescents. This is a serious problem that could severely hamper the widespread adoption and usage of web services. DOS attacks are probably the biggest concern.

Developers' Perspectives on the SOA

The service-oriented architecture has been praised for how it enables the deployment of large, complex systems of applications. It is an equally useful framework for application developers. Here, a service provider performs several activities that are part of the development realm:

- Designing and describing the service's interface
- Writing code to implement the service, assembling it into a deployable package, and subsequently deploying it
- Publishing XML and non-XML artifacts (i.e., WSDL files, usage documentations, specifications, etc.) for the service to a service registry or other interested parties

All of these activities, with the possible exception of the last one, fall squarely in the world of development. IBM defines the development aspect of the SOA as an "end-to-end" development lifecycle that consists of four steps or phases: build, deploy, run, and manage. Since the service provider performs most of these steps, we'll start with it.

Service provider

In many cases, the implementation for our web service is already built: we have a backend application (or maybe even a web application) and only need to put a web service frontend onto it. With the application already in hand, we only need to create a service description. Most serious Java-based web services platforms include tools for producing this description directly from a class using reflection.

If a service provider doesn't have an existing implementation, it needs to start by developing and testing the web services implementation, developing the service interface description, and developing the service implementation description. Developing a new web service involves using the programming languages and models that are appropriate for the service provider's environment.

Next, the developer needs to assemble the web service solution for deployment. Don't confuse deploying and publishing, as they are not synonymous. Deploying makes the web service visible to the outside world; publishing tells everyone it's there.

Finally, a service provider needs to maintain and enhance its web services. This maintenance phase covers ongoing management and administration of the web service application.

Service requestor

Developers build the service implementations that service requestors consume. Once coded, this service implementation plays the role of provider, and you or another developer craft a piece of software that acts as a requestor. Binding to a service means that the developer has a blueprint for using the service and a mechanism for executing the service. The blueprint contains both a definition of the service's interface and any requirements for using the service.

The P2P Model

The SOA provides a powerful framework for building next-generation applications. However, for some enterprises, the centralized hub-and-spoke structure of the SOA is too inflexible. Some enterprises want to build web service solutions that require real-time views of work in progress, inventories, logistics, etc. Other businesses want to exploit highly successful peer-to-peer (P2P) applications, such as instant messaging and content distribution.

The P2P approach differs from the SOA in that no attempt is made to define explicit roles. Any node, or *peer*, can operate in any role it knows about or can discover through other peers on the P2P network. We often think that this "be whatever you can discover" capability makes the P2P model more suitable for doing web services than the SOA.

Despite its legal problems, looking at an application such as Napster (or its close relative, Gnutella) from a web services perspective is useful. Users publish the files they are willing to share and these files are listed in a registry. (Napster had a centralized database that served as a registry and Gnutella has a distributed searching mechanism, which is essentially a virtual registry.) Other users can search the registry (physical or virtual) and download files directly from the provider. This process maps nicely onto the SOA, except that there's no clear distinction between provider and requestor or even (in the case of Gnutella) requestor and directory. Peers establish ad hoc, short-term relationships with one another; at any time, a peer can be provider, requestor, or both.

Advocates of P2P computing have often failed to come up with a business model that works in such a decentralized environment. However, that shouldn't prevent us from looking at the technical advantages of the peer-to-peer model and seeing how it might apply to web services. Here are some compelling reasons for considering the P2P approach:

More efficient use of network bandwidth. The concentrated, localized traffic congestion typical of today's Web doesn't apply to P2P networking. There is no server as such; interactions are between individual peers, with no centralized bottlenecks. If that peer experiences a hardware failure, another peer can handle the request. If a peer is too busy, it will be slow in replying to a request, and another peer will handle it.

Greater availability. In a P2P network, a peer can obtain content from multiple servers, ideally reaching one that is running nearby. The peer that first provided some content need not service every resource request; in fact, it does not even have to be running.

Although a detailed discussion of P2P frameworks is beyond the bounds of this book; we'll point you in the direction of two of the most promising projects: Project JXTA (*http://www.jxta.org*) and BEEP (*http://www.beepcore.org*). Both projects are open source works in progress. Although they haven't yet become part of the computing mainstream, dynamic and exciting developer communities have grown up around them. We won't mention them again in this book, but you should be aware of them and decide whether they're appropriate for the applications you're developing.

CHAPTER 3

SOAP: The Cornerstone of Interoperability

Much like web services, the broad definition of the Simple Object Access Protocol (SOAP) means various things to different people. It's a wire protocol. It's an RPC mechanism. It's an interoperability standard. It's a document exchange protocol. It's a universal business-to-business communications language. It's everything you would ever need. It's not nearly enough.

Actually, it's all of the above. Perhaps the best way to understand what it is and what it isn't is to break down the acronym into its parts and analyze where each one fits.

Simple

For starters, the "S" in SOAP stands for "simple." The basic approach of expressing data as XML and transporting it across the Internet using HTTP is simple. In the SOAP protocol, everything that goes across the wire is expressed in terms of HTTP or SMTP headers, MIME encoding, and a special XML grammar for encoding application data and objects.

However, a full understanding of the details and rules of SOAP is not for the faint of heart. For instance, the idea of expressing a SOAP document with attachments using the email and MIME metaphor is simple. Is MIME simple? It is simple only because it uses a data formatting convention that is already in widespread use, is familiar to most IT people, and is conceptually understood by less technical people. Perhaps the "S" should stand for "simpler."

Is XML simple? It can be as simple or as complex as you want it to be. XML provides a way to add semantic meaning to data shipped over the wire. Through XML-Schema, we have a way of describing a complex document such as a purchase order. But XML-Schema is far from simple. SOAP provides conventions for creating "envelopes" for your data. SOAP has explicit rules for encoding application data—even for such things as arrays of binary data—so it can be expressed in an ASCII human-readable form. It isn't all that simple, but it is explainable.

We don't mean to scare anybody off by representing SOAP as overly complex; we will walk you through it and explain it in detail. The good news is that tools and frameworks are already coming to the rescue. In the end, most of us will not worry about how a purchase order gets encoded or how it is sent over the wire. We will all code to a PO object and click on a "Save" button. However, for those of you who consider the best tool of trade to be vi, emacs, or Notepad, we must press on. Even those who like to take advantage of productivity tools and infrastructure need to understand what lies beneath.

Perhaps the "S" should stand for "straightforward." In SOAP, nothing is hidden intentionally. Every aspect of a SOAP request is intended to be completely self-describing and largely based on a conglomeration of proven, well-established conventions. That's the real beauty behind SOAP; the platforms and programming languages on both sides of a SOAP conversation are independent of one another, yet they can communicate as long as each side of the conversation can:

- Send and receive data transmissions across a network using either HTTP or SMTP[*]
- Understand MIME encoding rules and base the means of constructing and deconstructing binary attachments on those rules
- Construct and deconstruct XML documents that conform to the enveloping and encoding rules established by SOAP
- Perform the required action, if an action is indicated in the SOAP document

Also, simple doesn't necessarily connote "weak" or "lame." SOAP is powerful enough to represent any datatype, object serialization, method invocation, or document exchange.

Simple does mean that SOAP is missing some important things, such as security, reliability, routing, and rules of engagement for interaction among multiple parties. These items, however, will be added eventually. Let's just conclude that in its infancy, SOAP was "simpler" than its predecessors.

Object

The "O" in SOAP stands for "object" and has to do with its roots as a way of invoking COM objects across the Internet. As with its close cousin XML-RPC, SOAP is fully capable of describing a remote procedure call or method invocation. Here's a typical SOAP document that describes a method invocation on a remote object:

```
POST /StockQuote HTTP/1.1
Host: www.example.org
Content-Type: text/xml; charset="utf-8"
```

---

[*] Even this characterization is somewhat of a misnomer, as we will see when we talk about bindings and higher-level protocols built on top of SOAP.

```
Content-Length: nnnn
SOAPAction: "http://example.org/2001/06/quotes"

<env:Envelope xmlns:env="http://www.w3.org/2001/09/soap-envelope" >
 <env:Body>
  <m:GetLastTradePrice
        env:encodingStyle="http://www.w3.org/2001/09/soap-encoding"
        xmlns:m="http://example.org/2001/06/quotes">
    <symbol>DIS</symbol>
  </m:GetLastTradePrice>
 </env:Body>
</env:Envelope>
```

The section "Anatomy of a SOAP Message" discusses the details of this SOAP request. For now, it should suffice to say that the two most important parts are the method name, GetLastTradePrice, and its parameter, the ticker symbol DIS.

Access

A key feature of SOAP and web services is their accessibility. The initial developers of SOAP intended for all SOAP conversations to be carried out via a "binding" to another lower-level protocol, and that binding would most likely be HTTP or SMTP. These protocols were chosen because they are almost universally available. Most firewalls have been trained to allow HTTP sessions and SMTP exchanges, so SOAP conversations can easily cross corporate boundaries.

It's possible to create a SOAP binding for almost any protocol—however, for the time being, HTTP is the de facto binding (and most widely used). Other bindings, such as SOAP over RMI, or SOAP over JMS (for improved reliability), are emerging.

Protocol

Put all these factors together and we have a protocol. SOAP is an XML based protocol used to exchange information throughout a distributed environment.

Message-Based Document Exchange and RPC

SOAP has its roots in synchronous remote procedure calls over HTTP—although you wouldn't know it by reading the specification these days. In fact, the specification seems to go out of its way to distance itself from that association. Although special provisions are available for performing synchronous RPC calls in SOAP, there is also an asynchronous, message-based document exchange model. Actually, the document exchange model is the default method of exchanging data between two endpoints. An RPC call is a specialized case of combining multiple one-way asynchronous messages into a request-response.

The introduction to Section 2 of the SOAP 1.2 specification says it well:

> SOAP messages are fundamentally one-way transmissions from a SOAP sender to a SOAP receiver; however, SOAP messages are often combined to implement patterns such as request/response.

> SOAP implementations can be optimized to exploit the unique characteristics of particular network systems. For example, the HTTP binding ... provides for SOAP response messages to be delivered as HTTP responses, using the same connection as the inbound request.[*]

Because SOAP can represent some fairly complex data structures in both the request and response messages, the lines between the two models are blurred. This chapter presents the information that is germane to either model first. The RPC-specific concepts built on the more generic concepts are explained at the end. We use Apache SOAP 2.2 for our examples, which follows a similar design.

Anatomy of a SOAP Message

The SOAP specification describes four major components: formatting conventions for encapsulating data and routing directions in the form of an envelope, a transport or protocol binding, encoding rules, and an RPC mechanism. The envelope defines a convention for describing the contents of a message, which in turn has implications on how it gets processed. A protocol binding provides a generic mechanism for sending a SOAP envelope via a lower-level protocol such as HTTP. Encoding rules provide a convention for mapping various application datatypes into an XML tag-based representation. Finally, the RPC mechanism provides a way to represent remote procedure calls and their return values. Throughout this book, we'll refer to these four areas collectively as a *SOAP message*.

How XML Becomes SOAP

We start this discussion by focusing on the document exchange model. To clarify this topic, we use a simple purchase order document, *PO.xml*. This document is overly simplified because it contains only two things—a ship-to address and an item entry:

```
<?xml version="1.0" encoding="UTF-8"?>
<PurchaseOrder xmlns="urn:oreilly-jaws-samples">
    <shipTo country="US">
        <name>Joe Smith</name>
        <street>14 Oak Park</street>
        <city>Bedford</city>
        <state>MA</state>
        <zip>01730</zip>
    </shipTo>
```

---

[*] SOAP 1.2 Specification: *http://www.w3.org/TR/2001/WD-soap12-part1-20011002/*.

```
    <items>
        <item partNum="872-AA">
            <productName>Candy Canes</productName>
            <quantity>444</quantity>
            <price>1.68</price>
            <comment>I want candy!</comment>
        </item>
    </items>
</PurchaseOrder>
```

PO.xml is not yet a SOAP document; it's just a vanilla XML document. What makes it become a SOAP document is:

- The wrapping of the XML inside of a SOAP body
- The wrapping of the SOAP body within a SOAP envelope
- The optional inclusion of a SOAP header block
- Namespace declarations
- Encoding style directives for the serialization of data
- The binding of the whole thing to a protocol

As illustrated in Figure 3-1, a SOAP envelope contains two primary components: a header and a body. Both the header and the body can contain multiple blocks of information.

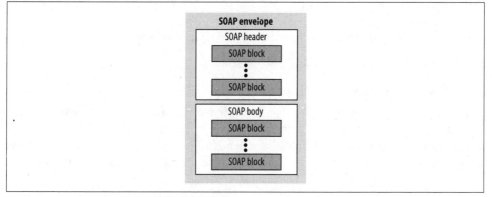

Figure 3-1. Block structure of a SOAP envelope

The following listing shows *PO.xml* wrapped by an envelope to make it conform to SOAP:

```
<?xml version='1.0' encoding='UTF-8'?>
<SOAP-ENV:Envelope
    xmlns:SOAP-ENV="http://schemas.xmlsoap.org/soap/envelope/"
    xmlns:xsi="http://www.w3.org/1999/XMLSchema-instance"
    xmlns:xsd="http://www.w3.org/1999/XMLSchema">
<SOAP-ENV:Header>
    ...
</SOAP-ENV:Header>
```

```
<SOAP-ENV:Body>
<PurchaseOrder xmlns="urn:oreilly-jaws-samples">
        <shipTo country="US">
                <name>Joe Smith</name>
                <street>14 Oak Park</street>
                <city>Bedford</city>
                <state>MA</state>
                <zip>01730</zip>
        </shipTo>
        <items>
                <item partNum="872-AA">
                        <productName>Candy Canes</productName>
                        <quantity>444</quantity>
                        <price>1.68</price>
                        <comment>I want candy!</comment>
                </item>
        </items>
</PurchaseOrder>
</SOAP-ENV:Body>
</SOAP-ENV:Envelope>
```

The SOAP Envelope

The SOAP envelope declaration is simply the outermost XML tag that delineates the
boundaries of the SOAP document. The following envelope tag shows three required
attributes, which specify the namespace and the schema to be used for this envelope:

```
<SOAP-ENV:Envelope
    xmlns:SOAP-ENV="http://schemas.xmlsoap.org/soap/envelope/"
    xmlns:xsi="http://www.w3.org/1999/XMLSchema-instance"
    xmlns:xsd="http://www.w3.org/1999/XMLSchema">
...
</SOAP-ENV:Envelope>
```

Let's examine the syntax of this tag. The first attribute, xmlns:SOAP-ENV="http://
schemas.xmlsoap.org/soap/envelope/", is a namespace declaration. The namespace
declaration prevents tag name conflicts when XML fragments are combined to form
composite documents. It's analogous to the use of the package keyword in Java.

At first, it may seem that "<SOAP-ENV:Envelope xmlns:SOAP-ENV" is nothing but a
string of special keywords. Actually, :Envelope and xmlns: are, but the use of the
string SOAP-ENV is completely arbitrary. What's really important is its relationship to
the :Envelope and xmlns: keywords. The URL *http://schemas.xmlsoap.org/soap/
envelope/* is a special URI reserved for the namespace defined by SOAP. Its purpose
in life is to be a unique string. A common convention is to use a URI that represents
a real URL owned by the organization that authors the document. This convention
ensures that the URI is globally unique. It could just as well have looked like this:

```
<abbr:Envelope
    xmlns:abbr="http://schemas.xmlsoap.org/soap/envelope/"
    xmlns:xsi="http://www.w3.org/1999/XMLSchema-instance"
    xmlns:xsd="http://www.w3.org/1999/XMLSchema">
```

```
    ...
    </abbr:Envelope>
```

In this version of the envelope element, `xmlns:abbr` declares a prefix that is an abbreviation to be used in place of the much more lengthy "http://schemas.xmlsoap.org/ soap/envelope/". The `<abbr:Envelope...>` tag and the closing `</abbr:Envelope>` tag indicate that this namespace is scoped to the entire envelope.

Next, the `xmlns:xsi=http://www.w3.org/1999/XMLSchema-instance` attribute declares the XML schema instance namespace. The prefix, `xsi`, must be prepended to all elements and attributes defined in this namespace. An example of such an attribute is `xsi:type`, which specifies the type of an element for encoding purposes.

Finally, `xmlns:xsd=http://www.w3.org/1999/XMLSchema` is just another namespace declaration, akin to `xsi` and `SOAP-ENV`. This declaration defines the XMLSchema namespace. Elements from this namespace are used as values for the `xsi:type` attribute—for example, `xsd:string` or `xsd:boolean`. The schema for the SOAP document is not referenced from the SOAP envelope.

The SOAP Header

The SOAP header and body are syntactically similar. SOAP 1.1 and SOAP 1.2 have no conventions for what is supposed to be in the header; it is simply a place to put directives to the SOAP processor that receives the message. The sending and receiving parties need to agree on which elements go there and what they mean. Higher- level protocols built on top of SOAP, such as ebXML Message Service (MS), have formalized the use of the SOAP header by defining specific elements such as a `<MessageHeader>`, which contains such specific things as `<From>`, `<To>`, and `<MessageId>`. The SOAP body is intended for the actual data, or message payload, to be consumed and processed by the ultimate receiver.

When using SOAP for RPC, the distinction between the header and the body is similar. The `<Body>` is reserved purely for the method call and its parameters, and the `<Header>` is used for things targeted at the underlying infrastructure, such as a transaction ID. A transaction ID clearly should not belong to the method signature; it's intended for the SOAP processor that receives the message, which could very well be a J2EE server with a transaction manager.

Here's the syntactic form of a SOAP header:

```
<SOAP-ENV:Envelope
    xmlns:SOAP-ENV="http://schemas.xmlsoap.org/soap/envelope/"
    xmlns:xsi="http://www.w3.org/1999/XMLSchema-instance"
    xmlns:xsd="http://www.w3.org/1999/XMLSchema">
<SOAP-ENV:Header>
    <jaws:MessageHeader xmlns:jaws="urn:oreilly-jaws-samples">
        <From>Me</From>
        <To>You</To>
        <MessageId>9999</MessageId>
```

```
    ...
    </jaws:MessageHeader>
  </SOAP-ENV:Header>
  <SOAP-ENV:Body>
  ...
  </SOAP-ENV:Body>
</SOAP-ENV:Envelope>
```

The SOAP Protocol Binding

At this point, we need to add only one thing to make *PO.xml* into a SOAP message: the additional information needed by the protocol that it is bound to. The following listing shows the HTTP header information that is prepended to the message when it is bound to the HTTP protocol:

```
SOAPAction = "urn:soaphttpclient-action-uri"
Host = localhost
Content-Type = text/xml; charset=utf-8
Content-Length = 701

<?xml version='1.0' encoding='UTF-8'?>
<SOAP-ENV:Envelope
    xmlns:SOAP-ENV="http://schemas.xmlsoap.org/soap/envelope/"
    xmlns:xsi="http://www.w3.org/1999/XMLSchema-instance"
    xmlns:xsd="http://www.w3.org/1999/XMLSchema">
...
</SOAP-ENV:Envelope>
```

The SOAPAction header is somewhat strange. In SOAP 1.1, it was a required part of the HTTP protocol binding. Its intent was to allow something that does routing or dispatching to make decisions without any knowledge of SOAP or the means to parse the SOAP envelope. For example, a dumb CGI script or servlet whose only purpose is to route requests to other processes shouldn't have to process the SOAP envelope to get routing information. This concept is great, but it is tied to the HTTP protocol.

In SOAP 1.2, SOAPAction has become optional. It's not up to SOAP to dictate extensions to an underlying protocol. Hindsight is 20/20. In this case, who can blame anyone for taking an existing HTTP header such as Action and creating something like it called SOAPAction? What's really needed is a generic mechanism for specifying sideband data independent of the protocol. If such a thing existed, the people responsible for creating a standard mapping to HTTP might just as well have chosen to have a SOAPAction header. However, the semantics of the first mapping shouldn't dictate how the rest of the mappings are done.

Sending and Receiving SOAP Messages

We have seen the building blocks of a SOAP message. The next steps are to understand how a message is built and how it is then communicated between two endpoints. To discuss these topics, we present a simple SOAP sender and a SOAP receiver using Apache SOAP and the Apache Tomcat servlet engine.* You may find it refreshing to discover that the additional pieces are not placed in the SOAP document by hand. The SOAP-ification is accomplished by using APIs that take care of the dirty work.

Before we look at the code of our first SOAP example, let's run it and observe its behavior. This example consists of a simple HTTP sender class that reads an XML file, wraps it in a SOAP envelope, and sends it to a URL destination. The destination is a simple HTTP servlet that takes the contents of the message and dumps it to the screen. As we progress through concepts such as dynamic headers, SOAP with Attachments, and SOAP-RPC, these examples will become progressively more sophisticated. For now, lets run the simple one. From the command line, run the command:

```
java SimpleGenericHTTPSoapClient -df ./PO.xml
```

 If this command doesn't work, make sure that *SimpleGenericHTTP-SoapClient.class* is on the classpath and *PO.xml* is in the current directory.

You should see the following output:

```
Starting SimpleGenericHTTPSoapClient:
    host url       = http://localhost:8080/examples/servlet/SimpleHTTPReceive
    data file      = ./PO.xml


Sent SOAP Message with Apache HTTP SOAP Client.
Waiting for response....
HTTP POST was successful.
```

In the command shell running the Tomcat servlet engine, you should see:

```
Received request.
----------------------
  SOAPAction = "urn:oreilly-jaws-samples"
  Host = localhost
  Content-Type = text/xml; charset=utf-8
  Content-Length = 695
----------------------
<?xml version='1.0' encoding='UTF-8'?>
<SOAP-ENV:Envelope xmlns:SOAP-ENV="http://schemas.xmlsoap.org/soap/envelope/" xm
lns:xsi="http://www.w3.org/1999/XMLSchema-instance" xmlns:xsd="http://www.w3.org
/1999/XMLSchema">
```

---

* While we use Apache SOAP, this chapter is not intended to be a tutorial on Apache SOAP or Tomcat. The intent is to talk about SOAP and its behavior whenever possible. The installation and set up of Apache SOAP, Tomcat, and the example files are not discussed. Installation is covered by the *readme* file included with the examples, which is available from *http://www.oreilly.com/catalog/javawebserv/examples*.

```
<SOAP-ENV:Body>
<PurchaseOrder xmlns="urn:oreilly-jaws-samples">
        <shipTo country="US">
                <name>Joe Smith</name>
                <street>14 Oak Park</street>
                <city>Bedford</city>
                <state>MA</state>
                <zip>01730</zip>
        </shipTo>
        <items>
                <item partNum="872-AA">
                        <productName>Candy Canes</productName>
                        <quantity>444</quantity>
                        <price>1.68</price>
                        <comment>I want candy!</comment>
                </item>
        </items>
</PurchaseOrder>
</SOAP-ENV:Body>
</SOAP-ENV:Envelope>
```

The SOAP Sender

We will soon examine the source code and some of the APIs used to create and send this message. But first, here is a listing of the simple SOAP sender in its entirety:

```java
import java.io.*;
import java.util.*;

public class SimpleGenericHTTPSoapClient
{
    /////////////////
    //Default values used if no command line parameters are set
    private static final String DEFAULT_HOST_URL =
        "http://localhost:8080/examples/servlet/SimpleHTTPReceive";

    private static final String DEFAULT_DATA_FILENAME   = "./PO.xml";

    private static final String URI = "urn:oreilly-jaws-samples";
    /////////////////
    //Member variables
    private String m_hostURL;
    //data file that will be the body content of a soap envelop
    private String m_dataFileName;

    public SimpleGenericHTTPSoapClient(String hostURL, String dataFileName)
        throws Exception
    {
        m_hostURL = hostURL;
        m_dataFileName      = dataFileName;
```

```
        System.out.println( );
        System.out.println("_____");
        System.out.println("Starting SimpleGenericHTTPSoapClient:");
        System.out.println("    host url       = " + m_hostURL);
        System.out.println("    data file      = " + m_dataFileName);
        System.out.println("_____");
        System.out.println( );
    }

    public void sendSOAPMessage( )
    {
        try
        {
            // get soap body to include in the SOAP envelope
            FileReader fr = new FileReader (m_dataFileName);
            javax.xml.parsers.DocumentBuilder xdb =
                org.apache.soap.util.xml.XMLParserUtils.getXMLDocBuilder( );
            org.w3c.dom.Document doc =
                xdb.parse (new org.xml.sax.InputSource (fr));
            if (doc == null) {
                throw new org.apache.soap.SOAPException
                    (org.apache.soap.Constants.FAULT_CODE_CLIENT, "parsing error");
            }

            //Create the SOAP envelope
            org.apache.soap.Envelope envelope = new org.apache.soap.Envelope( );

            // create a vector for collecting the body elements
            Vector bodyElements = new Vector( );

            //obtain the top-level DOM element and place it into the vector
            bodyElements.add(doc.getDocumentElement ( ));

            //Create the SOAP body element
            org.apache.soap.Body body = new org.apache.soap.Body( );
            body.setBodyEntries(bodyElements);

            //Add the SOAP body element to the envelope
            envelope.setBody(body);

            // Build the Message.
            org.apache.soap.messaging.Message msg
                = new org.apache.soap.messaging.Message( );

            msg.send (new java.net.URL(m_hostURL), URI, envelope);
            System.out.println("Sent SOAP Message with Apache HTTP SOAP Client.");

            // receive response from the transport and dump it to the screen
            System.out.println("Waiting for response....");
            org.apache.soap.transport.SOAPTransport st = msg.getSOAPTransport ( );
            BufferedReader br = st.receive ( );
            String line = br.readLine( );
```

```
            if(line == null)
            {
                System.out.println("HTTP POST was successful. \n");
            }
            else
            {
                while (line != null)
                {
                    System.out.println (line);
                    line = br.readLine( );
                }
            }
        }
        catch(Exception e)
        {
            e.printStackTrace( );
        }
    }

    //
    // NOTE: the remainder of this deals with reading arguments
    //
    /** Main program entry point. */
    public static void main(String args[]) {

        // not relevant ...
    }
}
```

The main( ) method is responsible for parsing the command-line arguments, running the constructor, and calling the sendSOAPMessage( ) method:

```
/** Main program entry point. */
public static void main(String args[]) {

...

    // Start the HTTPSoapClient
    try
    {
        SimpleGenericHTTPSoapClient soapClient =
            new SimpleGenericHTTPSoapClient(hostURL, dataFileName);
        soapClient.sendSOAPMessage( );

    }
...
}
```

The constructor simply stores some local member variables and prints things on the screen. All the real work happens in sendSOAPMessage( ). After reading the *PO.xml* document, sendSOAPMessage( ) parses the document into a DOM tree. We get a parser by calling the Apache getXMLDocBuilder( ) method, which returns a DocumentBuilder object. This parser is represented by a javax.xml.parsers. DocumentBuilder interface, which is part of the Java API for XML Processing (JAXP) package. While we chose to use the Xerces parser, the actual parser could be any parser that implements the interface. Once a suitable parser is obtained, the parser is invoked; it returns an `org.w3c.dom.Document` object:

```
public void sendSOAPMessage( )
{
    try
    {
        // get soap body to include in the SOAP envelope
        FileReader fr = new FileReader (m_dataFileName);
        javax.xml.parsers.DocumentBuilder xdb =
            org.apache.soap.util.xml.XMLParserUtils.getXMLDocBuilder( );
        org.w3c.dom.Document doc
            = xdb.parse (new org.xml.sax.InputSource (fr));
        if (doc == null) {
            throw new org.apache.soap.SOAPException
                (org.apache.soap.Constants.FAULT_CODE_CLIENT, "parsing error");
        }
```

Next, we need to create a SOAP envelope to hold everything and place the document into it. To associate the document with the envelope, place the top-level DOM element into a Vector, then attach the Vector to a Body object. Then place the body in the envelope using the setBody( ) method. In this simple case, only one top-level element, the <PurchaseOrder> tag, should be attached. The DOM parser has taken care of building and attaching the nodes underneath the main PurchaseOrder element:

```
//Create the SOAP envelope
org.apache.soap.Envelope envelope = new org.apache.soap.Envelope( );

// create a vector for collecting the body elements
Vector bodyElements = new Vector( );

//obtain the top-level DOM element and place it into the vector
bodyElements.add(doc.getDocumentElement ( ));

//Create the SOAP body element
org.apache.soap.Body body = new org.apache.soap.Body( );
body.setBodyEntries(bodyElements);

//Add the SOAP body element to the envelope
envelope.setBody(body);
```

Now that the envelope is constructed, it needs to be sent to a destination. In Apache SOAP, a Message object performs an asynchronous one-way send:

```
// Build the Message.
org.apache.soap.messaging.Message msg
    = new org.apache.soap.messaging.Message( );

msg.send (new java.net.URL(m_hostURL), URI, envelope);
System.out.println("Sent SOAP Message with Apache HTTP SOAP Client.");
```

The `Message.send( )` method takes three parameters: a URL that represents a destination, a URI that represents the value for the `SOAPAction` header, and the SOAP envelope that we just built. The `SOAPAction` URI is really part of the binding to HTTP. When we ran the example, the value *urn:oreilly-jaws-samples* appeared as part of the HTTP header information that the receiving servlet dumped. Later, we will see how to use the `SOAPAction` to map the request into either an Apache `MessageRouter` service or a `RPCRouter` service. For now, it suffices to say that this URI is used to determine which function or service is invoked when the message reaches its destination.

The `Message` interface is intended for asynchronous one-way communications; `Message.send( )` has a void return value. This value does not preclude it from being used in a two-way synchronous conversation. When the `Message` interface is implemented over a two-way transport protocol, such as HTTP, the `SOAPTransport.receive( )` method can be used to receive a response:

```
// receive response from the transport and dump it to the screen
System.out.println("Waiting for response....");
org.apache.soap.transport.SOAPTransport st = msg.getSOAPTransport ( );
BufferedReader br = st.receive ( );
String line = br.readLine( );
if(line == null)
{
    System.out.println("HTTP POST was successful. \n");
}
else
{
    while (line != null)
    {
        System.out.println (line);
        line = br.readLine( );
    }
}
```

`SOAPTransport.receive( )` blocks and waits for a response from the receiver. In the case of a `SOAPTransport` implemented over HTTP, the `receive( )` method blocks and waits for an error, a timeout on the HTTP request, or even a good return code, such as a "HTTP 1.0 200 OK". It is a good idea to look for a response, even if your application is not expecting anything. In this example, the sender does not expect any application-level response from the sender, but it calls `receive( )` to check for any underlying HTTP errors. In a more serious application, you would probably want to raise an alert when an error occurs and log the unexpected error to a logging service.

That's all you need to do to send a SOAP message—at least for now. We will revisit this example as we go along, building envelope headers dynamically, adding MIME attachments, and moving on to SOAP-RPC. Before we get too far along that path, though, let's become more familiar with our receiver.

The Simple Servlet Receiver

Here's a listing of SimpleHTTPReceive, which is the servlet that received the SOAP message you ran in the first example. So far, this is a plain Java servlet with no knowledge of SOAP, or even of XML; it simply receives the HTTP POST request and dumps out the HTTP headers to the screen, followed by the body of the message:

```java
import java.io.*;
import java.text.*;
import java.util.*;
import javax.servlet.*;
import javax.servlet.http.*;

public class SimpleHTTPReceive extends HttpServlet
{
    // Treat GET requests as errors.
    public void doGet(HttpServletRequest request, HttpServletResponse response)
        throws IOException, ServletException
    {
        System.out.println("Received GET request");
        response.setStatus(HttpServletResponse.SC_BAD_REQUEST);
    }

    // Our SOAP requests are going to be received as HTTP POSTS
    public void doPost(HttpServletRequest request, HttpServletResponse response)
        throws IOException, ServletException
    {
        System.out.println("_____");
        System.out.println("Received request.");
        System.out.println("-----------------------");

        // Traverse the HTTP headers and show them on the screen
        for(Enumeration enum = request.getHeaderNames();
          enum.hasMoreElements(); )
        {
            String header = (String)enum.nextElement();
            String value  = request.getHeader(header);

            System.out.println("  " + header + " = " + value);
        }

        System.out.println("-----------------------");

        // If there is anything in the body of the message,
        // dump it to the screen as well
        if(request.getContentLength() > 0)
        {
            try{
                java.io.BufferedReader reader = request.getReader();
                String line = null;
                while((line = reader.readLine()) != null)
                {
                    System.out.println(line);
                }
```

```
        }
        catch(Exception e)
        {
            System.out.println(e);
        }
    }

    System.out.println("_____");
    // Need this to prevent Apache SOAP from gacking
    response.setContentType("text/xml");
    }
}
```

The Servlet Receiver Becomes SOAP-Aware

While this generic servlet is useful for dumping the contents of an HTTP request, it is not very helpful for SOAP programming. Let's expand on it a bit and explore the SOAP-aware version, HTTPReceive. First, run the example again and direct the output to the HTTPReceive:

```
java SimpleGenericHTTPSoapClient -df ./PO.xml -url
    http://localhost:8080/examples/servlet/HTTPReceive
```

The output in the Tomcat window should be the same as it was before, with an important difference: the information is now being extracted using the inverse of the APIs that were used to construct the message. The SOAP-aware servlet looks exactly like the simple servlet until it gets to the processing of the request content. We start by getting a DocumentBuilder, just as we did in the sender:

```
public class HTTPReceive extends HttpServlet
{
    ...

    public void doPost(HttpServletRequest request, HttpServletResponse response)
        throws IOException, ServletException
    {
        ...

        if(request.getContentLength( ) > 0)
        {
            try
            {
                java.io.BufferedReader reader = request.getReader( );

                // get the document builder
                javax.xml.parsers.DocumentBuilder xdb =
                    org.apache.soap.util.xml.XMLParserUtils.getXMLDocBuilder( );
```

Next, we parse that document into a DOM tree, getting a Document object as the result:

```
                // parse it into a DOM
                org.w3c.dom.Document doc =
```

```
        xdb.parse (new org.xml.sax.InputSource (reader));
    if (doc == null)
    {
        // Error occured
        System.out.println("Doc is null!");
            throw new org.apache.soap.SOAPException
            (org.apache.soap.Constants.FAULT_CODE_CLIENT,
            "parsing error");
    }
    else
    {
```

In the sender, we created an envelope and populated it. In the receiver, we already have an envelope that was sent to us. The SOAP envelope is the outermost element of a SOAP document, and therefore its root element. We could just walk the DOM tree and obtain the envelope and its children directly. However, we choose to use the envelope and its associated interfaces because they help separate the details of the SOAP packaging from the raw processing of the document contents. We obtain an Envelope instance from the document object by calling unmarshall( ), which is a static method of the Envelope class:

```
// call static method to create the envelope from the document
org.apache.soap.Envelope env =
    org.apache.soap.Envelope.unmarshall(
        doc.getDocumentElement( ));
```

Now that we have an envelope, we do the inverse of what we did to populate it: we get the Vector of BodyEntrys from the Envelope and get the Body from the Vector:

```
org.apache.soap.Body body = env.getBody( );
java.util.Vector bodyEntries = body.getBodyEntries( );

java.io.StringWriter writer = new java.io.StringWriter( );
for (java.util.Enumeration e = bodyEntries.elements( );
    e.hasMoreElements( );)
{
    org.w3c.dom.Element el =
    (org.w3c.dom.Element)e.nextElement( );
```

In this case, only one entry, the <PurchaseOrder> element, is in the Vector. Now that we have the PurchaseOrder element, we have a DOM object that is identical to the raw DOM object that we built for *PO.xml* (before it got SOAPified). Since the goal of this example is to write the original XML document to the screen, we call the static method DOM2Writer.serializeAsXML( ). This method serializes the PurchaseOrder element and all of its children into a StringWriter object:

```
    org.apache.soap.util.xml.DOM2Writer.serializeAsXML(
        (org.w3c.dom.Node)el, writer);
    }
    System.out.println(writer.toString( ));
}
}
```

```
        catch(Exception e)
        {
            System.out.println(e);
        }
    }

    System.out.println("_____");

    response.setContentType("text/xml");
    }
}
```

 Apache SOAP provides a more straightforward way to go about this process. It has the notion of a service that can be deployed using a special message router service handler. In that model, a special method signature causes the Envelope object to get passed to the listener directly. We will discuss that model in more detail later. For this introductory example, we thought it would be appropriate to show how to handle the message using the DOM and the Envelope interfaces by themselves, in the event that you work with an infrastructure that is not Tomcat-based.

Adding a Header Block

So far, the construction of the SOAP envelope has relied on reading a file from disk to obtain the XML content and then running that file through a parser to build a DOM tree. That's an acceptable way to deal with the message body if the SOAP layer will interact with a backend system that produces and consumes raw XML documents. However, SOAP documents, or parts of them, need to be built dynamically in many cases. In this example, we construct a SOAP <Header> block dynamically. A SOAP header is not generally intended for application data but for carrying information specific to the SOAP processors that are at either endpoint in the conversation. Therefore, it is the most likely candidate for dynamic construction. To see it in action, run the following command:*

```
java GenericHTTPSoapClient -df ./PO.xml -url
    http://localhost:8080/examples/servlet/SimpleHTTPReceive
```

You should see the following output in the Tomcat servlet window. Note that the header information enclosed by the <SOAP-ENV:Header> tags is not formatted nicely, but it is all there:

```
Received request.
-----------------------
  SOAPAction = "urn:oreilly-jaws-samples"
```

---

* We have removed the word "Simple" from the SimpleGenericHTTPSoapClient sender class. We explicitly tell it to send the message to the SimpleHTTPReceive servlet, which dumps the raw content of the message to the console. We're still using SimpleHTTPReceive because we have not yet told our HTTPReceive servlet how to extract the header.

```
  Host = localhost
  Content-Type = text/xml; charset=utf-8
  Content-Length = 869
-----------------------
<?xml version='1.0' encoding='UTF-8'?>
<SOAP-ENV:Envelope xmlns:SOAP-ENV="http://schemas.xmlsoap.org/soap/envelope/" xm
lns:xsi="http://www.w3.org/1999/XMLSchema-instance" xmlns:xsd="http://www.w3.org
/1999/XMLSchema">
<SOAP-ENV:Header>
<jaws:MessageHeader xmlns:jaws="urn:oreilly-jaws-samples"><From>Me</From><To>You
</To><MessageId>9999</MessageId></jaws:MessageHeader>
</SOAP-ENV:Header>
<SOAP-ENV:Body>
<PurchaseOrder xmlns="urn:oreilly-jaws-samples">
        <shipTo country="US">
                <name>Joe Smith</name>
                <street>14 Oak Park</street>
                <city>Bedford</city>
                <state>MA</state>
                <zip>01730</zip>
        </shipTo>
        <items>
                <item partNum="872-AA">
                        <productName>Candy Canes</productName>
                        <quantity>444</quantity>
                        <price>1.68</price>
                        <comment>I want candy!</comment>
                </item>
        </items>
</PurchaseOrder>
</SOAP-ENV:Body>
</SOAP-ENV:Envelope>
```

Let's examine the code that puts the header there. Here's an excerpt from
GenericHTTPSoapClient. It is identical to its "simple" sibling, with the addition of the
code in sendSoapMessage(). This method reads the *PO.xml* document and parses it,
just as in the previous example:

```
public void sendSOAPMessage()
{
    try
    {
        // get soap body to include in the SOAP envelope
        FileReader fr = new FileReader (m_dataFileName);
        javax.xml.parsers.DocumentBuilder xdb =
            org.apache.soap.util.xml.XMLParserUtils.getXMLDocBuilder();
        org.w3c.dom.Document doc =
            xdb.parse (new org.xml.sax.InputSource (fr));
        if (doc == null) {
            throw new org.apache.soap.SOAPException
                (org.apache.soap.Constants.FAULT_CODE_CLIENT, "parsing error");
        }
```

Next, it creates a Vector for holding the header elements, similar to the way the body elements are handled:

```
// create a vector for collecting the header elements
Vector headerElements = new Vector( );
```

The org.w3c.dom.Document object is used as a factory to create all nodes in the DOM tree. We create a tag with the name MessageHeader, which has its own namespace, using the namespace prefix jaws:. To create this tag, we use createElementNS( ). It takes two parameters: the namespace URI and the qualified name (Qname) of the element:

```
// Create a header element in a namespace
org.w3c.dom.Element headerElement =
    doc.createElementNS("urn:oreilly-jaws-samples",
    "jaws:MessageHeader");
```

The <MessageHeader> element contains three subelements: <From>, <To>, and <MessageId>. An element is created to represent the <From> tag. Another node is created under that tag to represent the text within the tag. The objects Element, Text, and Node are all members of the tree; Element and TextNode both extend Node, which is the base object responsible for the linkage to parents, children, and siblings:

```
// Create subnodes within the MessageHeader
org.w3c.dom.Element ele = doc.createElement("From");
org.w3c.dom.Text textNode = doc.createTextNode("Me");
org.w3c.dom.Node tempNode = ele.appendChild(textNode);

tempNode = headerElement.appendChild(ele);

ele = doc.createElement("To");
textNode = doc.createTextNode("You");
tempNode = ele.appendChild(textNode);

tempNode = headerElement.appendChild(ele);

ele = doc.createElement("MessageId");
textNode = doc.createTextNode("9999");
tempNode = ele.appendChild(textNode);

tempNode = headerElement.appendChild(ele);
```

Now that this subtree is constructed, place it in the document using the Envelope APIs. The APIs for creating the Header and attaching it to the envelope are analogous to the Body APIs that we have already seen:

```
headerElements.add(headerElement);

...

//Create the SOAP envelope
org.apache.soap.Envelope envelope = new org.apache.soap.Envelope( );
```

```
//Add the SOAP header element to the envelope
org.apache.soap.Header header = new org.apache.soap.Header();
header.setHeaderEntries(headerElements);
envelope.setHeader(header);

//Create the SOAP body element
org.apache.soap.Body body = new org.apache.soap.Body();
body.setBodyEntries(bodyElements);
//Add the SOAP body element to the envelope
envelope.setBody(body);

...
}
```

The Apache SOAP Routing Service

Before moving on to the rest of the examples, we need to make a quick note about Apache SOAP's routing and service capability. It's a concept that is likely to be applicable to other SOAP infrastructures you may use in the future. If you have poked around with Apache (or you looked ahead at the rest of the chapter), you may have noticed that many samples use a common URL, which either looks like http://localhost:8080/soap/servlet/messagerouter or http://localhost:8080/soap/servlet/rpcrouter. These special URLs point to Apache's routing and dispatching mechanism. This mechanism looks at the content of the SOAP envelope and decides which class to load and which method to call within that class. Apache refers to this destination as a *service*. The service is registered with the servlet engine in a two-step process. First, an XML deployment descriptor is created, specifying details about the class name of the service, its associated method call, and the target URI. Then a special `org.apache.soap.server.ServiceManagerClient` class is invoked to register the service with Apache SOAP.

Using the RPC router, any Java class and method can be registered as a service; the Apache SOAP infrastructure will call the method with the appropriate parameters. An example of SOAP-RPC can be found in Chapter 4. Using the message router, the method name is the tag name of the body entry in the SOAP envelope, and the method always conforms to the following signature:

```
public void anyMessageMethod(Envelope requestEnvelope,
    SOAPContext requestContext, SOAPContext responseContext)
```

for which *anyMessageMethod* is specified in the deployment descriptor for the service and is also the tag name of the body entry in the SOAP envelope.

The Apache TunnelGui Application

Sending SOAP messages to the `SimpleHTTPReceive` servlet is an excellent way of dumping raw output to the screen. A more convenient way to see the raw output from the sender and the receiver is to use the TunnelGui included with Apache

SOAP. TunnelGui is a simple utility that intercepts the HTTP request, displays it in a window on the screen, and forwards the request to the ultimate destination. It's a great tool for analyzing and debugging problems that have to do with unexpected output. To launch the Apache TunnelGui utility, issue the following command:

```
java org.apache.soap.util.net.TcpTunnelGui 5555 localhost 8080
```

5555 is the port on which TunnelGui listens; 8080 is the port to which it forwards requests (8080 also happens to be the default port for Tomcat). To send a SOAP request through TunnelGui, specify port 5555 instead of 8080 in the destination URL. For example, issue the following command:

```
java GenericHTTPSoapClient -df ./PO.xml -url
    http://localhost:5555/examples/servlet/SimpleHTTPReceive
```

This command displays the expected output in the Tomcat server window and shows the request and response in the TunnelGui window (Figure 3-2).

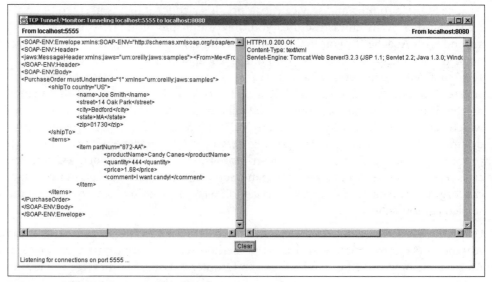

Figure 3-2. The Apache TunnelGui utility

The SOAP-Aware Servlet Becomes a Message Router

In the previous example, we promised to show another way to set up a servlet that passes the SOAP envelope directly to the receiver. To do this, we'll use Apache's message router service. For this example, we can use the GenericHTTPClient without any modifications; simply override the destination URL on the command line:

```
java GenericHTTPSoapClient -url http://localhost:8080/soap/servlet/messagerouter
```

Here's what you should see in the command window for the sender:

```
Starting GenericHTTPSoapClient:
    host url        = http://localhost:8080/soap/servlet/messagerouter
    data file       = ./PO.xml
```

```
Sent SOAP Message with Apache HTTP SOAP Client.
Waiting for response....
<PurchaseOrderResponse>Accepted</PurchaseOrderResponse>
```

In the Tomcat console window, you should see:

```
Received a PurchaseOrder!!

Header==>
<jaws:MessageHeader xmlns:jaws="urn:oreilly:jaws:samples"><From>Me</From><To>You
</To><MessageId>9999</MessageId></jaws:MessageHeader>
Body====>
<PurchaseOrder xmlns="urn:oreilly-jaws-samples">
        <shipTo country="US">
                <name>Joe Smith</name>
                <street>14 Oak Park</street>
                <city>Bedford</city>
                <state>MA</state>
                <zip>01730</zip>
        </shipTo>
        <items>
                <item partNum="872-AA">
                        <productName>Candy Canes</productName>
                        <quantity>444</quantity>
                        <price>1.68</price>
                        <comment>I want candy!</comment>
                </item>
        </items>
</PurchaseOrder>
```

This example works partly because of the information in the deployment descriptor for this service. The class name of the receiver is PurchaseOrderAcceptor. The method name is PurchaseOrder, which is also the name of the main tag in the SOAP body. Here's the deployment descriptor:

```
<isd:service xmlns:isd="http://xml.apache.org/xml-soap/deployment"
             id="urn:oreilly-jaws-samples" type="message">
  <isd:provider type="java" scope="Application"
             methods="PurchaseOrder PurchaseOrderWithAttachment">
    <isd:java class="PurchaseOrderAcceptor"/>
  </isd:provider>
  <isd:faultListener>org.apache.soap.server.DOMFaultListener</isd:faultListener>
</isd:service>
```

If you are going to experiment with creating your own Apache services, remember that the URI represented by the id attribute of the service tag in the deployment descriptor must match the target URI used in the `Message.send( )` call—something that's not obvious from reading the Apache documentation.

Here's a listing of the `PurchaseOrderAcceptor` class and its `PurchaseOrder( )` method. It uses the Envelope, Header, and Body APIs to pick apart the header and body of the message:

```
import org.apache.soap.Envelope;
import org.apache.soap.Constants;
import org.apache.soap.SOAPException;

import org.apache.soap.rpc.SOAPContext;

public class PurchaseOrderAcceptor
{

    public void PurchaseOrder(Envelope requestEnvelope, SOAPContext requestContext,
                              SOAPContext responseContext)
      throws SOAPException
    {
      System.out.println("Received a PurchaseOrder!!");

      java.io.StringWriter writer = new java.io.StringWriter( );

      org.apache.soap.Header header = requestEnvelope.getHeader( );
      java.util.Vector headerEntries = header.getHeaderEntries( );

      writer.write("\nHeader==>\n");
      for (java.util.Enumeration e = headerEntries.elements( ); e.hasMoreElements( );)
      {
          org.w3c.dom.Element el = (org.w3c.dom.Element)e.nextElement( );
          org.apache.soap.util.xml.DOM2Writer.serializeAsXML(
              (org.w3c.dom.Node)el, writer);
      }

      org.apache.soap.Body body = requestEnvelope.getBody( );
      java.util.Vector bodyEntries = body.getBodyEntries( );

      writer.write("\nBody====>\n");
      for (java.util.Enumeration e = bodyEntries.elements( ); e.hasMoreElements( );)
      {
          org.w3c.dom.Element el = (org.w3c.dom.Element)e.nextElement( );
          org.apache.soap.util.xml.DOM2Writer.serializeAsXML(
              (org.w3c.dom.Node)el, writer);
      }
      System.out.println(writer.toString( ));
      try
      {
        //should really be better XML with declaration and namespaces
        responseContext.setRootPart(
          "<PurchaseOrderResponse>Accepted</PurchaseOrderResponse>", "text/xml");
      }
      catch(Exception e)
```

```
    {
      throw new SOAPException(Constants.FAULT_CODE_SERVER,
        "Error writing response", e);
    }
  }
}
```

SOAP with Attachments

While XML and SOAP are very good at describing data, many kinds of application data aren't well-suited for XML—for example, a piece of binary data such as an image, or a CAD file that contains schematic diagrams of parts being ordered electronically. SOAP with Attachments (SwA) was born in recognition of this limitation. SwA combines the SOAP protocol with the MIME format to allow any arbitrary data to be included as part of a SOAP message. The model is exactly the same as the model used for including email attachments.

Parts Is Parts

The MIME protocol allows multiple arbitrary blocks of data to be strung together in a message, with each block separated by a MIME header. The MIME headers delineate where each part begins and the previous part ends. The next example shows what a MIME header looks like. In SwA, the entire message consists of multiple MIME parts; the first part (part 0) is the SOAP envelope, and the remaining parts (1 through n) are the attachments. All parts are wrapped by the underlying protocol, as illustrated by Figure 3-3.

To construct and deconstruct SwA messages, use the Apache SOAP and JavaMail APIs. Before running the example, note that the example archive contains a text file called *attachment.txt*. It is a simple text file that contains the string "This is an attachment." There is also a file called *poWithAttachment.xml* that is identical to *PO.xml*, except that the root level tag is `<PurchaseOrderWithAttachment>`. The other modification we have made is the addition of an element with the name of attachment. This element contains an href attribute:

```
<attachment href="cid:the-attachment"/>
```

This element helps identify the attachment when processing the document. Now run the example from the command line:

```
java GenericHTTPSWAClient -df ./poWithAttachment.xml -at attachment.txt
```

In addition to the purchase order, you should see the following output in the Tomcat console window:

```
Content-ID = the-attachment
The attachment is...
This is an attachment.
```

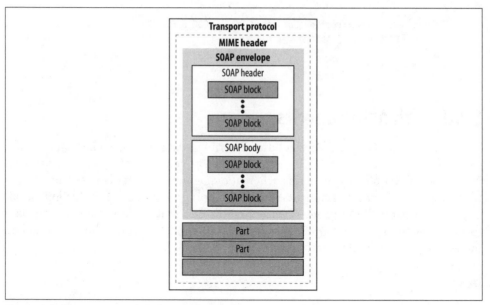

Figure 3-3. The structure of a SOAP with Attachments message

Let's see the raw output from our client by redirecting it at the `SimpleHTTPReceive` servlet. Run the following command:

```
java GenericHTTPSWAClient -url
    http://localhost:8080/examples/servlet/SimpleHTTPReceive
    -df ./poWithAttachment.xml -at attachment.txt
```

You should see the following output:

```
Received request.
-----------------------
  SOAPAction = "urn:oreilly-jaws-samples"
  Host = localhost
  Content-Type = multipart/related; boundary="----=_Part_0_252212802.10059402721
20"; type="text/xml"; start="1730639424.1005940272280.apache-soap.nbchappell3"
  Content-Length = 1283
-----------------------
------=_Part_0_252212802.1005940272120
Content-Type: text/xml; charset=utf-8
Content-Transfer-Encoding: 8bit
Content-ID: <1730639424.1005940272280.apache-soap.nbchappell3>
Content-Length: 869

<?xml version='1.0' encoding='UTF-8'?>
<SOAP-ENV:Envelope xmlns:SOAP-ENV="http://schemas.xmlsoap.org/soap/envelope/" xm
lns:xsi="http://www.w3.org/1999/XMLSchema-instance" xmlns:xsd="http://www.w3.org
/1999/XMLSchema">
<SOAP-ENV:Header>
<jaws:MessageHeader xmlns:jaws="urn:oreilly-jaws-samples"><From>Me</From><To>You
```

```
</To><MessageId>9999</MessageId></jaws:MessageHeader>
</SOAP-ENV:Header>
<SOAP-ENV:Body>
<PurchaseOrder xmlns="urn:oreilly-jaws-samples">
    ... same as before ...
  <attachment href="cid:the-attachment"/>
</PurchaseOrder>
</SOAP-ENV:Body>
</SOAP-ENV:Envelope>

------=_Part_0_252212802.1005940272120
Content-Type: text/plain; charset=us-ascii
Content-Transfer-Encoding: 7bit
Content-ID: the-attachment

This is an attachment.
------=_Part_0_252212802.1005940272120--
```

Note the Content-Type = multipart/related in the HTTP header itself and the individual part boundaries and their associated MIME headers for each of the parts.

Constructing SOAP with Attachments

GenericHTTPSWAClient is identical to GenericHTTPClient, with the addition of the code used to construct the MIME attachments. For that reason, we'll look only at the changes. First, we need an import statement to allow the use of the MimeBodyPart class, which is included in the JavaMail APIs:

```
import javax.mail.internet.MimeBodyPart;
```

Next, there are some parts we won't get into, which relate to parsing the command line for the attachment file and passing the file to the constructor. The SOAP envelope is created and populated as before, complete with the <header> and <body> constructs. The message is created as usual. Here's the additional code for creating a MimeBodyPart object and setting its content as the text that we read from the attachment file:

```
// Build the Message.
org.apache.soap.messaging.Message msg =
new org.apache.soap.messaging.Message();

//Attach any attachments
if(m_attachment != null)
{
    BufferedReader attachmentReader =
    new BufferedReader(new FileReader(m_attachment));
    StringBuffer buffer = new StringBuffer();
    for(String line = attachmentReader.readLine(); line != null;
        line = attachmentReader.readLine())
    {
        buffer.append(line);
    }
```

```
MimeBodyPart attachment = new MimeBodyPart( );
attachment.setText(buffer.toString( ));
```

Next, we need a way for the receiver to reference the attachment. To enable the receiver to dissect the message, we add an element in the XML document with an href value of the-attachment. We use that value for this attachment part's content-id:

```
attachment.setHeader("Content-ID", "the-attachment");
```

Finally, we add the attachment part to the message and send it. Apache SOAP knows that you have added an attachment to the message and formats the message appropriately:

```
        msg.addBodyPart(attachment);
    }

    msg.send (new java.net.URL(m_hostURL), URI, envelope);
    System.out.println("Sent SOAP Message with Apache HTTP SOAP Client.");
```

Receiving the SOAP with Attachments Message

The method PurchaseOrderAcceptor.PurchaseOrderWithAttachment( ) is similar to PurchaseOrderAcceptor.PurchaseOrder( ), with the addition of the MIME code:

```
//import statements
...

public class PurchaseOrderAcceptor
{
...

  public void PurchaseOrderWithAttachment(Envelope requestEnvelope,
                                          SOAPContext requestContext,
                                          SOAPContext responseContext)
    throws SOAPException
  {
    System.out.println("Received a PurchaseOrderWithAttachment!!");

    String cid = null;
    java.io.StringWriter writer = new java.io.StringWriter( );

    // process SOAP header - nothing new here
    ...

    // process SOAP body
    org.apache.soap.Body body = requestEnvelope.getBody( );
    java.util.Vector bodyEntries = body.getBodyEntries( );

    writer.write("\nBody====>\n");
    for (java.util.Enumeration e = bodyEntries.elements( ); e.hasMoreElements( );)
    {
        org.w3c.dom.Element el = (org.w3c.dom.Element)e.nextElement( );
        org.apache.soap.util.xml.DOM2Writer.serializeAsXML(
            (org.w3c.dom.Node)el, writer);
```

Remember the `<attachment href="cid:the-attachment"/>` element that we put into *poWithAttachment.xml*? We now use it to find the attachment. First, we retrieve the `<attachment>` element by name. Then we extract the value of the content-id stored in the href attribute. Once we have the ID, we can use the getBodyPart( ) method on the SOAPContext object to retrieve the MIME attachment by content-id:

```
org.w3c.dom.Element attachmentEl =
    (org.w3c.dom.Element)el.getElementsByTagName("attachment").item(0);
if (attachmentEl != null)
{
    writer.write("\nAttachment==>\n");
    cid = attachmentEl.getAttribute("href").substring(4);//get rid of cid:
    writer.write("Content-ID = "+cid+"\n");
    MimeBodyPart attachment = requestContext.getBodyPart(cid);
    try
    {
        writer.write(
            "The attachment is...\n"+attachment.getContent( )+"\n");
    }catch(Exception ex)
    {
        throw new SOAPException(Constants.FAULT_CODE_SERVER,
            "Error writing response", ex);
    }
}else
    writer.write("The Content-ID is null!\n");
}
System.out.println(writer.toString( ));
...
  }
}
```

Now that we've had a closer look at SOAP and how it structures XML messages and the types of processing it can perform as part of message handling, let's study SOAP more deeply. SOAP message passing is important in its own right (and, as we've already seen, the SOAP specification stresses it's message-passing foundations), but most developers see SOAP as a mechanism for remote procedure call (RPC). In Chapter 4, we'll look at SOAP-RPC in more detail and discuss the Fault mechanism and the MustUnderstand header.

CHAPTER 4

SOAP-RPC, SOAP-Faults, and Misunderstandings

SOAP-RPC

SOAP-RPC defines a model for representing an RPC and an RPC response using the SOAP infrastructure. It is not necessarily bound tightly to a synchronous request/ reply model, or to the HTTP protocol. In fact, both the SOAP 1.1 and 1.2 specifications explicitly state that the use of SOAP-RPC is orthogonal to the protocol binding. The specifications do concede that when SOAP-RPC is bound to HTTP, an RPC invocation maps naturally to an HTTP request, and an RPC return maps naturally to an HTTP response, but this natural mapping is purely coincidental. One of the goals of the SOAP 1.2 effort was to distance itself from the point of view that SOAP is inherently an RPC mechanism. As a result, SOAP-RPC was moved into the optional "Adjuncts" portion of the specification.

That said, what's really important is that SOAP defines a uniform model for representing an RPC and its return value or values. The fundamental requirements for an RPC call are that the body element contains the method name and the parameters and that the parameters are accessible via accessors.* In addition, SOAP has provisions for encoding the method signature, header data, and the URI that represents the destination.

In the next example, we'll look at a SOAP-RPC client that calls a remote service that returns the value of a book at Barnes & Noble. The service is hosted and available at *www.xmethods.net*. Let's start by running the client and examining its output:

```
java GetBookPrice
```

The default settings look up the price of O'Reilly's *Java Message Service*, using its ISBN number.

---

* Accessors as defined in SOAP-encoding. They can be referenced by either a tag or an ordinal value such as an array index.

You should see the following output:

```
Starting GetBookPrice:
    service url    = http://services.xmethods.com:80/soap/servlet/rpcrouter
    ISBN#          = 0596000685
```

```
The price for O'Reilly's The Java Message Service book is 34.95
```

Congratulations! You have just executed a SOAP-RPC invocation over the Internet and received a response with a return value. Let's examine the SOAP messages that just went over the wire and the code that made it happen. To see what the SOAP looks like, we can reroute the transaction to our SimpleHTTPReceiver with this command:

```
java GetBookPrice -url http://localhost:8080/examples/servlet/SimpleHTTPReceive
    -isbn 0596000686
```

You will see the following output in the Tomcat servlet window (we have reformatted some of the output for readability):

```
Received request.
----------------------
  SOAPAction = ""
  Host = localhost
  Content-Type = text/xml; charset=utf-8
  Content-Length = 461
----------------------
<?xml version='1.0' encoding='UTF-8'?>
<SOAP-ENV:Envelope xmlns:SOAP-ENV="http://schemas.xmlsoap.org/soap/envelope/"
    xmlns:xsi="http://www.w3.org/1999/XMLSchema-instance"
    xmlns:xsd="http://www.w3.org/1999/XMLSchema">
<SOAP-ENV:Body>
    <ns1:getPrice xmlns:ns1="urn:xmethods-BNPriceCheck"
      SOAP-ENV:encodingStyle="http://schemas.xmlsoap.org/soap/encoding/">
        <isbn xsi:type="xsd:string">0596000686</isbn>
    </ns1:getPrice>
</SOAP-ENV:Body>
</SOAP-ENV:Envelope>
```

When using SOAP-RPC, the body of the envelope contains the method name and the parameters for the procedure call. In this SOAP message, <ns1:getPrice> is an automatically generated tag that represents the method name. The parameter <isbn> is represented by the type xsd:string and has a value of 0596000686.

The SOAP-Encoding Attribute

SOAP encoding is a set of rules that designates how datatypes are encoded, or serialized, over the wire. In this message, the encodingStyle attribute is set to the value *http://schemas.xmlsoap.org/soap/encoding/*. This particular URL defines the encoding rules based on the schema for SOAP 1.1. If you look at that URL directly, you'll see that it is an actual XML Schema document. Among other things, it defines the xsd: string type used for the <isbn> tag. If this SOAP call used SOAP 1.2, the encodingStyle attribute would be set to *http://www.w3.org/2001/09/soap-encoding*.

The SOAP encoding covers rules for serializing any datatype, ranging from simple scalar types such as int, float, and string, to complex datatypes such as structures, arrays, and sparse arrays.*

SOAP-RPC Method Signatures

The rules for method signatures simply state that the <body> element contains a single SOAP struct. The elements in the struct each have to be referenceable by an accessor. In SOAP, an element with an accessor can be identified directly by a named tag (for example, <isbn>) or by an ordinal value (as in an array value). If multiple parameters exist, they must appear in the same order as they appear in the signature of the receiving method. Finally, the types have to match. If this example used a second parameter, such as a book title, the body might look like this:†

```
<SOAP-ENV:Body>
    <ns1:getPrice xmlns:ns1="urn:xmethods-BNPriceCheck"
      SOAP-ENV:encodingStyle="http://schemas.xmlsoap.org/soap/encoding/">
        <isbn xsi:type="xsd:string">0596000686</isbn>
        <title xsi:type="xsd:string">Java And Web Services</isbn>
    </ns1:getPrice>
</SOAP-ENV:Body>
```

The rules for the response are similar. The response is also a named struct that can contain multiple values. In the SOAP document itself, no direct correlation exists between the request and the response. By convention, the name of the return value should be the same as the name of the request method with the string "Response" appended; for example, getPriceResponse would be the return value for getPrice. However, this role is only a convention, not a requirement. Furthermore, the association between the format of the request and the format of the response is also arbitrary; there is no way to dictate in the request which parameters are [in] parameters and which are [in|out] parameters. As we will see, this deficiency is addressed by WSDL. A WSDL definition can include the complete XML Schema for the request and the response.

SOAP 1.2 imposes two additional rules: the name of the return value accessor is result, and it is namespace-qualified with the namespace identifier http://www.w3.org/2001/09/soap-rpc.

---

* A subset of an array, for which only the "sparsely populated" portions of the array are relevant.

† If you actually try to add a second parameter with the existing service, you may learn about handling SOAP Faults sooner than you think.

The SOAP-RPC Sender—Remote Service

Here's a complete listing of the SOAP-RPC client that we used to look up a book price on Barnes & Noble:

```java
import java.io.*;
import java.util.*;

public class GetBookPrice {

    // default values to be used if not supplied on the command line
    private static final String DEFAULT_SERVICE_URL =
        "http://services.xmethods.com:80/soap/servlet/rpcrouter";
    private static final String DEFAULT_BOOK_ISBN = "0596000685";
    private String m_serviceURL;
    private String m_bookISBN;

    public GetBookPrice (String serviceURL, String bookISBN) throws Exception
    {
        //this section displays the status of the call to the service
        m_serviceURL = serviceURL;
        m_bookISBN   = bookISBN;

        System.out.println();
        System.out.println(
            "_____");
        System.out.println("Starting GetBookPrice:");
        System.out.println("    service url    = " + m_serviceURL);
        System.out.println("    ISBN#          = " + m_bookISBN);
        System.out.println(
            "_____");
        System.out.println();
    }

    public static float sendSoapRPCMessage (String url, String isbn)
                            throws Exception
    {

      //Build the call.
      org.apache.soap.rpc.Call call = new org.apache.soap.rpc.Call ();

      //This service uses standard SOAP encoding
      String encodingStyleURI = org.apache.soap.Constants.NS_URI_SOAP_ENC;
      call.setEncodingStyleURI(encodingStyleURI);

      //Set the target URI
      call.setTargetObjectURI ("urn:xmethods-BNPriceCheck");

      //Set the method name to invoke
      call.setMethodName ("getPrice");

      //Create the parameter objects
      Vector params = new Vector ();
```

```
    params.addElement (new org.apache.soap.rpc.Parameter("isbn",
                          String.class, isbn, null));

    //Set the parameters
    call.setParams (params);

    //Invoke the service
    org.apache.soap.rpc.Response resp = call.invoke (new java.net.URL(url),"");

    //Check the response
    if (resp.generatedFault ()) {
       org.apache.soap.Fault fault = resp.getFault();
       System.err.println("Generated fault: ");
       System.out.println("  Fault Code   = " + fault.getFaultCode());
       System.out.println("  Fault String = " + fault.getFaultString());
       return 0;
    } else {
       org.apache.soap.rpc.Parameter result = resp.getReturnValue ();
       Float FL = (Float) result.getValue();
       return FL.floatValue();
    }
}

public static void main(String args[]) {

    // Argument parsing stuff
    ...

    try
    {
        GetBookPrice soapClient = new GetBookPrice(serviceURL, bookISBN);

        // call method that will perform RPC call using supplied Service
        // url and the book ISBN number to query on
        float f = soapClient.sendSoapRPCMessage(serviceURL, bookISBN);

        // output results of RPC service call
        if (bookISBN != DEFAULT_BOOK_ISBN) {
          System.out.println(
            "The Barnes & Noble price for this book is " + f);
        }else {
          System.out.println(
            "The price for O'Reilly's The Java Message Service book is " + f);
        }

    } catch(Exception e) {
        System.out.println(e.getMessage());
    }
}
...
}
```

Let's examine the code in detail, paying particular attention to the pieces that do the real work. The code starts with several import statements, which import some standard Java packages plus some Apache packages we used for handling the SOAP messages. After the import statements, the class declaration, and some field declarations, we have the constructor—which sets some default parameters and does some runtime reporting:

```java
import java.io.*;
import java.util.*;

public class GetBookPrice {

    // default values to be used if not supplied on the command line
    private static final String DEFAULT_SERVICE_URL =
        "http://services.xmethods.com:80/soap/servlet/rpcrouter";
    private static final String DEFAULT_BOOK_ISBN = "0596000685";
    private String m_serviceURL;
    private String m_bookISBN;

    public GetBookPrice (String serviceURL, String bookISBN) throws Exception
    {
        ...
    }
```

The real workhorse of this application is sendSoapRPCMessage( ). This method builds the SOAP Call object and populates it with the information necessary for remote service. This client calls the Barnes & Noble service and provides it with an ISBN number for a book. The service returns the retail value for that book. In Apache SOAP, the key to making this work is specifying the correct target URI for the call object that the service uses to identify itself. The service creator specifies this value in a deployment descriptor when it registers the service. setMethodName( ) sets the name of the method you want to call; this method must exist in the service referenced in the URN. Finally, the client creates parameter objects for the call. The number of parameters and their types must match the parameters that the service expects:

```java
public static float sendSoapRPCMessage (String url, String isbn)
                        throws Exception
{

    //Build the call.
    org.apache.soap.rpc.Call call = new org.apache.soap.rpc.Call ();

    //This service uses standard SOAP encoding
    String encodingStyleURI = org.apache.soap.Constants.NS_URI_SOAP_ENC;
    call.setEncodingStyleURI(encodingStyleURI);

    //Set the target URI
    call.setTargetObjectURI ("urn:xmethods-BNPriceCheck");

    //Set the method name to invoke
    call.setMethodName ("getPrice");

    //Create the parameter objects
    Vector params = new Vector ();
```

```
params.addElement (new org.apache.soap.rpc.Parameter("isbn",
                       String.class, isbn, null));

//Set the parameters
call.setParams (params);
```

The service is then invoked by calling the Call object's invoke( ) method, passing the URL of the service and the SOAP action, if more than one exists. This RPC call is synchronous, meaning that invoke( ) blocks until a response is returned. When the response is received, sendSoapRPCMessage( ) first checks whether the call returned a SOAP fault. (More information on SOAP faults can be found in the "Error Handling with SOAP Faults" section of this chapter.) If the call was successful, it extracts the return value from the response object and displays it:

```
//Invoke the service
org.apache.soap.rpc.Response resp = call.invoke (new java.net.URL(url),"");

//Check the response
if (resp.generatedFault ( )) {
    org.apache.soap.Fault fault = resp.getFault( );
    System.err.println("Generated fault: ");
    System.out.println("  Fault Code   = " + fault.getFaultCode( ));
    System.out.println("  Fault String = " + fault.getFaultString( ));
    return 0;
} else {
    org.apache.soap.rpc.Parameter result = resp.getReturnValue ( );
    Float FL = (Float) result.getValue( );
    return FL.floatValue( );
}
}
```

Another SOAP-RPC Sender: Local Service

That example was cool. Let's look at how to do the server portion. Unfortunately, we don't have access to the Barnes & Noble's server, so we have to run another RPC example on a local machine so we can watch what's going on. In this example, we'll look at a SOAP-RPC client that calls a local service we deploy using a Tomcat server. The service accepts an item number and returns the stock on hand for that item. Here's a listing of the client, CheckStock:

```
import java.net.*;
import java.util.*;

public class CheckStock {

    private static final String DEFAULT_HOST_URL
        = "http://localhost:8080/soap/servlet/rpcrouter";
    private static final String DEFAULT_ITEM = "Test";
    private static final String URI = "urn:oreilly-jaws-samples";
```

```
//Member variables
private String m_hostURL;
private String m_item;

public CheckStock (String hostURL, String item) throws Exception
{
    m_hostURL = hostURL;
    m_item    = item;
    // print stuff to the console
    ...
}

public void checkStock( ) throws Exception {

  //Build the call.
  org.apache.soap.rpc.Call call = new org.apache.soap.rpc.Call ( );

  //This service uses standard SOAP encoding
  String encodingStyleURI = org.apache.soap.Constants.NS_URI_SOAP_ENC;
  call.setEncodingStyleURI(encodingStyleURI);

  //Set the target URI
  call.setTargetObjectURI ("urn:stock-onhand");

  //Set the method name to invoke
  call.setMethodName ("getQty");

  //Create the parameter objects
  Vector params = new Vector ( );
  params.addElement (new org.apache.soap.rpc.Parameter("item",
                        String.class, m_item, null));

  //Set the parameters
  call.setParams (params);

  //Invoke the service
  org.apache.soap.rpc.Response resp
      = call.invoke ( new java.net.URL(m_hostURL),"urn:go-do-this");

  //Check the response
  if (resp != null) {
    if (resp.generatedFault ()) {
       org.apache.soap.Fault fault = resp.getFault ( );
       System.out.println ("Call failed due to a SOAP Fault: ");
       System.out.println ("  Fault Code   = " + fault.getFaultCode ());
       System.out.println ("  Fault String = " + fault.getFaultString ());
    } else {
       org.apache.soap.rpc.Parameter result = resp.getReturnValue ( );
       Integer intresult = (Integer) result.getValue();
       System.out.println ("The stock-on-hand quantity for this item is: "
           + intresult );
    }
  }
}
```

```
/** Main program entry point. */

public static void main(String args[]) {
    // Command line parsing
    ...

    // Start the CheckStock client
    try
    {
        CheckStock stockClient = new CheckStock(hostURL, item);
        stockClient.checkStock();
    }catch(Exception e){
        System.out.println(e.getMessage());
    }
}
...
}
```

This client is similar to our previous client for looking up book prices, GetBookPrice. Thus, rather than reviewing how to write a simple client, we'll concentrate on the service side of the application.

The SOAP-RPC Service

Here's a listing of the SOAP-RPC service:

```
import java.net.*;
import java.io.*;
import java.util.*;

public class StockQuantity{

  public int getQty (String item)
    throws org.apache.soap.SOAPException {

    int inStockQty = (int)(java.lang.Math.random() * (double)1000);

    return inStockQty;
  }
  // main() for command line testing
  ...
}
```

This program is obviously very simple and doesn't require much explanation. However, you should note the class name and method name. These names are important when you register the service with the server, and in turn when you call the service from the sender. In our case, the class name (StockQuantity) and method name (getQty) are used in the Deployment Descriptor, which describes the service to the Apache SOAP server.

The Deployment Descriptor

Here is a listing of the Deployment Descriptor used to register the service with the server. Use the appropriate server manager to register the Deployment Descriptor:

```
<isd:service xmlns:isd="http://xml.apache.org/xml-soap/deployment"
             id="urn:stock-onhand">
  <isd:provider type="java"
                scope="Application"
                methods="getQty">
    <isd:java class="StockQuantity"/>
  </isd:provider>
  <isd:faultListener>org.apache.soap.server.DOMFaultListener</isd:faultListener>
</isd:service>
```

The Deployment Descriptor contains information that the server needs to call the service successfully, such as the service and provider elements. The service element contains the namespace with which this descriptor is associated (i.e., the namespace that defines the tags used within the descriptor) and the URN used by the service to identify itself to the server. The caller uses this value in the setTargetObjectURI( ) method of the Call object.

The provider element contains information about the type of service, the scope of the service (i.e., Request, Session, or Application), and the methods exposed by the service. In our case, the service is clearly a Java service; we specify Application scope, which means that a single instance of the service class is created when the server starts; and we have only one service exposed and accessible, getQty. Finally, we specify the class name associated with the service. Class location needs to be accessible to the server.

Error Handling with SOAP Faults

SOAP errors are handled using a specialized envelope known as a Fault Envelope. If an error occurs while the server processes a SOAP message, it constructs a SOAP Fault and sends it back to the client. Here's a typical SOAP 1.1 Fault:

```
<?xml version='1.0' encoding='UTF-8'?>
<SOAP-ENV:Envelope xmlns:SOAP-ENV="http://schemas.xmlsoap.org/soap/envelope/" xmlns:
xsi="http://www.w3.org/1999/XMLSchema-instance" xmlns:xsd="http://www.w3.org/1999/
XMLSchema">

<SOAP-ENV:Body>
    <SOAP-ENV:Fault>
        <faultcode>SOAP-ENV:Server</faultcode>
        <faultstring>Test Fault</faultstring>
        <faultactor>/soap/servlet/rpcrouter</faultactor>
        <detail>
            <stackTrace>[SOAPException: faultCode=SOAP-ENV:Server; msg=Test Fault]
            at StockQuantity.getQty(StockQuantity.java:21)
```

```
            at java.lang.reflect.Method.invoke(Native Method)
            at org.apache.soap.server.RPCRouter.invoke(RPCRouter.java:146)
            ...
            at org.apache.tomcat.util.ThreadPool$ControlRunnable.run(
                ThreadPool.java:501)
            at java.lang.Thread.run(Thread.java:498)
        </stackTrace>
        </detail>
     </SOAP-ENV:Fault>
  </SOAP-ENV:Body>
  </SOAP-ENV:Envelope>
```

A SOAP Fault is a special element that must appear as an immediate child of the SOAP body element. The <faultcode> and <faultstring> elements are required. The <faultactor> and <detail> elements are optional. Table 4-1 lists the possible values for the faultcodes and their meanings.

Table 4-1. SOAP faultcodes

Faultcode	Meaning
VersionMismatch	The SOAP node processing the request encountered a version mismatch. The namespace identifier of the SOAP envelope determines version compatibility.
MustUnderstand	An immediate child element of the SOAP header (i.e., <MessageHeader>) contained a MustUnderstand attribute with a setting of true or 1. The SOAP processor was not able to recognize the element or was not capable of processing it.
DTDNotSupported	Introduced in SOAP 1.2 Working Draft 12/17/2001. It is an error for a SOAP 1.2 envelope to contain a DTD.
DataEncodingUnknown	The soapEncodingStyle attribute specified is unknown or not supported. It was also introduced in SOAP 1.2 WD 12/17/2001.
Client	The content generated by the client is incorrect or malformed. Therefore, resending the same data will result in the same error. In SOAP 1.2, this fault is being changed to Sender.
Server	The content sent by the client is perfectly acceptable, but the SOAP processor is unable to process it for some reason, such as an unavailable service. Resending the message at a later time could result in success. In SOAP 1.2, this fault is being changed to Receiver.

The body and Fault elements are namespace-qualified to the envelope's namespace—for example, <SOAP-ENV:body> and <SOAP-ENV:Fault>. The <faultcode> element uses the local namespace (it has no namespace prefix), and the <faultcode> value that the element contains is a qualified name using the envelope's namespace—for example, <faultcode>SOAP-ENV:Client</faultcode>.

The SOAP Fault from the previous listing was achieved by making a slight modification to the StockQuantity service. In Apache SOAP, having the service throw an exception is all that's needed to generate a fault; Apache takes care of the rest:

```
public class StockQuantity{

  public int getQty (String item)
    throws org.apache.soap.SOAPException {
```

```
    int inStockQty = (int)(java.lang.Math.random( ) * (double)1000);

    if (item.equalsIgnoreCase("Fail"))
        throw new org.apache.soap.SOAPException
        (org.apache.soap.Constants.FAULT_CODE_SERVER,
                "Test Fault");

    return inStockQty;
    }
...
}
```

In Apache SOAP 2.2, this code is all that is necessary to send a complete SOAP 1.1 Fault message back to the sender. To view the full output of the Fault message, redirect the CheckStock RPC call through the TunnelGui utility by using the command:

```
java CheckStock -url http://localhost:5555/soap/servlet/rpcrouter -item Fail
```

In this command, 5555 is the port on which the TunnelGui is listening. The RPC request and the corresponding SOAP Fault can be viewed in the TunnelGui window, as shown in Figure 4-1.

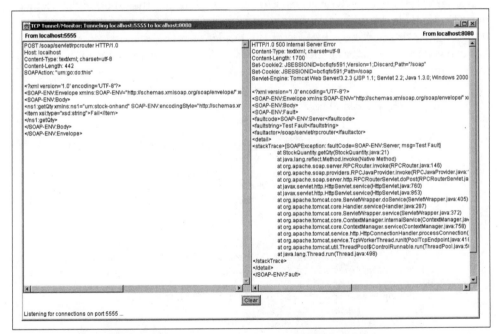

Figure 4-1. A SOAP Fault viewed through the Apache TunnelGui utility

The sending client can trap the Fault programatically and take appropriate action. Apache SOAP has a Fault object that can be used to access the pieces of the Fault message, as indicated in this excerpt from CheckStock:

```
//Invoke the service
Response resp = call.invoke (url,"urn:go-do-this");
```

```
            //Check the response
            if (resp != null) {
                if (resp.generatedFault ()) {
                    Fault fault = resp.getFault ();
                    System.out.println ("Call failed due to a SOAP Fault: ");
                    System.out.println ("  Fault Code   = " + fault.getFaultCode ());
                    System.out.println ("  Fault String = " + fault.getFaultString ());
```

While the ability to generate a fault by throwing an exception is handy, you may want more control over what goes into a fault message. For example, Apache SOAP, by default, puts the current stacktrace into the <detail> element of the SOAP fault. That may not be what you want. We will explore how to build your own Fault message in the context of the mustUnderstand attribute.

Soap Faults and the mustUnderstand Attribute

To appreciate the meaning and role of the mustUnderstand or misUnderstood fault codes, one must first understand the intent of the mustUnderstand attribute. This attribute can be placed in any top-level header element. The presence of the mustUnderstand attribute with a value of true or 1 means that the header element must be recognizable by the receiving SOAP processor. If the SOAP processor does not recognize or know how to process the header element, it must generate a Fault. We can generate a header element with a mustUnderstand attribute by adding the following line of code to our GenericHTTPSoapClient:

```
            // Create a header element in a namespace
            org.w3c.dom.Element headerElement =
                doc.createElementNS(URI,"jaws:MessageHeader");

            headerElement.setAttributeNS(URI,"SOAP-ENV:mustUnderstand","1");

            // Create subnodes within the MessageHeader
            org.w3c.dom.Element ele = doc.createElement("From");
            org.w3c.dom.Text textNode = doc.createTextNode("Me");
```

This code creates a SOAP envelope that looks like this:

```
        <SOAP-ENV:Envelope xmlns:SOAP-ENV="http://schemas.xmlsoap.org/soap/envelope/"
            xmlns:xsi="http://www.w3.org/1999/XMLSchema-instance"
            xmlns:xsd="http://www.w3.org/1999/XMLSchema">
        <SOAP-ENV:Header>
            <jaws:MessageHeader xmlns:jaws="urn:http://oreilly/jaws/samples"
                SOAP-ENV:MustUnderstand="1" >
                <From>Me</From>
                <To>You</To>
                <MessageId>9999</MessageId>
                ...
            </jaws:MessageHeader>
        </SOAP-ENV:Header>
        <SOAP-ENV:Body>
```

```
...
</SOAP-ENV:Body>
</SOAP-ENV:Envelope>
```

This envelope requires the server to understand the <MessageHeader> element. Since the server doesn't understand these elements, it returns a SOAP 1.1 Fault message:

```
<?xml version='1.0' encoding='UTF-8'?>

<SOAP-ENV:Envelope xmlns:SOAP-ENV="http://schemas.xmlsoap.org/soap/envelope/" xmlns:
xsi="http://www.w3.org/1999/XMLSchema-instance" xmlns:xsd="http://www.w3.org/1999/
XMLSchema">
    <SOAP-ENV:Body>
        <SOAP-ENV:Fault>
        <faultcode>SOAP-ENV:MustUnderstand</faultcode>
        <faultstring>Unsupported header: jaws:MessageHeader</faultstring>
        <faultactor>/examples/servlet/FaultServlet</faultactor>
        </SOAP-ENV:Fault>
    </SOAP-ENV:Body>
</SOAP-ENV:Envelope>
```

The code used to generate this fault is in the following listing of the FaultServlet class. FaultServlet is a variation of our HTTPReceive class. As part of the header's processing, we look for the existence of a mustUnderstand attribute:

```
public class FaultServlet extends HttpServlet
{
...

    public void doPost(HttpServletRequest request, HttpServletResponse response)
        throws IOException, ServletException
    {
    ...
        // Get the header and check it for mustunderstand
        Header header = env.getHeader();
        java.util.Vector headerEntries = header.getHeaderEntries();

        screenWriter.write("\nHeader==>\n");
        for (java.util.Enumeration e = headerEntries.elements();
                    e.hasMoreElements();)
        {
            org.w3c.dom.Element el = (org.w3c.dom.Element)e.nextElement();
            org.apache.soap.util.xml.DOM2Writer.serializeAsXML(
              (org.w3c.dom.Node)el, screenWriter);

        // process mustUnderstand
            String mustUnderstand=
                    el.getAttributeNS(Constants.NS_URI_SOAP_ENV,
                "mustUnderstand");
            screenWriter.write("\nMustUnderstand: "
             + mustUnderstand + "\n");

            String tagName = el.getTagName();
            screenWriter.write("Tag Name: " + tagName + "\n");
```

FaultServlet doesn't support the <MessageHeader> tag; it supports only the <IOnlyUnderstandThis> tag. Therefore, we must generate a fault when it sees the message header tag combined with the mustUnderstand attribute. To construct the fault, we create a SOAPException and use it to create a new Fault object:

```
if(!tagName.equalsIgnoreCase("IOnlyUnderstandThis"))
{
    //generate a fault.
    screenWriter.write("Unsupported header: " + tagName + "\n");
    screenWriter.write("Generating Fault....\n");
    SOAPException se =
    new SOAPException(Constants.FAULT_CODE_MUST_UNDERSTAND,
            "Unsupported header: " + tagName);
    Fault fault = new Fault(se);
    fault.setFaultActorURI (request.getRequestURI ());

    String respEncStyle = Constants.NS_URI_SOAP_ENC;
```

Next, we create a Response object and supply it with the Fault object that we created:

```
org.apache.soap.rpc.Response soapResponse =
new org.apache.soap.rpc.Response (
        null,          // targetObjectURI
        null,          // methodName
        fault,
        null,          // params
        null,          // headers
        respEncStyle, // encodingStyleURI
        null);         // SOAPContext
```

Finally, we create an Envelope from the Response object and marshall it into the PrintWriter attached to the servlet's HTTPResponse:

```
Envelope faultEnvelope = soapResponse.buildEnvelope();

org.apache.soap.encoding.SOAPMappingRegistry smr
    = new org.apache.soap.encoding.SOAPMappingRegistry();

PrintWriter resW = response.getWriter();

faultEnvelope.marshall(resW, smr,
    soapResponse.getSOAPContext());
response.setContentType(request.getContentType());
response.setStatus(response.SC_INTERNAL_SERVER_ERROR);
    ...
}
}
```

Note that in the SOAP 1.2 effort, there has been much debate over whether mustUnderstand also means "MustExecute" or "MustProcess."

SOAP 1.2 clarifies the use of the SOAP header in Fault processing. The general idea is that the body of a Fault message should contain only the errors that resulted from processing the body of the message that caused the Fault. Likewise, detailed information about any errors that occur as the result of processing a header block should be placed in the header block of the resulting Fault message. The <Fault> and <Faultcode> elements still appear in the body. However, the <Misunderstood> element in the header carries detailed information about which header element could not be recognized.

The SOAP 1.2 Fault message (generated from not being able to understand the <MessageHeader> element in our previous example) would look like this:

```
<env:Envelope xmlns:env='http://www.w3.org/2001/09/soap-envelope'
        xmlns:f='http://www.w3.org/2001/09/soap-faults' >
    <env:Header>
        <f:misunderstood qname="jaws:MessageHeader"
            xmlns:jaws="urn:http://oreilly/jaws/samples" />
    </env:Header>
    <env:Body>
        <env:Fault>
                    <faultcode>env:mustUnderstand</faultcode>
                    <faultstring>
                One or more mandatory headers not understood
            </faultstring>
            </env:Fault>
    </env:Body>
</env:Envelope>
```

SOAP 1.2 adds an additional set of fault codes. These RPC fault codes use the new namespace identifier *http://www.w3.org/2001/09/soap-rpc* with the namespace prefix of *rpc:*. The new codes are listed in Table 4-2.

Table 4-2. SOAP 1.2 RPC fault codes

Fault code	Meaning
rpc:ProcedureNotPresent	The server can't find the specified procedure.
rpc:BadArguments	The server can't parse the arguments (or the arguments don't match what the server is expecting for the procedure call).
env:DataEncodingUnknown	The encodingStyle attribute contained in either the header or body is not supported.

SOAP Intermediaries and Actors

The world of interapplication communication usually involves more than two parties talking with one another in a point-to-point fashion. A SOAP envelope that represents a business transaction may move from place to place as it goes through the various stages of a business process. Each stage in a multihop process may act upon the envelope, modify its contents, and route it along to the next step in a process.

Recognizing that messages may take many hops as they travel from the sender to their final destination, SOAP defines a Message Exchange Model. As illustrated in Figure 4-2, this model defines terminology and roles such as SOAP Node, Intermediary, Actor, the initial SOAP sender, and the ultimate receiver. A node is any object or process performing any of these roles. An intermediary is any node that sits between the initial SOAP sender and the ultimate receiver. An actor is any node that receives a SOAP envelope for processing and can be either an intermediary or the ultimate receiver.

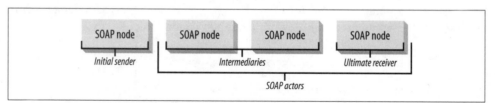

Figure 4-2. Multihop processing terminology

The actor attribute may be used to specify which blocks of information are intended for each step in the process. Each node in a multihop process is responsible for digesting and interpreting the meaning of the actor attribute for each SOAP block and possibly re-inserting it into the SOAP block and forwarding it on to the next node for processing. Any SOAP receiver that encounters a header block without an actor attribute, or an actor attribute equivalent to the special URI *http://www.w3. org/2001/09/soap-envelope/actor/next*, has to interpret that header block as being intended for it (the current SOAP node). If the current SOAP node cannot fulfill the mustUnderstand requirements, it must generate a SOAP Fault.

An actor attribute with the special value of *http://www.w3.org/2001/09/soap-envelope/actor/none* indicates that this header is not targeted at anything in particular. This indication is useful for sharing header information across multiple nodes.

Note on URIs, URNs, and URLs

There's a lot of confusion about URIs, URNs, and URLs, which are seemingly similar concepts used throughout web services and are gradually infiltrating Internet programming in general. In 2001, the W3C published a document that attempts to clarify these three commonly misused acronyms. The full document can be found at *http://www.w3.org/TR/2001/NOTE-uri-clarification-20010921/*.

1 URI Partitioning

There is some confusion in the web community over the partitioning of URI space, specifically, the relationship among the concepts of URL, URN, and URI. The confusion owes to the incompatibility between two different views of URI partitioning, which we call the "classical" and "contemporary" views.

1.1 Classical View

During the early years of discussion of web identifiers (early to mid 90s), people assumed that an identifer type would be cast into one of two (or possibly more) classes. An identifier might specify the location of a resource (a URL) or its name (a URN) independent of location. Thus a URI was either a URL or a URN. There was discussion about generalizing this by addition of a discrete number of additional classes; for example, a URI might point to metadata rather than the resource itself, in which case the URI would be a URC (citation). URI space was thus viewed as partitioned into subspaces: URL and URN, and additional subspaces, to be defined. The only such additional space ever proposed was URC and there never was any buy-in; so without loss of generality it's reasonable to say that URI space was thought to be partitioned into two classes: URL and URN. Thus for example, "*http:*" was a URL scheme, and "*isbn:*" would (someday) be a URN scheme. Any new scheme would be cast into one or the other of these two classes.

1.2 Contemporary View

Over time, the importance of this additional level of hierarchy seemed to lessen; the view became that an individual scheme does not need to be cast into one of a discrete set of URI types such as "URL", "URN", "URC", etc. Web-identifer schemes are in general URI schemes; a given URI scheme may define subspaces. Thus "*http:*" is a URI scheme. "*urn:*" is also a URI scheme; it defines subspaces, called "namespaces". For example, the set of URNs of the form "*urn:isbn:n-nn-nnnnnn-n*" is a URN namespace. ("*isbn*" is an URN namespace identifier. It is not a "URN scheme" nor a "URI scheme").

Further according to the contemporary view, the term "URL" does not refer to a formal partition of URI space; rather, URL is a useful but informal concept: a URL is a type of URI that identifies a resource via a representation of its primary access mechanism (e.g., its network "location"), rather than by some other attributes it may have. Thus as we noted, "*http:*" is a URI scheme. An http URI is a URL. The phrase "URL scheme" is now used infrequently, usually to refer to some subclass of URI schemes which exclude URNs.

1.3 Confusion

The body of documents (RFCs, etc.) covering URI architecture, syntax, registration, etc., spans both the classical and contemporary periods. People who are well-versed in URI matters tend to use "URL" and "URI" in ways that seem to be interchangable. Among these experts, this isn't a problem. But among the Internet community at large, it is. People are not convinced that URI and URL mean the same thing, in documents where they (apparently) do. When one sees an RFC that talks about URI schemes (e.g., *[RFC 2396]*), another that talks about URL schemes (e.g., *[RFC 2717]*), and yet another that talks of URN schemes (*[RFC 2276]*) it is natural to wonder what's the difference, and how they relate to one another. While RFC 2396 1.2 attempts to address the distinction between URIs, URLs and URNs, it has not been successful in clearing up the confusion.

We hope this clears it up for everyone. The summarized description that we feel is generally acceptable in the industry is this:

A Universal Resource Identifier (URI) is a generic representation that can either be a Universal Resource Locator (URL) or a Universal Resource Name (URN). A URL is something that represents a physical network location and contains things that pertain to a particular protocal, such as *http://* or *ftp://*. A URN is something that does not necessarily resolve to any physical location; generally, it is intended to be used to identify something uniquely, such as a SOAP action or a namespace.

CHAPTER 5
Web Services Description Language

In the previous two chapters, we talked extensively about SOAP and the structure it delivers to web services. Not surprisingly, the adoption of SOAP's messaging formats brought about a need to describe operational information in an equally structured way. WSDL was introduced to address this need.

WSDL is an XML grammar for describing a web service as a collection of access endpoints* capable of exchanging messages in a procedure- or document-oriented fashion. A WSDL document is a recipe used to automate the details involved in application-to-application communication.

On one level, WSDL is not that different from CORBA IDL or Microsoft IDL. They are all used to define the interfaces (method signatures) and datatypes for a discreet piece of programming logic.

On another level, WSDL is an altogether different beast, offering a degree of extensibility that has no parallel in the IDL specification. This extensibility allows WSDL to be used to:

- Describe endpoints and their messages, regardless of the message format or network protocol used to exchange them.
- Treat messages as abstract descriptions of the data being exchanged.
- Treat port types as abstract collections of a web services' operations. A port type can then be mapped to a concrete protocol and data format.

If you are feeling a bit dazed after reading these bullet items, it's just the WSDL specification talking! We'll offer fewer "scientific" definitions as we go along; don't let the terms scare you away from this technology.

---

* URLs to which service requests are sent.

Introduction to WSDL

As the number of communication formats and protocols used on the Internet continues to increase, finding a standard way of describing how two machines should communicate with one another has become increasingly important. WSDL describes what a service does, how to invoke its operations, and where to find it. WSDL has created separate definitions and terminology for defining a web service, the communication endpoint where that web service exists, the legal format for input and output messages for the web service, and an abstract way to declare a binding to a concrete protocol and data format.

Everything defined within a WSDL file is abstract: it's just the definition of parameters and constraints for how communication should occur at runtime. The web service implementation has to adhere to the guidelines defined in the WSDL file but has some flexibility over specifics. WSDL also provides the ability to define a *binding* that attaches an abstract set of message definitions to a concrete protocol or data format. A *binding extension* is a type of binding defined for a major protocol. WSDL defines out-of-the-box binding extensions for SOAP 1.1, HTTP GET, HTTP POST, and MIME.

How a Service Description Begets Code

Since WSDL is just an abstract description of a web service's interface, it is conceivable that implementation code can be generated from a WSDL definition and that WSDL definitions can be created automatically from existing implementation code. From a programming perspective, using WSDL to generate code is one of its biggest values. Methods of generating WSDL from existing components have also been discovered. Both techniques are a boon to developers and nondevelopers alike and lend credibility to the notion of truly dynamic computing models.

The question that developers have to ask, however, is what they are going to build first. Will you build the service implementation first and then generate the interfaces automatically? Will you create the WSDL for a web service and then use a tool to create the matching J2EE base components necessary to implement the web service?

We feel that the model that will resonate most with developers is one that focuses on creating a web service and a specified set of input methods. Developers will create an implementation and make sure it works correctly; tools then take the basic implementation and generate WSDL files automatically. Most tools on the market today are capable of doing this. For example, Cape Clear's CapeConnect allows you to create a web service; it generates the WSDL automatically. BEA's WebLogic Server 6.1 allows you to create an EJB or a JMS Destination and provides Ant scripts to create the WSDL associated with the implementations. Sonic Software's SonicXQ allows you to generate WSDL that is mapped to various services, or endpoints, which could represent JMS destinations, calls to WebLogic EJB Server, or a J2EE

Connector. Other available industry tools available for working with WSDL include Systinet WASP, The Mind Electic's GLUE, and IBM's Web Services Toolkit.

Integration between Java and WSDL is discussed in more depth at the end of this chapter.

Anatomy of a WSDL Document

Let's take a detailed look at the individual parts of a WSDL document. The following code shows the major elements that may appear in a WSDL document. An asterisk (*) next to an element indicates that more than one of these elements may appear. Elements from WSDL binding extensions (i.e., SOAP, HTTP, etc.) were not included here, to keep things simpler:

```
<definitions>
    <import>*
    <types>
        <schema></schema>*
    </types>
    <message>*
        <part></part>*
    </message>
    <PortType>*
        <operation>*
            <input></input>
            <output></output>
            <fault></fault>*
        </operation>
    </PortType>
    <binding>*
        <operation>*
            <input></input>
            <output></output>
        </operation>
    </binding>
    <service>*
        <port></port>*
    </service>
</definitions>
```

In the next few sections, we define each of the major WSDL elements and present a real-life example as part of the explanation. Finding a WSDL file sophisticated enough to cover the various facets of the specification while still remaining readable was not simple. The following sections present the WSDL document that defines a web service for the translation of the Z39.50 ASN.1 specification. Z39.50/XER (XML Encoding Rules) allows information described in ASN.1 to be carried in XML. It describes the datatypes and operations that one would need to perform real-time conversions between ASN.1-encoded data structures and XML-encoded data structures.

The *ez3950-PortTypes.wsdl* file in the examples directory contains the WSDL for this example. This file also depends upon *ez3950.xsd*, which is in the same directory.

<definitions> Element

The <definitions> element in a WSDL document acts as a container for the service description. It provides a place to do global declarations of namespaces that are intended to be visible throughout the rest of the document. Here is the <definitions> element from the XML Encoding Rules. Note that some of the namespaces defined in this element have prefixes (xsd, soap, soapenc, xer, etc.), and some do not. These prefixes are bound to a particular namespace but do not govern which schemas are actually available to a schema processor:

```
<definitions
    targetNamespace="urn:3950"
    xmlns="http://schemas.xmlsoap.org/wsdl/"
    xmlns:xsd="http://www.w3.org/2001/XMLSchema"
    xmlns:soap="http://schemas.xmlsoap.org/wsdl/soap/"
    xmlns:soapenc="http://schemas.xmlsoap.org/soap/encoding/"
    xmlns:tns="urn:3950"
>
```

What's an XML Namespace?

If you aren't familiar with the concept of an XML namespace, just think of it as a name that qualifies element and attribute names. Most XML grammars used in the web services technology stack have an XML Schema (*.xsd*) document that governs the elements and attributes used in them, their datatypes, and valid values. A namespace provides an alias (code name) to use within the current XML document for referring to the rules defined in a separate XML Schema document.

A namespace is used as a qualifier for tags. For example, if two XML Schema documents each define the <car> tag with different subelements, how would an XML file that uses both schemas know which <car> definition to refer to? The namespace alias is used as a prefix to qualify an XML tag as coming from a particular XML Schema document. For example, the <car> tag might be modified to be <ford:car> (to indicate that the <car> tag definition that is valid is the one defined in the XML Schema document with the ford alias).

A namespace definition is valid for the element it is defined in and for all subelements. Subelements can have additional or overriding namespace definitions.

Are the addresses specified in these namespace URIs real? Some of them are and some of them are not. It's a common practice to post the XML Schema document that the namespace URI refers to at the real URL. Many organizations don't follow this practice, however. Namespaces frequently contain URIs that are just references to XML Schema documents that aren't located on the Internet. Connect to the Internet and try entering *http://schemas.xmlsoap.org/wsdl/soap/* in your browser. If you use Internet Explorer 5, you should see the XML Schema document for the SOAP binding extension for WSDL. Can you get the XML schema for all namespace URIs?

The `targetNamespace` attribute of the `<definitions>` element defines the namespace definition that this document is creating. This attribute is used in lieu of the name attribute on the `<definitions>` element. The target namespace creates a new, unique identifier within which any types or abstract definitions defined by the document fall. The default namespace allows you to use tags without prepending the namespace alias to the beginning of the tag. The URI for the `targetNamspace` attribute must be an absolute reference, not a relative one. Here, *http://asf.gils.net/xer* is specified as the target and *http://schemas.xmlsoap.org/wsdl/* is used as the default namespace.

Given this description, keep the following issues in mind when working with namespaces:

- A namespace is qualified in an XML document through a QNAME. The QNAME is the value following `xmlns:` in an XML document. It is a value used to qualify an element within the XML document. If two elements imported from different namespaces have the same name, they are qualified by using the QNAME followed by a colon.

- The default namespace used on elements (also known as the default qualifier) is the namespace that follows the `xmlns=` attribute in an XML definition. If two conflicting elements come from different namespaces, the element defined in the namespace identified by `xmlns=` is used.

- The `targetNamespace` creates a unique identifier of the namespace created in the WSDL document. Since the WSDL document defines new elements and attributes, the value of this attribute is the identifier given to the namespace to which those elements belong.

- It is common practice to further qualify the target namespace by creating a QNAME named `tns` that points to the same value of `targetNamespace`. Thus, `targetNamespace` creates a new namespace, and `tns` becomes the QNAME for identifying "this namespace" within the same WSDL document.

Table 5-1 lists the namespace prefixes and URIs that you'll see most frequently in WSDL documents. Of course, many namespaces aren't listed in this table.

Table 5-1. Common namespace prefixes

Prefix	Namespace URI	Synopsis
wsdl	*http://schemas.xmlsoap.org/wsdl/*	Namespace of WSDL grammar.
soap	*http://schemas.xmlsoap.org/wsdl/soap/*	Namespace of WSDL extension binding for SOAP message.
http	*http://schemas.xmlsoap.org/wsdl/http/*	Namespace of WSDL extension binding HTTP protocol.

Table 5-1. Common namespace prefixes (continued)

Prefix	Namespace URI	Synopsis
mime	*http://schemas.xmlsoap.org/wsdl/mime/*	Namespace of WSDL extension binding for MIME protocol.
soapenc	*http://schemas.xmlsoap.org/soap/encoding/*	Namespace of schema governing SOAP 1.1 encoding.
soapenv	*http://schemas.xmlsoap.org/soap/envelope/*	Namespace of schema governing SOAP 1.1 envelopes.
xsi	*http://www.w3.org/2000/10/XMLSchema-instance*	Namespace of schema governing XML Schema instances. An instance is an XML document that conforms to a given XML Schema (.*xsd*) file.
xsd	*http://www.w3.org/2000/10/XMLSchema*	Namespace of schema governing XML Schema (.*xsd*) files.
tns	(application or context-dependent)	Namespace convention used to refer to the current WSDL document. The prefix is an acronym for "this namespace." Assigning the targetNamespace value to this prefix is customary.

\<import> Element

After the \<definitions> element, we see an \<import> element:

```
<definitions
    targetNamespace="urn:3950"
    xmlns="http://schemas.xmlsoap.org/wsdl/"
    xmlns:xsd="http://www.w3.org/2001/XMLSchema"
    xmlns:soap="http://schemas.xmlsoap.org/wsdl/soap/"
    xmlns:soapenc="http://schemas.xmlsoap.org/soap/encoding/"
    xmlns:tns="urn:3950"
>
    <import namespace="http://asf.gils.net/xer"
            location="http://asf.gils.net/xer/ez.xsd"/>
```

The \<import> element serves a purpose similar to the #include directive in the C/C++ programming language. It lets you separate the elements of a service definition into independent documents and include them in the main document, where appropriate. Effective use of the \<import> element promotes the modularization of WSDL documents and creates an environment of reuse that can create clear service definitions. WSDL documents structured in this way are easier to use and maintain, but require any WSDL parsing engine to perform additional I/O operations to import any externally referenced resource. You can have zero or more \<import> elements.

The \<import> element imports the namespace of another file, not the file itself. Elements in an XML file are identified by a namespace declaration. A namespace declaration can occur at any element in the file and then applies for any subelements, assuming that an overriding namespace isn't applied. When an \<import> statement is used, all elements for that given namespace are included at the location of the \<import> element in the parent document.

In the *ez3950-PortTypes.wsdl* file that we have provided, an \<import> tag is used to include information located in another XML file. In this case, the \<import> tag imports the file located at *http://asf.gils.net/xer/ez.xsd*. Even though this file is local, the WSDL file is placed on the Internet, so it is important to provide an absolute URL for the location of the imported file. The *ez.xsd* file is located in the examples directory and contains the schema definitions required for this WSDL file. The schema definitions are further defined in the next section.

<types> Element

The <types> element in a WSDL document acts as a container for defining the datatypes used in <message> elements. <message> elements define the format of messages interchanged between a client and a web service. Currently, XML Schema Definitions (XSD) is the most widely used data typing method, but WSDL allows the inclusion of other XML typing approaches.

For the most part, a study of the <types> element is a study of XML Schema. The <types> element has zero or more <schema> subelements, which must follow the rules for XML Schema documents. The <schema> element of our WSDL document is surprisingly simple, but long.

If you look at the *ez3950-PortTypes.wsdl* file provided in this chapter, a <types> element is not included. Rather, the schema definitions required for the WSDL document are included via the <import> element. What is interesting is that if you look at the *ez3950.xsd* file, that file does not have a <types> element. Since the namespace being imported is a schema definition, the WSDL parser automatically understands that the included elements must be included as part of the <types> definition. The <types> section listed here appears as it would if the <import> statement did not exist in the WSDL document and the WSDL contained all schema definitions inline.

The <types> section is presented in several portions to illustrate some of the different kinds of syntax available with XML Schema. XML Schema can be very complex. This chapter provides some rudimentary explanations of XML Schema notation, but we're assuming that you already have a basic understanding of what XML Schemas are and how they work. We start with the <type> tag itself, followed by the definition of a single complex type:

```
<types>
  <xsd:schema xmlns:xsd="http://www.w3.org/2001/XMLSchema">
    <xsd:element name="PDU" type="PDU"/>
      <xsd:complexType name="PDU">
        <xsd:choice>
          <xsd:element name="initRequest" type="InitializeRequest" />
          <xsd:element name="initResponse" type="InitializeResponse" />
          <xsd:element name="searchRequest" type="SearchRequest" />
          <xsd:element name="searchResponse" type="SearchResponse" />
          <xsd:element name="presentRequest" type="PresentRequest" />
          <xsd:element name="presentResponse" type="PresentResponse" />
          <xsd:element name="deleteResultSetRequest"
            type="DeleteResultSetRequest" />
          <xsd:element name="deleteResultSetResponse"
            type="DeleteResultSetResponse" />
```

```
            <xsd:element name="accessControlRequest"
                type="AccessControlRequest" />
            <xsd:element name="accessControlResponse"
                type="AccessControlResponse" />
            <xsd:element name="resourceControlRequest"
                type="ResourceControlRequest" />
            <xsd:element name="resourceControlResponse"
                type="ResourceControlResponse" />
            <xsd:element name="triggerResourceControlRequest"
                type="TriggerResourceControlRequest" />
            <xsd:element name="resourceReportRequest"
                type="ResourceReportRequest" />
            <xsd:element name="resourceReportResponse"
                type="ResourceReportResponse" />
            <xsd:element name="scanRequest" type="ScanRequest" />
            <xsd:element name="scanResponse" type="ScanResponse" />
            <xsd:element name="sortRequest" type="SortRequest" />
            <xsd:element name="sortResponse" type="SortResponse" />
            <xsd:element name="segmentRequest" type="Segment" />
            <xsd:element name="extendedServicesRequest"
                type="ExtendedServicesRequest" />
            <xsd:element name="extendedServicesResponse"
                type="ExtendedServicesResponse" />
            <xsd:element name="close" type="Close" />
        </xsd:choice>
    </xsd:complexType>
```

XML Schema is a language used to define the structure and restrictions for new elements and attributes. New elements are defined through the <simpleType> and
<complexType> elements. A <simpleType> defines the format of a single element, while
<complexType> defines an element with subelements. The <xsd:complexType> element
(which starts at the fourth line of the preceding code) defines a complex datatype that
uses a <choice> model group. This model group ensures that the value assigned to an
instance of this datatype corresponds to exactly one of the possible values for it.

The next element, <xsd:simpleType>, defines a simple datatype that represents an
enumeration. It starts with the definition of a predefined schema datatype, xsd:
string, and then restricts the behavior to a form that meets our needs:

```
        <xsd:simpleType name="KnownProximityUnit">
            <xsd:restriction base="xsd:string">
                <xsd:enumeration value="character" />
                <xsd:enumeration value="word" />
                <xsd:enumeration value="sentence" />
                <xsd:enumeration value="paragraph" />
                <xsd:enumeration value="section" />
                <xsd:enumeration value="chapter" />
                <xsd:enumeration value="document" />
                <xsd:enumeration value="element" />
                <xsd:enumeration value="subelement" />
                <xsd:enumeration value="elementType" />
                <xsd:enumeration value="byte" />
            </xsd:restriction>
        </xsd:simpleType>
```

The base xsd:string type allows a string value to have any combination of characters and any length. The new type, named KnownProximityUnit, creates a new string type that allows only the values defined in the <xsd:enumeration> elements to appear as values; the value of a KnownProximityUnit must be of type xsd:string and must have one of the specified values.

The next part of the file defines several additional types derived by restriction:

```
<xsd:simpleType name="ReferenceId">
    <xsd:restriction base="xsd:hexBinary" />
</xsd:simpleType>
<xsd:simpleType name="GeneralString">
    <xsd:restriction base="xsd:string" />
</xsd:simpleType>
<xsd:simpleType name="InternationalString">
    <xsd:restriction base="GeneralString" />
</xsd:simpleType>
<xsd:simpleType name="OID">
    <xsd:restriction base="xsd:string">
        <xsd:pattern value="\d*{\.\d*}*" />
    </xsd:restriction>
</xsd:simpleType>
<xsd:simpleType name="ANY">
    <xsd:restriction base="xsd:anyType" />
</xsd:simpleType>
```

As you can see, <simpleType> datatypes can be derived from a variety of existing base types. The ReferenceId and GeneralString types are derived from the xsd:hexBinary and xsd:string base types, respectively. The user-defined type InternationalString is derived in turn from GeneralString. Likewise, the user-defined type ANY is derived by restriction from xsd:anyType. This type can represent any value that conforms to nearly any type. In toolkits that map XML Schema to Java, xsd:anyType elements are typically mapped to java.lang.Object classes.

The next part of the WSDL file takes us for a whirlwind ride through almost every XML Schema structure and type you're likely to come across regularly:

```
<xsd:element name="SortRequest" type="SortRequest" />
<xsd:complexType name="SortRequest">
    <xsd:sequence>
        <xsd:element name="referenceId" type="ReferenceId" minOccurs="0" />
        <xsd:element name="inputResultSetNames">
          <xsd:simpleType>
              <xsd:list itemType="InternationalString" />
          </xsd:simpleType>
        </xsd:element>
        <xsd:element name="sortedResultSetName"
          type="InternationalString" />
        <xsd:element name="sortSequence">
          <xsd:complexType>
              <xsd:sequence minOccurs="0" maxOccurs="unbounded">
                  <xsd:element name="SortKeySpec" type="SortKeySpec" />
```

```
                    </xsd:sequence>
                </xsd:complexType>
            </xsd:element>
            <xsd:element name="otherInfo" type="OtherInformation"
                minOccurs="0" />
        </xsd:sequence>
    </xsd:complexType>
    <xsd:element name="SortResponse" type="SortResponse" />
    <xsd:complexType name="SortResponse">
        <xsd:sequence>
            <xsd:element name="referenceId" type="ReferenceId"
                minOccurs="0" />
            <xsd:element name="sortStatus">
                <xsd:simpleType>
                    <xsd:restriction base="xsd:string">
                        <xsd:enumeration value="success" />
                        <xsd:enumeration value="partial-1" />
                        <xsd:enumeration value="failure" />
                    </xsd:restriction>
                </xsd:simpleType>
            </xsd:element>
            <xsd:element name="resultSetStatus" minOccurs="0">
                <xsd:simpleType>
                    <xsd:restriction base="xsd:string">
                        <xsd:enumeration value="empty" />
                        <xsd:enumeration value="interim" />
                        <xsd:enumeration value="unchanged" />
                        <xsd:enumeration value="none" />
                    </xsd:restriction>
                </xsd:simpleType>
            </xsd:element>
            <xsd:element name="diagnostics" minOccurs="0">
                <xsd:complexType>
                    <xsd:sequence minOccurs="0" maxOccurs="unbounded">
                        <xsd:element name="DiagRec" type="DiagRec" />
                    </xsd:sequence>
                </xsd:complexType>
            </xsd:element>
            <xsd:element name="otherInfo" type="OtherInformation"
                minOccurs="0" />
        </xsd:sequence>
    </xsd:complexType>
```

The <xsd:list> element introduces a list element. This element is a datatype whose
values consist of a finite-length sequence of values of an atomic datatype (i.e., xsd:
string, derived restriction, etc.). It has an attribute named itemType, which specifies
the atomic datatype for the items that make up the list. For the most part, the rest of
the lines contain datatypes we have already discussed (user-defined complex types,
user-defined simple types, or enumerations).

The last block introduces the <xsd:element> element's ref attribute:

```
        <xsd:complexType name="EXTERNAL">
            <xsd:sequence>
```

```
<xsd:element name="External">
    <xsd:complexType>
        <xsd:sequence>
            <xsd:element name="direct-reference"
                type="xsd:string" />
            <xsd:element name="encoding">
                <xsd:complexType>
                    <xsd:choice>
                        <xsd:element ref="single-ASN1-type" />
                        <xsd:element ref="octet-aligned" />
                    </xsd:choice>
                </xsd:complexType>
            </xsd:element>
        </xsd:sequence>
    </xsd:complexType>
</xsd:element>
        </xsd:sequence>
    </xsd:complexType>
<xsd:element name="single-ASN1-type">
    <xsd:complexType>
        <xsd:sequence>
            <xsd:element ref="motd" minOccurs="0" maxOccurs="unbounded" />
            <xsd:element ref="DBName" minOccurs="0"
                maxOccurs="unbounded" />
        </xsd:sequence>
    </xsd:complexType>
</xsd:element>
<xsd:element name="octet-aligned" type="xsd:string" />
<xsd:element name="motd" type="xsd:string" />
<xsd:element name="DBName" type="xsd:string" />
<xsd:complexType name="DatabaseNames">
    <xsd:sequence minOccurs="0" maxOccurs="unbounded">
        <xsd:element ref="DatabaseName" />
    </xsd:sequence>
</xsd:complexType>
<xsd:element name="databaseNames" type="DatabaseNames" />
<xsd:element name="DatabaseName" type="xsd:string" />
</xsd:schema>
    </types>
```

As implied by its name, this attribute allows you to reference a user-defined type (either complex or simple) defined elsewhere within the schema document. For example, the ref="DatabaseName" attribute indicates that the element definition in which it appears (<DatabaseNames>) can include a <DatabaseName> element, which is defined elsewhere in the document. The definition for <DatabaseName> appears at the end of this block of code; it is defined as an xsd:string type with no restrictions.

A complete discussion of XML Schema would be a book in itself.* It suffices to say that XML Schema is a pretty intense body of work. Unfortunately, developers still have to

---

* The XML Schema recommendation has three parts: a primer (*http://www.w3.org/TR/xmlschema-0/*), structures (*http://www.w3.org/TR/xmlschema-1/*), and datatypes (*http://www.w3.org/TR/xmlschema-2/*).

do some XML Schema mangling, which requires you to understand the details of this complex specification. However, many web services and XML Schema toolkits are becoming adept at processing <schema> elements and providing interfaces that abstract the details of XML Schema definitions provided by developers. If you want to know more about XML Schema, see Eric van der Vlist's *XML Schema* (O'Reilly).

<message> Element

The <message> element is used to model the data exchanged as part of a web service. <message> elements reference the types defined in the <types> section. The data contained within a <message> element typed by a <message> element is abstract. A message consists of one or more <part> subelements. A <part> subelement identifies the individual pieces of data that are part of this data message and the datatypes that the pieces adhere to. The following <message> element is contained in the *ez3950-PortTypes.wsdl* file:

```
<message name="soapHeader">
  <part type="xsd:string" name="id"/>
  <part type="xsd:string" name="timeout"/>
</message>
```

In the previous code, the <message> element is uniquely identified by the name attribute. This message is named soapHeader; it has two <part> subelements, of which the first is named id and the second is named timeout. In this case, each part is typed as an XML Schema string (xsd:string). But the types used in part definitions aren't required to come from XML Schema; they could just as well be defined in the <types> element of the existing WSDL document itself.

The rest of the <message> elements contained in our sample WSDL file follow. Note that multiple parts are used if the message contains multiple logical parts, such as parameters in an RPC request. Each part can be a simple type or a structure. You can define the part structure here within the message using the <element> tag, or you can refer to the typed structures defined in the <types> section:

```
<message name="initRequest">
    <part type="xer:initRequest" name="initRequest"/>
</message>
<message name="initResponse">
    <part type="xer:initResponse" name="initResponse"/>
</message>
<message name="searchRequest">
    <part type="xer:searchRequest" name="searchRequest"/>
</message>
<message name="searchResponse">
    <part type="xer:searchResponse" name="searchResponse"/>
</message>
<message name="presentRequest">
    <part type="xer:presentRequest" name="presentRequest"/>
</message>
```

```
<message name="presentResponse">
    <part type="xer:presentResponse" name="presentResponse"/>
</message>
<message name="sortRequest">
    <part type="xer:sortequest" name="sortRequest"/>
</message>
<message name="sortResponse">
    <part type="xer:sortResponse" name="sortResponse"/>
</message>
<message name="scanRequest">
    <part type="xer:sortRequest" name="scanRequest"/>
</message>
<message name="scanResponse">
    <part type="xer:scanResponse" name="scanResponse"/>
</message>
<message name="deleteRequest">
    <part type="xer:scanRequest" name="deleteRequest"/>
</message>
<message name="deleteResponse">
    <part type="xer:scanResponse" name="deleteResponse"/>
</message>
<message name="accessControlRequest">
    <part type="xer:accessControlRequest" name="accessControlRequest"/>
</message>
<message name="accessControlResponse">
    <part type="xer:accessControlResponse" name="accessControlResponse"/>
</message>
<message name="triggerResourceControlRequest">
    <part type="xer:triggerResourceControlRequest"
        name="triggerResourceControlRequest"/>
</message>
<message name="resourceControlRequest">
    <part type="xer:resourceControlRequest" name="resourceControlRequest"/>
</message>
<message name="resourceControlResponse">
    <part type="xer:resourceControlResponse" name="resourceControlResponse"/>
</message>
<message name="resourceReportRequest">
    <part type="xer:resourceReportRequest" name="resourceReportRequest"/>
</message>
<message name="resourceReportResponse">
    <part type="xer:resourceReportResponse" name="resourceReportResponse"/>
</message>
<message name="extendedServicesRequest">
    <part type="xer:extendedServicesRequest" name="extendedServicesRequest"/>
</message>
<message name="extendedServicesResponse">
    <part type="xer:extendedServicesResponse" name="extendedServicesResponse"/>
</message>
<message name="close">
    <part type="xer:close" name="close"/>
</message>
```

<portType> Element

The <portType> element specifies a subset of operations supported for an endpoint of a web service. In a sense, a <portType> element provides a unique identifier to a group of actions that can be executed at a single endpoint.

The <operation> element represents an operation. This element is an abstract definition of an action supported by a web service. A WSDL <operation> element is analogous to a Java method definition. A WSDL operation can have input and output messages as part of its action. The <operation> tag defines the name of the action by using a name attribute, defines the input message by the <input> subelement, and defines the output message by the <output> subelement. The <input> and <output> elements reference <message> elements defined in the same WSDL document or an imported one. A <message> element can represent a request, response, or a fault.

Continuing with the Z39.50 ASN.1 sample, the WSDL file defines a single <portType> element:

```
<portType name="ez3950PortTypes">
```

This element declares that this endpoint has a set of operations that are jointly referenced as ez3950PortTypes. The following lines define the <operation> elements for this <portType>:

```
<!-- Request-response Operations (client initiated) -->
    <operation name="init">
        <input message="initRequest"/>
        <output message="initResponse"/>
    </operation>
    <operation name="search">
        <input message="searchRequest"/>
        <output message="searchResponse"/>
    </operation>
    <operation name="present">
        <input message="presentRequest"/>
        <output message="presentResponse"/>
    </operation>
    <operation name="sort">
        <input message="sortRequest"/>
        <output message="sortResponse"/>
    </operation>
    <operation name="scan">
        <input message="scanRequest"/>
        <output message="scanResponse"/>
    </operation>
    <operation name="delete">
        <input message="deleteRequest"/>
        <output message="deleteResponse"/>
    </operation>
    <operation name="resourceReport">
        <input message="resourceReportRequest"/>
        <output message="resourceReportResponse"/>
    </operation>
```

```
        <operation name="extendedServices">
            <input message="extendedServicesRequest"/>
            <output message="extendedServicesResponse"/>
        </operation>
        <operation name="close">
            <output message="close"/>
            <input message="close"/>
        </operation>

    <!-- Solicit-response Operation (Server initiated) -->
        <operation name="accessControl">
            <output message="accessControlResponse"/>
            <input message="accessControlRequest"/>
        </operation>
        <operation name="resourceControl">
            <output message="resourceControlResponse"/>
            <input message="resourceControlRequest"/>
        </operation>
        <operation name="close">
            <output message="close"/>
            <input message="close"/>
        </operation>

    <!-- Notification Operations (Server initiated)-->
        <operation name="segment">
            <output message="segmentRequest"/>
        </operation>

    <!-- One-way Operations (Client initiated) -->
        <operation name="triggerResourceControl">
            <input message="triggerResourceControlRequest"/>
        </operation>

    </portType>
```

These <operation> elements are grouped according to their behavior. When an operation is defined in a WSDL document, it is made to be abstract; it is purely an operation definition, but how that operation is mapped to a real function is defined later (i.e., the operation can behave in a number of different ways depending on the actual definition). The WSDL specification defines the following behavioral patterns as transmission primitives:

- Request-response
- Solicit-response
- One-way
- Notification

First, the operation can follow a request-response model, in which a web service client invokes a request and expects to receive a synchronous response message. This model is defined by the presence of both <input> and <output> elements. The <input> element must appear before the <output> element. This order indicates that the operation first accepts an input message (request) and then sends an output message (response). This model is similar to a normal procedure call, in which the calling method blocks until the called method returns its result.

Second, the operation can follow a solicit-response model, in which the web service solicits a response from the client, expecting to receive a response. This model is defined as having both <input> and <output> elements. The <output> element must appear before the <input> element. This order indicates that the operation first sends an output message (solicit) and then receives an input message (response).

Third, the operation can be a one-way invocation, in which the web sevice client sends a message to the web service without expecting to receive a response. This model is defined by a single <input> message with no <output> message. This model indicates that the operation receives input messages (one-way invocation), but doesn't deliver a response to the client.

Fourth, the operation can be a notification, in which the web services sends a one-way message to the client without expecting a response. This model is defined by a single <output> message and no <input> message. It indicates that the operation sends output messages asynchronously; i.e., the messages are not in response to a request, but can be sent at any time. The operation doesn't expect a response to the messages it sends.

> For the request-response and solicit-response models, an optional <fault> element can be included. This element refers to another message. A <fault> message will be transmitted if any processing, system, or application errors occur. The <fault> message is delivered to the client in a request-response model and to the web service in the solicit-response model.

The value assigned to the name attribute of each <operation> element must be unique within the scope of the <portType>. The names of the input and output messages must be unique within the <portType>, not just the <operation>. The value assigned to the message attribute of an <input> or <output> element must match one of the names of the <message> elements defined in the same WSDL document or in an imported one.

<binding> Element

A <binding> element is a concrete protocol and data format specification for a <portType> element. It is where you would use one of the standard binding extensions—HTTP, SOAP, or MIME—or create one of your own.

Each protocol has its own wire format. For example, HTTP has a simple header/body format. SOAP, which can exist inside of HTTP and other protocols, has its own header and body. A SOAP message can have attachments included as part of a message.

Our WSDL document has already defined the <operation> elements for this web service. A <binding> element takes the abstract definition of the operations and their input/output messages and maps them to the concrete protocol that the web service uses. Should the <input> element defined in a WSDL document be located in the SOAP header? Should it be in the SOAP body? Should it be in the attachment? Also, how should the data be encoded? Should the supplied schema be used for encoding rules or should literal encoding be used? The <binding> element provides this mapping.

The SOAP binding extension

The SOAP 1.1 binding extension in the WSDL 1.1 specification allows you to use SOAP-specific grammar in the <binding> element. Table 5-2 lists the SOAP-specific elements that are part of the SOAP binding extension.

Table 5-2. SOAP binding extension elements

Element	Synopsis
<soap:binding>	This element signifies that the binding is bound to the SOAP protocol format. It has a transport attribute that specifies the network transport protocol (i.e., HTTP, SMTP, etc.) in which the SOAP message will travel. It also has a style attribute that specifies the default style of each operation in the binding. The possible values for this attribute are rpc and document.
<soap:operation>	This element overrides the style attribute; it identifies the SOAPAction attribute in an HTTP SOAP binding and identifies the encoding system used. Like the <soap:binding> element, it also has a style attribute that indicates the operation's orientation (i.e., rpc, document). If no style attribute is specified, the style from the <soap:binding> element is inherited. It also has a soapAction attribute, which specifies the value to use for this operation's SOAPAction HTTP header. It is very important to set the encoding rules. Encoding rules are defined through the use attribute. use=literal means that the type or element definitions referenced by the parts attribute specify the concrete schema for this message. use=encoded means that the message parts refer to abstract types and the concrete schema must be derived from the encoding style defined by the encodingStyle attribute. The advantage of using use=encoded is that you don't need to follow the XML Schema schemas precisely when serializing the data. For example, though a schema says there's an element <a> with two children, <b> and <c>, and these are both integers, when encoded use is in effect, SOAP encoding can make <b> a reference to an integer even though the reference may be a string.
<soap:body>	This element specifies how the message parts appear inside the SOAP body element. It is used in both RPC and document-oriented messages, but the style of the enclosing operation has important effects on how the body section is structured.
	For RPC-oriented messages, each part is a parameter or a return value and appears inside a wrapper element within the body.
	For document-oriented messages, there are no additional wrappers, so the message parts appear directly under the SOAP body element.
<soap:fault>	This element specifies the contents of the SOAP Fault details element and is patterned after the <soap:body> element.
<soap:header>	This element specifies how header information would appear in the SOAP Header element. These entries are transmitted in the <SOAP-ENC:Header> element of the SOAP envelope. It is patterned after the <soap:body> element.

Table 5-2. SOAP binding extension elements (continued)

Element	Synopsis
`<soap:headerfault>`	This element is used to specify a fault that will contain the contents of the SOAP Fault details elements associated with a `<soap:header>` element. These faults will probably be `mustUnderstand` faults.
`<soap:address>`	This element provides the address (a URI) for a `<port>` child element of the `<service>` element. A port can have only one address; if the service is written in Java, with a J2EE-based toolkit or library, its address is usually the address of a servlet or JSP. The URI scheme specified for the address must correspond to the transport specified by the `<soap:binding>` element.

Demonstrating a binding through example

The WSDL file we are working through uses the SOAP binding extension, so it provides an excellent example for explaining how the SOAP binding extension works in reality. This example is fairly long, so it is broken up in various places with explanations of how the binding extension works. It starts with a `<binding>` tag:

```
<binding name="ez3950SOAPBinding" type="tns:ez3950PortTypes">
```

The `<binding>` tag indicates that we will map a `<portType>` to a particular protocol. The `name` attribute defines a unique identifier for this binding; the value of the `type` attribute must be the name of one of the `<portType>` elements contained within the same WSDL document or in an imported one. Note that the `tns:` namespace is used to reference a port type in the existing WSDL:

```
<soap:binding style="rpc"
        transport="http://schemas.xmlsoap.org/soap/http"/>
```

The `<soap:binding>` element is a child of the `<binding>` element. This element indicates that we will use the SOAP binding extensions to map the operations. To use the HTTP GET/POST binding extension, replace this tag with `<http:binding>`. To use the MIME binding extension, use the tag `<mime:binding>`.

The value of the `style` attribute can be `document` or `rpc`. The value given in this tag is used as the default value and applied to the `style` attribute of each subsequent operation, if a style isn't defined within the operation itself. The `style` attribute defaults to document if one is not provided. The `transport` attribute specifies the SOAP transport protocol that will be used. Is the SOAP packet embedded within HTTP, FTP, SMTP, or something else? In our example, the SOAP transport is HTTP.

Next, we look at the `<operation>` tag:

```
<operation name="init">
    <soap:operation soapAction=""/>
        <input>
            <soap:body use="encoded"
                    encodingStyle="http://schemas.xmlsoap.org/soap/encoding/"/>
        </input>
        <output>
            <soap:header message="soapHeader"
                    part="id"
```

```
                             use="encoded"
                             encodingStyle="http://schemas.xmlsoap.org/soap/encoding/"/>
                  <soap:header message="soapHeader"
                             part="timeout"
                             use="encoded"
                             encodingStyle="http://schemas.xmlsoap.org/soap/encoding/"/>
                  <soap:body use="encoded"
                             encodingStyle="http://schemas.xmlsoap.org/soap/encoding/"/>
               </output>
        </operation>
```

We must include an <operation> here for each <operation> that was defined as part of the <portType> tag. The WSDL file must map the <input>, <output>, and <fault> elements of each element to a SOAP envelope.

The <operation> tag has a <soap:operation> subelement. The <soap:operation> element has a soapAction attribute that defines the value of the SOAPAction header. The URI used for this header represents the action that should occur when the message arrives at its destination. It is not the URI of the web service's endpoint. In this case, the URI is the empty string (" ").

Since the first operations defined in the WSDL document follow the request-response model, this <soap:operation> defines <input> and <output> tags. The <input> tag has a <soap:body> subelement. The <soap:body> element defines how the message parts should appear inside of a SOAP body. The required use attribute defines how the data is encoded inside of the SOAP packet. If the value is encoded, as in this example, then the value of the encodingStyle attribute references a URI that indicates how the data should be encoded. If the value of the use attribute is literal, then the definition of the message provided within the WSDL document is written into the SOAP body without using another encoding mechanism.

In addition to defining a single <soap:body> element, the <input> and <output> elements can have zero or more <soap:header> elements. The <soap:header> element defines the content that should be included in a SOAP header as part of an envelope. Our example identifies two items included in the SOAP header for the output message. The use and encodingStyle attributes operate the same way as they do for the <soap:body> element. Individual parts, as opposed to whole messages, are included in a SOAP header. The value of the message attribute refers-0.75 to an abstract <message> already defined in the same WSDL document. The value of the part attribute identifies the part of the <message> element that should be included within the SOAP header.

If you refer to the <message> definitions earlier in this chapter, one of the messages was named soapHeader. The soapHeader message had two parts defined: id and timeout. Both parts are included as part of the SOAP header for the output message. Though our example pulled all of the SOAP header fields from a single message definition, you can pull the fields from any other message contained in the same WSDL document.

The next few pages continue the listing of the `<binding>` for the Z39.50 ASN.1 sample. It shows how each operation behavior is represented using the SOAP binding extension elements:

```
<operation name="search">
    <soap:operation soapAction=""/>
    <input>
        <soap:header message="soapHeader" part="id" use="encoded"
            encodingStyle="http://schemas.xmlsoap.org/soap/encoding/"/>
        <soap:body use="encoded"
            encodingStyle="http://schemas.xmlsoap.org/soap/encoding/"/>
    </input>
    <output>
        <soap:header message="soapHeader" part="id" use="encoded"
            encodingStyle="http://schemas.xmlsoap.org/soap/encoding/"/>
        <soap:header message="soapHeader" part="timeout" use="encoded"
            encodingStyle="http://schemas.xmlsoap.org/soap/encoding/"/>
        <soap:body use="encoded"
            encodingStyle="http://schemas.xmlsoap.org/soap/encoding/"/>
    </output>
</operation>

<operation name="present">
    <soap:operation soapAction=""/>
    <input>
        <soap:header message="soapHeader" part="id" use="encoded"
            encodingStyle="http://schemas.xmlsoap.org/soap/encoding/"/>
        <soap:body use="encoded"
            encodingStyle="http://schemas.xmlsoap.org/soap/encoding/"/>
    </input>
    <output>
        <soap:header message="soapHeader" part="id" use="encoded"
            encodingStyle="http://schemas.xmlsoap.org/soap/encoding/"/>
        <soap:header message="soapHeader" part="timeout" use="encoded"
            encodingStyle="http://schemas.xmlsoap.org/soap/encoding/"/>
        <soap:body use="encoded"
            encodingStyle="http://schemas.xmlsoap.org/soap/encoding/"/>
    </output>
</operation>

<operation name="sort">
    <soap:operation soapAction=""/>
    <input>
        <soap:header message="soapHeader" part="id" use="encoded"
            encodingStyle="http://schemas.xmlsoap.org/soap/encoding/"/>
        <soap:body use="encoded"
            encodingStyle="http://schemas.xmlsoap.org/soap/encoding/"/>
    </input>
    <output>
        <soap:header message="soapHeader" part="id" use="encoded"
            encodingStyle="http://schemas.xmlsoap.org/soap/encoding/"/>
        <soap:header message="soapHeader" part="timeout" use="encoded"
            encodingStyle="http://schemas.xmlsoap.org/soap/encoding/"/>
```

```
          <soap:body use="encoded"
              encodingStyle="http://schemas.xmlsoap.org/soap/encoding/"/>
      </output>
  </operation>

  <operation name="scan">
      <soap:operation soapAction=""/>
      <input>
          <soap:header message="soapHeader" part="id" use="encoded"
              encodingStyle="http://schemas.xmlsoap.org/soap/encoding/"/>
          <soap:body use="encoded"
              encodingStyle="http://schemas.xmlsoap.org/soap/encoding/"/>
      </input>
      <output>
          <soap:header message="soapHeader" part="id" use="encoded"
              encodingStyle="http://schemas.xmlsoap.org/soap/encoding/"/>
          <soap:header message="soapHeader" part="timeout" use="encoded"
              encodingStyle="http://schemas.xmlsoap.org/soap/encoding/"/>
          <soap:body use="encoded"
              encodingStyle="http://schemas.xmlsoap.org/soap/encoding/"/>
      </output>
  </operation>

  <operation name="delete">
      <soap:operation soapAction=""/>
      <input>
          <soap:header message="soapHeader" part="id" use="encoded"
              encodingStyle="http://schemas.xmlsoap.org/soap/encoding/"/>
          <soap:body use="encoded"
              encodingStyle="http://schemas.xmlsoap.org/soap/encoding/"/>
      </input>
      <output>
          <soap:header message="soapHeader" part="id" use="encoded"
              encodingStyle="http://schemas.xmlsoap.org/soap/encoding/"/>
          <soap:header message="soapHeader" part="timeout" use="encoded"
              encodingStyle="http://schemas.xmlsoap.org/soap/encoding/"/>
          <soap:body use="encoded"
              encodingStyle="http://schemas.xmlsoap.org/soap/encoding/"/>
      </output>
  </operation>

  <operation name="resourceReport">
      <soap:operation soapAction=""/>
      <input>
          <soap:header message="soapHeader" part="id" use="encoded"
              encodingStyle="http://schemas.xmlsoap.org/soap/encoding/"/>
          <soap:body use="encoded"
              encodingStyle="http://schemas.xmlsoap.org/soap/encoding/"/>
      </input>
      <output>
          <soap:header message="soapHeader" part="id" use="encoded"
              encodingStyle="http://schemas.xmlsoap.org/soap/encoding/"/>
          <soap:header message="soapHeader" part="timeout" use="encoded"
              encodingStyle="http://schemas.xmlsoap.org/soap/encoding/"/>
```

```
            <soap:body use="encoded"
                  encodingStyle="http://schemas.xmlsoap.org/soap/encoding/"/>
      </output>
</operation>

<operation name="extendedService">
      <soap:operation soapAction=""/>
      <input>
            <soap:header message="soapHeader" part="id" use="encoded"
                  encodingStyle="http://schemas.xmlsoap.org/soap/encoding/"/>
            <soap:body use="encoded"
                  encodingStyle="http://schemas.xmlsoap.org/soap/encoding/"/>
      </input>
      <output>
            <soap:header message="soapHeader" part="id" use="encoded"
                  encodingStyle="http://schemas.xmlsoap.org/soap/encoding/"/>
            <soap:header message="soapHeader" part="timeout" use="encoded"
                  encodingStyle="http://schemas.xmlsoap.org/soap/encoding/"/>
            <soap:body use="encoded"
                  encodingStyle="http://schemas.xmlsoap.org/soap/encoding/"/>
      </output>
</operation>

<operation name="close">
      <soap:operation soapAction=""/>
      <input>
            <soap:header message="soapHeader" part="id" use="encoded"
                  encodingStyle="http://schemas.xmlsoap.org/soap/encoding/"/>
            <soap:body use="encoded"
                  encodingStyle="http://schemas.xmlsoap.org/soap/encoding/"/>
      </input>
      <output>
            <soap:header message="soapHeader" part="id" use="encoded"
                  encodingStyle="http://schemas.xmlsoap.org/soap/encoding/"/>
            <soap:body use="encoded"
                  encodingStyle="http://schemas.xmlsoap.org/soap/encoding/"/>
      </output>
</operation>

<operation name="close">
      <soap:operation soapAction=""/>
      <output>
            <soap:header message="soapHeader" part="id" use="encoded"
                  encodingStyle="http://schemas.xmlsoap.org/soap/encoding/"/>
            <soap:header message="soapHeader" part="timeout" use="encoded"
                  encodingStyle="http://schemas.xmlsoap.org/soap/encoding/"/>
            <soap:body use="encoded"
                  encodingStyle="http://schemas.xmlsoap.org/soap/encoding/"/>
      </output>
      <input>
            <soap:header message="soapHeader" part="id" use="encoded"
                  encodingStyle="http://schemas.xmlsoap.org/soap/encoding/"/>
            <soap:body use="encoded"
                  encodingStyle="http://schemas.xmlsoap.org/soap/encoding/"/>
```

```
        </input>
    </operation>

    <operation name="accessControl">
        <soap:operation soapAction=""/>
        <output>
            <soap:header message="soapHeader" part="id" use="encoded"
                encodingStyle="http://schemas.xmlsoap.org/soap/encoding/"/>
            <soap:header message="soapHeader" part="timeout" use="encoded"
                encodingStyle="http://schemas.xmlsoap.org/soap/encoding/"/>
            <soap:body use="encoded"
                encodingStyle="http://schemas.xmlsoap.org/soap/encoding/"/>
        </output>
        <input>
            <soap:header message="soapHeader" part="id" use="encoded"
                encodingStyle="http://schemas.xmlsoap.org/soap/encoding/"/>
            <soap:body use="encoded"
                encodingStyle="http://schemas.xmlsoap.org/soap/encoding/"/>
        </input>
    </operation>

    <operation name="resourceControl">
        <soap:operation soapAction=""/>
        <output>
            <soap:header message="soapHeader" part="id" use="encoded"
                encodingStyle="http://schemas.xmlsoap.org/soap/encoding/"/>
            <soap:header message="soapHeader" part="timeout" use="encoded"
                encodingStyle="http://schemas.xmlsoap.org/soap/encoding/"/>
            <soap:body use="encoded"
                encodingStyle="http://schemas.xmlsoap.org/soap/encoding/"/>
        </output>
        <input>
            <soap:header message="soapHeader" part="id" use="encoded"
                encodingStyle="http://schemas.xmlsoap.org/soap/encoding/"/>
            <soap:body use="encoded"
                encodingStyle="http://schemas.xmlsoap.org/soap/encoding/"/>
        </input>
    </operation>

    <operation name="segment">
        <soap:operation soapAction=""/>
        <output>
            <soap:header message="soapHeader" part="id" use="encoded"
                encodingStyle="http://schemas.xmlsoap.org/soap/encoding/"/>
            <soap:header message="soapHeader" part="timeout" use="encoded"
                encodingStyle="http://schemas.xmlsoap.org/soap/encoding/"/>
            <soap:body use="encoded"
                encodingStyle="http://schemas.xmlsoap.org/soap/encoding/"/>
        </output>
    </operation>

    <operation name="triggerResourceControl">
        <soap:operation soapAction=""/>
```

```
    <input>
        <soap:header message="soapHeader" part="id" use="encoded"
            encodingStyle="http://schemas.xmlsoap.org/soap/encoding/"/>
        <soap:body use="encoded"
            encodingStyle="http://schemas.xmlsoap.org/soap/encoding/"/>
    </input>
</operation>

</binding>
```

This section discusses only the SOAP binding extension; extensions and elements are also defined for the HTTP and MIME binding extensions. They are similar to the SOAP binding extensions, but use different elements to reference different portions of their packets. Refer to the WSDL specification to learn how each of these binding extensions operates.

<service> Element

Even though there was a lot of text in the <binding> element and its subelements, a careful eye might notice that the binding never referenced the URL at which the web service is actually located! The <service> element typically appears at the end of a WSDL document and identifies a web service. Please note that some WSDL documents do not contain a <service> definition. The primary purpose of a WSDL document is to describe the abstract interface. A <service> element is used only when describing the actual endpoint of a service.

A web service is a grouping of one or more <port> elements. A <port> element represents a single endpoint (or access point) for the web service. Given this definition, you can create a web service that is conceptually whole, but operates out of several different URLs. Here is the <service> definition for the Z39.50 ASN.1 sample:

```
<service name="Oxford University Libraries">
    <documentation>
        Z39.50 Server for Oxford University Libraries
    </documentation>
    <port name="OLIS" binding="ez:ez3950SOAPBinding">
        <soap:address location="http://jafer.las.ox.ac.uk/ez3950"/>
    </port>
</service>
```

A <service> element has an optional <documentation> subelement that describes the web service. It also contains one or more <port> subelements. The <port> element has a name attribute that provides a unique identifier for this endpoint. It also contains a binding attribute that references the name of a <binding> element contained within the same WSDL document or in an imported one.

The <port> element has a <soap:address> subelement—an element defined as part of the SOAP binding extension. The <soap:address> element identifies the URL of the web service. If this service used a different binding extension, this element would be different as well.

The end of the example!

That's it! We have made it to the end of the WSDL sample—a complete, working WSDL file. We didn't leave out any portions of this file along the way, so if you have been able to follow up to this point, you are well on your way to becoming a WSDL master.

Best Practices, Makes Perfect

One of the biggest mistakes that many developers make when working with WSDL is defining operations and messages that are too fine-grained. By doing so, developers usually define more than they really need. You need to ensure that your web service is coarse-grained and that the messages being defined are more business oriented than programmatic. You shouldn't define a web service operation for every Java method you want to expose. Rather, you should define an operation for each action you need to expose. Deciding what to expose in your web service requires a methodological rather than a technical mindset.

The natural tendency for a developer is to treat a WSDL document like code because it describes the operations and types for the web service. It's not code, though—it's metadata about code. Take care not to include anything that a service requestor doesn't need to know to invoke the web service.

For maximum interoperability and platform neutrality, use XML Schema as your type system whenever possible. If your WSDL is publicly visible, imagine that it is part of a workflow that you do not get to define. It is entirely feasible that the web service your WSDL describes is upstream or downstream of other actions and that a tool uses the WSDL document to instrument it. Realize that your service hasn't necessarily succeeded when the particular application you're developing works; the real test of a successful web service is when other applications that you didn't anticipate use your service.

Where Is All the Java?

You might have noticed that there wasn't much Java in this chapter. Most Java web service frameworks do a very good job of hiding the details of WSDL from the web service clients that they provide. You're not likely to write a WSDL file yourself; you're more likely to read a WSDL file to understand and debug an interoperability problem.

Conceptually, a Java toolkit can work with an existing WSDL file in two ways. First, given a WSDL file, Java code could be generated that is capable of accessing the web service defined within the WSDL file. This type of code seems convenient, but it would contain classes and interfaces specific to the WSDL file. A client that used these classes would have to be recompiled or even rewritten each time the WSDL file was modified and the Java code was regenerated. The advantage of using a system like this is that it would provide Java objects for each WSDL type, message, and operation. Compile-time checking would provide a more reliable application.

The JAX-RPC specification, which is part of the Java Web Services Pack available from *http://java.sun.com*, allows both models. A tool that is compliant with JAX-RPC may generate statically defined stub interfaces, or it may generate a more generic stub that uses a dynamic invocation interface (DII) based on Java reflection to build a request object. JAX-RPC is discussed in more depth in Chapter 7.

Second, a Java web service invocation mechanism can import a WSDL file and then make an invocation on an operation dynamically. The advantage of this model is that the client code would not have to be recompiled each time the WSDL is modified, nor would Java code have to be generated each time the WSDL file is modified. The drawback to this approach is that no compile-time checking of data is used. The toolkit would formulate messages dynamically at runtime, so any typing problems that might arise could be more difficult to track down.

IBM's Web Service Invocation Framework (WSIF) and Systinet WASP use this model. The WSIF is a toolkit (*http://www.alphaworks.ibm.com/tech/wsif*) that provides a simple API for invoking web services, no matter how or where the services are provided. The WSIF's API is driven by the abstract service description in WSDL. It is completely divorced from the actual Java client stub/proxy used. This invocation API is WSDL-oriented because it uses WSDL terms to refer to message parts, operations, etc.

Systinet WASP provides dynamic access to any service described by WSDL. It creates a dynamic Java proxy based on the WSDL description. WASP can also dynamically access any J2EE resource, such as a JMS Destination, JDBC driver, EJB, or J2EE CA adapter by creating a dynamic proxy.

The binding of Java to WSDL is discussed in more depth in upcoming chapters. Chapter 6, which discusses UDDI, has a section that talks about how WSDL documents should be placed within a UDDI registry. The next chapters also discuss JAX-RPC and how it absorbs WSDL documents to facilitate the invocation of web services in a standardized way.

CHAPTER 6

UDDI: Universal Description, Discovery, and Integration

The Universal Description, Discovery, and Integration (UDDI) Project provides a standardized method for publishing and discovering information about web services. The UDDI Project is an industry initiative that attempts to create a platform-independent, open framework for describing services, discovering businesses, and integrating business services. UDDI focuses on the process of *discovery* in the service-oriented architecture.

The UDDI Project is an initiative that communicates with the public through *www.uddi.org*. The UDDI Community runs the UDDI Project. The Community consists of a group of Working Group members who develop the specifications and Advisory Group members who provide requirements and review the specifications. The Working Group is an invitation-based group and the Advisory Group is open to everyone.

Web services are becoming the basis for electronic commerce of all forms. Companies invoke the services of other companies to accomplish a business transaction. In an environment in which only a few companies participate, managing the discovery of business partners manually would be simple. After all, how difficult would it be to figure out if one of your few business partners has an access point that adheres to your requirements? This model breaks down, however, as the number of companies that you need to interact with grows, along with the number and types of interfaces they export. How do you discover all the business partners that you can do business with? If you attempted to account for them manually, you could never be sure that you discovered every partner. UDDI is a single conceptual registry distributed among many nodes that replicate the participating businesses' data with one another. The UDDI registry of services (hosted by different businesses on the Internet) attempts to solve this problem.

This chapter presents an overview of UDDI and how to put it to work. It includes a discussion about the information stored in a UDDI registry, the different potential uses of UDDI, and its technical architecture; the specifications that comprise the UDDI effort, with a focus on their relevance to developers and a list of different Java approaches for programming with UDDI; and an introduction to interacting with a UDDI registry programmatically. The following sections cover the UDDI data structures and XML APIs available for accessing a registry.

UDDI Overview

Prior to the UDDI project, no industry-wide approach was available for businesses to reach their customers and partners with information about their products and web services. Nor was there a uniform method that detailed how to integrate the systems and processes that are already in place at and between business partners. Nothing attempted to cover both the business and development aspects of publishing and locating information associated with a piece of software on a global scale.

Conceptually, a business can register three types of information into a UDDI registry. The specification does not call out these types specifically, but they provide a good summary of what UDDI can store for a business:

White pages
> Basic contact information and identifiers about a company, including business name, address, contact information, and unique identifiers such as D-U-N-S numbers or tax IDs. This information allows others to discover your web service based upon your business identification.

Yellow pages
> Information that describes a web service using different categorizations (taxonomies). This information allows others to discover your web service based upon its categorization (such as being in the manufacturing or car sales business).

Green pages
> Technical information that describes the behaviors and supported functions of a web service hosted by your business. This information includes pointers to the grouping information of web services and where the web services are located.

How UDDI Is Used

UDDI has several different uses, based on the perspective of who is using it. From a business analyst's perspective, UDDI is similar to an Internet search engine for business processes. Typical search engines, such as AskJeeves, organize and index URLs for web sites. However, a business exporting a web service needs to expose much more than a simple URL. A business analyst can browse one or more UDDI registries to view the different businesses that expose web services and the specifications of those services. However, business users probably won't browse a UDDI registry directly, since the information stored within it is not necessarily reader friendly. A series of marketplaces and business search portals could crop up to provide business analysts with a more user-oriented approach to browsing the services and businesses hosted in a UDDI registry.

Software developers use the UDDI Programmer's API to publish services (i.e., put information about them in the registry) and query the registry to discover services matching various criteria. It is conceivable that software will eventually discover a service dynamically and use it without requiring human interaction.

 Even though the API provided by UDDI allows random searching for businesses, it's not feasible for a program to select new business partners dynamically. Realistically, it's more likely that business analysts with specific knowledge of the problem at hand will use UDDI portals to discover potentially interesting services and partners, and technologists will write programs to use the services from companies that have already been discovered. We'll probably see programs that update the data in a UDDI registry, but most publicly available registries already have a user-friendly interface that allows human users to update information in a registry.

Even though the registries have human-friendly interfaces for direct access, humans should never have to interface with a repository directly. The web service tool you use should automate interaction with a UDDI registry. For example, if you use a tool that creates a web service, that tool should be able to not only deploy the web service into production, but add it to the UDDI registry for you on your behalf.

Both business analysts and software developers can publish new business entities and services. Business analysts can use portals attached directly to a particular UDDI server or to a more general search portal that supports UDDI. Figure 6-1 depicts the relationship between business analysts and technologists.

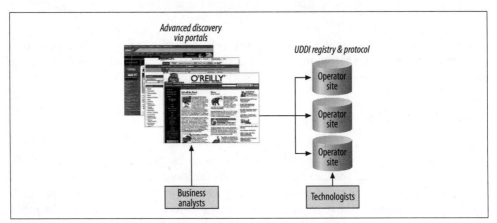

Figure 6-1. Relationship between business analysts and technologists

Technical Architecture

Figure 6-2 depicts the makeup of the UDDI project. The UDDI Business Registry (UBR), also known as the Public Cloud, is a conceptually single system built from multiple nodes that has their data synchronized through replication. A series of operator nodes each hosts a copy of the content. The global grouping of operator nodes is jointly known as the UBR. Operator nodes replicate content among one another. Accessing any individual operator node provides the same information and quality of service as any other operator node. Content inserted into the UBR is done at a single node, and that operator node becomes the master owner of that content. Any subsequent updates or deletes of the data must occur at the operator node where the data was inserted.

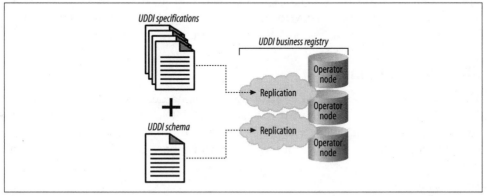

Figure 6-2. The UDDI initiative

Note that the scope of the UDDI project is much more than the UBR; a company can provide a private operator node that is not part of the UBR. Private nodes do not have data synchronized with the UBR, so the information contained within is distinct. A grouping of companies can also create a "private cloud" of nodes that have information replicated between their private nodes, but that replication sequence will not have any interaction with the UBR nodes.

The UBR has widely accessible inquiry services, but services may be published only by authenticated entities. Any business can create an operator node and make it available over the Internet and part of the UBR. Private operator nodes can define the access rules for their nodes on a case-by-case basis. They can follow the same model as the UBR or make the restrictions looser or tighter.

Companies will likely set up private UDDI nodes. Even though use of these nodes will probably be limited in the near future, quite a few companies are showing interest in setting up private registries for internal or B2B operations. Industry groups are also discussing options for meeting the demands of their individual sector.

Many products have either been created or are being expanded to allow companies to create their own public and private UDDI registries. For example, BEA WebLogic Server and IBM WebSphere both intend to ship a fully compliant UDDI Server embedded within the application server sometime in 2002. Other companies, such as Systinet, HP, Oracle, SAP, Cape Clear, The Mind Electric, and Silverstream, have created J2EE-compliant UDDI implementations that work with existing application servers, including Tomcat, BEA, and IBM. Microsoft has an implementation based upon .NET. Additionally, two open source J2EE UDDI projects are in development: Bowstreet's jUDDI (*http://www.juddi.org*) and JP Moresmau's pudding (*http://www.opensorcerer.org*).

UDDI Specifications and Java-Based APIs

This section discusses the different specifications that make up the UDDI initiative and the options available to developers writing Java programs that interact with a UDDI registry.

UDDI Specifications

The UDDI project also defines a set of XML Schema definitions that describe the data formats used by the various specification APIs. These documents are all available for download at *http://www.uddi.org*. The UDDI project releases their specifications in unison. The current version of all specification groups is Version 2.0. The specifications include:

UDDI replication
> This document describes the data replication processes and interfaces to which a registry operator must conform to achieve data replication between sites. This specification is not a programmer's API; it defines the replication mechanism used among UBR nodes.

UDDI operators
> This document outlines the behavior and operational parameters required by UDDI node operators. This specification defines data management requirements to which operators must adhere. For example, node operators are responsible for durable recording and backup of all data, ensuring that each business registration has a valid email address associated with it, and the integrity of the data during deletions (e.g., deleting a business means that all of its service entries must also be deleted). This document is not a programmer's API and private registries are not required to support it.

UDDI Programmer's API
> This specification defines a set of functions that all UDDI registries support for inquiring about services hosted in a registry and for publishing information about a business or a service to a registry. This specification defines a series of SOAP messages containing XML documents that a UDDI registry accepts, parses, and responds to. This specification, along with the UDDI XML API schema and the UDDI Data Structure specification, makes up a complete programming interface to a UDDI registry.

UDDI data structures

This specification covers the specifics of the XML structures contained within the SOAP messages defined by the UDDI Programmer's API. This specification defines five core data structures and their relationships to one another.

The UDDI XML API schema is not contained in a specification; rather, it is stored as an XML Schema document that defines the structure and datatypes of the UDDI data structures.

Java-Based APIs

The UDDI specifications do not directly define a Java-based API for accessing a UDDI registry. The Programmer's API specification only defines a series of SOAP messages that a UDDI registry can accept. Thus, a Java developer who wishes to access a UDDI registry can do so in a number of ways:

Using a Java-based SOAP API

A Java programmer can use an API that creates SOAP messages containing a UDDI XML document. The Java programmer would be have to create each XML document by hand and insert this document into the body of each SOAP message. This approach would require that a developer understand the ordering of the SOAP messages that a UDDI registry accepts and format each SOAP message properly.

Using a custom Java-based UDDI client API

Some companies, such as Systinet, have created client APIs for accessing a UDDI registry. These APIs have classes and constructs that represent the data structures and messages supported by UDDI. These APIs also allow you to interact with a UDDI registry without knowing the specifics of SOAP or the XML messages and data structures that UDDI interacts with. These custom libraries work with any UDDI registry, so you can use Systinet's library to access Microsoft's UBR node.

Using JAXR

The JAXR specification defines a standardized way for Java programs to access a registry. JAXR allows developers to write code that can access several different registries, including UDDI and the ebXML Registry/Repository. JAXR's programming constructs don't mimic those used by UDDI, but this API gives you a common way to access a variety of different registry types, whereas a custom Java-based UDDI client API can access only a UDDI registry. The trade-off for portability is dealing with the additional layer of abstraction required by JAXR. JAXR is currently in an early preview release

To get you up to speed with UDDI, this chapter presents a simple UDDI example implemented three times—one time for each technique. Apache SOAP is used to develop a client that uses a Java-based SOAP API, Systinet WASP UDDI Client Package demonstrates a custom Java-based UDDI client API, and a JAXR client shows how JAXR's abstract approach looks to the developer. However, as more details of

UDDI are explained, the examples use the Apache SOAP implementation because it allows us to focus on the details of XML and UDDI.

Programming UDDI

Two APIs are described by the UDDI specification: the inquiry API and the Publishing API. They are accessed using the same techniques but use different XML documents, data structures, and access points. The inquiry API locates information about a business, the services a business offers, the specifications of those services, and information about what to do in a failure situation. Any read operation from a UDDI registry uses one of the inquiry API's messages. The inquiry API does not require authenticated access and is subsequently accessed using HTTP.

The Publishing API is used to create, store, or update information located in a UDDI registry. All functions in this API require authenticated access to a UDDI registry; the UDDI registry must have a logon identity, and the security credentials for this identity must be passed as a parameter of the XML document for each UDDI invocation. Because publishing requires authenticated access, it is accessed over HTTPS, with a different URL than the one used with the inquiry access point. Table 6-1 lists the inquiry and publishing access point URLs for some major operator nodes.

Table 6-1. Access point URLs for some operator nodes

Operator node	Inquiry URL	Publishing URL
HP	http://uddi.hp.com/inquire	https://uddi.hp.com/publish
IBM Production	http://www-3.ibm.com/services/uddi/inquiryapi	https://www-3.ibm.com/services/uddi/protect/publishapi
IBM Test	http://www-3.ibm.com/services/uddi/testregistry/inquiryapi	https://www-3.ibm.com/services/uddi/testregistry/protect/publishapi
Microsoft Production	http://uddi.microsoft.com/inquire	https://uddi.microsoft.com/publish
Microsoft Test	http://test.uddi.microsoft.com/inquire	https://test.uddi.microsoft.com/publish
SAP Test	http://udditest.sap.com/UDDI/api/inquiry/	https://udditest.sap.com/UDDI/api/publish/
Systinet	http://www.systinet.com/wasp/uddi/inquiry/	https://www.systinet.com/wasp/uddi/publishing/

Several primary information types construct the XML documents used as input and output to UDDI invocations. This section shows these data structures along with the major APIs as defined by the UDDI specifications.

UDDI APIs are designed to be simple. All operations that a UDDI registry performs are synchronous, meaning that the requesting client blocks and waits until it receives a response message. Additionally, all operations have a simple request/response mechanism that gives them a stateless behavior. Therefore, using the UDDI APIs doesn't require a lot of complex ordering.

UDDI Data Structures

To understand the structure of the messages that are part of the API, you need a basic appreciation for the different data structures and XML formats that are used. This section discusses the major data structures that are passed as input and output parameters for major API messages. Figure 6-3 shows the relationships between the primary UDDI data structures.

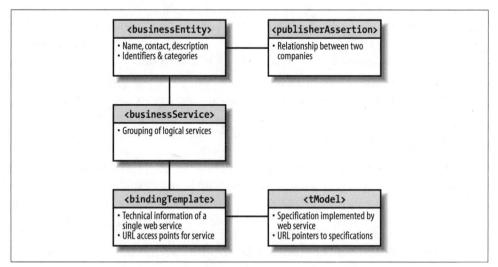

Figure 6-3. Relationship of primary UDDI data structures

A <businessEntity> structure represents a business's basic information. This information includes contact information, categorization, identifiers, descriptions, and relationships to other businesses. UDDI allows companies to establish relationships with one another. Many different types of relationships are possible. For example, a conglomerate can reference a subsidiary, or two companies can declare a partnership. In either case, each company must establish a unique <businessEntity> and separately establish its relationships to other companies that have their own <businessEntity> structures.

The <publisherAssertion> structure is used to establish public relationships between two <businessEntity> structures. A relationship between two <businessEntity> structures is visible only to the "public" when both companies have created the same assertion with two separate <publisherAssertion> documents independently. Thus, a company can claim a business relationship only if its partner asserts the same relationship. One company's assertion about a business relationship isn't visible to the public until its partner creates a similar, but separate, <publisherAssertion> document for its own <businessEntity> structure. Thus, if Company A asserts a relationship with Company B (fromKey=A, toKey=B), then the relationship will become public when Company B asserts a relationship with Company A (fromKey=B, toKey=A).

A `<businessEntity>` contains one or more `<businessService>` structures. A `<businessService>` represents a single, logical service classification. A `<businessService>` element is used to describe a set of services provided by the business. These services can be web services or manual services such as a nonelectronic service. A `<businessService>` document is reusable (i.e., a `<businessService>` element can be used by several `<businessEntity>` elements). For example, GE might create an HR web service and publish that service as part of an "HR web service" `<businessService>` structure. Additionally, GE might choose to list each of its subsidiaries as a separate `<businessEntity>`, since each subsidiary has its own IT infrastructure. Doing so would allow the `<businessEntity>` structure for the Plastics division to reference the same "HR web service" `<businessService>` as the Chemicals division.

A `<businessService>` contains one or more `<bindingTemplate>` structures. A `<bindingTemplate>` contains pointers to technical descriptions and the access point URL, but does not contain the details of the service's specifications. A `<bindingTemplate>` contains an optional text description of the web service, the URL of its access point, and a reference to one or more `<tModel>` structures. A `<tModel>` is an abstract description of a particular specification or behavior to which the web service adheres. A `<tModel>` is a type of digital "fingerprint" for determining the specifics of how to interact with a particular web service. The `<tModel>` structure does not provide the web service's specification directly. Instead, it contains pointers to the locations of the actual specifications. Companies can use the information pointed to by a `<tModel>` to determine whether a web service is compatible with their business requirements.

UUID

Instances of these data structures are identified and referenced by a universally unique identifier, known as a UUID. UUIDs are assigned when the data structure is first inserted into the UUID registry. They are hexadecimal strings whose structure and generation algorithm is defined by the ISO/IEC 11578:1996 standard. This standard virtually guarantees the generation of a unique identifier by concatenating the current time, hardware address, IP address, and random number in a specific fashion. The Inquiry API uses the UUID to request a particular structure on demand.

`<publisherAssertion>` documents do not have UUIDs, however.

Browsing Basic Information

A series of messages allow a program to retrieve basic information about a business, a web service, or metadata about a specification that a web service supports. These messages all have SOAP messages whose XML body element begins with find. Table 6-2 lists the messages that can be used to retrieve basic information for searching purposes. The "Message name" column lists the name of the XML root element

---

used as the body of the SOAP envelope on the call's request portion. The "Response document" column shows the name of the XML root element that is the body of the SOAP envelope for the response.

Table 6-2. XML documents used in browsing inquiry messages

Message name	Response document	Brief description
`<find_binding>`	`<bindingDetail>`	Given a UUID to a `<businessService>` structure, this message retrieves zero or more `<bindingTemplate>` structures within a single `<bindingDetail>` structure matching the criteria specified in the input arguments.
`<find_business>`	`<businessList>`	Given a regular expression, business category, business identifier, or `<tModel>`, this message retrieves zero or more `<businessInfo>` structures contained within a single `<businessList>` structure that meet the criteria specified in the input arguments.
`<find_relatedBusinesses>`	`<relatedBusinesses List>`	Given the UUID of a `<businessEntity>`, this message returns a list of UUIDs contained within a `<relatedBusinessList>` structure for the other businesses that have a relationship with this business.
`<find_service>`	`<serviceList>`	Given the UUID of a `<businessEntity>` and either the name of the service, the `<tModel>` of an implemented specification, or the service category, this message returns a list of all matching `<businessService>` documents contained within a `<serviceList>` structure.
`<find_tModel>`	`<tModelList>`	Given the a name, a category, or identifier, this message returns all matching `<tModel>` structures contained within a `<tModelList>` structure.

UDDI Response Structure

Many response messages return an XML document that contains zero or more of the primary UDDI data structures, rather than the data structures themselves. For example, the `<find_business>` message returns zero or more `<businessInfo>` structures, but does so in a `<businessList>` structure. The `<businessList>` structure is merely another data structure designed to hold zero or more other elements, similar to a Java Collection object. Don't confuse collection structures such as `<businessList>` with the primary UDDI data structures; they exist only for grouping.

The UDDI Programmer's API and UDDI Schema documents identify dozens of different structures used to make up the request and response messages. The Programmer's API identifies the structure of the request and response messages, paying particular attention to the input parameters for every request message. The UDDI Schema represents the same data structures, but provides datatyping and constraint information that can't be conveyed in the Programmer's API. When doing any development with UDDI, you should keep a copy of these two documents.

Traversing UDDI data structures can be complicated. To demonstrate this complexity, let's delve into the inner workings of the <find_business> message. The <find_business> message returns a <businessList> structure. Here's the definition of <businessList> from the UDDI Schema:

```
<element name="businessList" type="uddi:businessList" />
<complexType name="businessList">
  <sequence>
    <element ref="uddi:businessInfos" />
  </sequence>
  <attribute name="generic" use="required" type="string" />
  <attribute name="operator" use="required" type="string" />
  <attribute name="truncated" use="optional" type="uddi:truncated" />
</complexType>
```

This definition says that a <businessList> contains a single <businessInfos> subelement (defined in the same schema, as indicated by the preceding uddi:) and three attributes named generic, operator, and truncated. Doesn't tell us much, does it? So, let's delve further. The schema for the <businessInfos> structure is:

```
<element name="businessInfos" type="uddi:businessInfos" />
<complexType name="businessInfos">
  <sequence>
    <element ref="uddi:businessInfo" minOccurs="0" maxOccurs="unbounded" />
  </sequence>
</complexType>
```

This definition tells us that a <businessInfos> structure contains zero or more <businessInfo> subelements, which are also defined in the same schema document. minOccurs="0" and maxOccurs="unbounded" tell us that the included <businessInfo> elements can be repeated zero or more times. We now need to seek out the schema definition of the <businessInfo> structure, which is:

```
<element name="businessInfo" type="uddi:businessInfo" />
<complexType name="businessInfo">
  <sequence>
    <element ref="uddi:name" maxOccurs="unbounded" />
    <element ref="uddi:description" minOccurs="0" maxOccurs="unbounded" />
    <element ref="uddi:serviceInfos" />
  </sequence>
  <attribute name="businessKey" use="required" type="uddi:businessKey" />
</complexType>
```

This structure contains three subelements and an attribute. The attribute, businessKey, is the UUID for this business. The first subelement, <name>, gives the name of the business. The second subelement, <description>, is zero or more text elements that describe what the business does. The third subelement, <serviceInfos>, is a grouping of <businessService> documents. To figure out what a <businessService> document is, we must search the schema for the <serviceInfos> element.

Searching for this schema is left as the proverbial "exercise for the reader." At this stage, you should have an idea of the complexity of UDDI data structures and their navigation. An entire book could be dedicated to exploring every facet of the UDDI Programmers API. The rest of this chapter focuses on how to interact with UDDI and presents Java clients that demystify some of the complexity in the UDDI API and its data structures.

Finding a Business

Now it's finally time to pull everything that we have talked about together into a program. The examples in this chapter use Systinet WASP UDDI Standard. We selected this software because it is robust and free for development purposes. It includes:

- A "local" UDDI registry (server) that runs as a servlet under Apache Tomcat 3.2.3, WebLogic Server 6.1, or IBM WebSphere 4.0
- Database scripts for using Oracle, PostgreSQL, Cloudscape, Microsoft SQL Server, IBM DB2, and Sybase as the persistent store for the local UDDI registry
- A Java-based UDDI client API
- Sample code that illustrates how to use its custom client API in Java

We use Systinet WASP UDDI Standard primarily for its local registry, which allows you to run a registry locally on your computer for testing and development. We won't focus on the client API. Since a UDDI server accepts standard SOAP messages, we can use any Java-based SOAP client API to create the appropriate messages and direct them to a valid UDDI registry.

Our first UDDI client retrieves basic business information for a fictitious company called Demi Credit. The Systinet WASP UDDI registry comes with a preconfigured entry for Demi Credit. This example uses the Apache SOAP client library to create an appropriate SOAP message that has a `<find_business>` document as its body. We won't create this document programmatically, which would be an exercise in the use of the DOM or JDOM APIs; instead, we'll take the body for our SOAP request message from the file *Ch6_FindBusiness.xml*:

```
<uddi:find_business generic="2.0" maxRows="10">
  <uddi:name>
    Demi Credit
  </uddi:name>
</uddi:find_business>
```

The `<uddi:find_business>` tag indicates that this element is named `find_business` and defined in the `uddi` namespace. The contents of the tag must adhere to the schema for `find_business`, which defines a couple of different attributes. The `generic` attribute indicates the UDDI API version that is used (Version 2.0, in this case). `maxRows` indicates how many matching `<businessInfo>` structures should be returned if the query matches more than one company.

This `<find_business>` element has a single subelement, `<name>`, which is the meat of our request. The value of the `<name>` element is a simple regular expression used to search the names of different businesses. The percentage sign (%) can be used for wildcard matching. In this example, we know the name of the company we are searching for: Demi Credit.

Before looking at the code for the client, let's run it and observe its behavior. The client reads an XML file, wraps it in a SOAP envelope, and sends it to a URL destination, adding various UDDI and Systinet namespace declarations that are required to make the SOAP message comply to the UDDI specification. The destination is the URL of an endpoint configured to accept UDDI inquiry messages. Run the command:

```
java UDDISoapClient -df ./Ch6_FindBusiness.xml
```

You should see the following output:

```
Starting UDDISoapClient:
    host url     = http://localhost:8080/wasp/uddi/inquiry/
    data file    = Ch6_FindBusiness.xml

Sent SOAP Message with Apache HTTP SOAP Client.
Waiting for response....

<?xml version="1.0" encoding="UTF-8"?>
<SOAP-ENV:Envelope xmlns:SOAP-ENV="http://schemas.xmlsoap.org/soap/envelope/">
  <SOAP-ENV:Body>
    <businessList xmlns="urn:uddi-org:api_v2" generic="2.0" operator="SYSTINET">
      <businessInfos>
        <businessInfo businessKey="892ac280-c16b-11d5-85ad-801eef208714">
          <name xml:lang="en">
            Demi Credit
          </name>
          <description xml:lang="en">
            A smaller demo credit agency used for illustrating UDDI inquiry.
          </description>
```

```
          <serviceInfos>
            <serviceInfo serviceKey="860eca90-c16d-11d5-85ad-801eef208714"
              businessKey="9a26b6e0-c15f-11d5-85a3-801eef208714">
              <name xml:lang="en">
                DCAmail
              </name>
            </serviceInfo>
          </serviceInfos>
        </businessInfo>
      </businessInfos>
    </businessList>
  </SOAP-ENV:Body>
</SOAP-ENV:Envelope>
```

This output is saved as *Ch6_FindBusiness_OUTPUT.xml* and is included with the examples provided for this chapter. Other examples that use this program have their response documents saved in the same format.

Let's pick apart the response to see what it contains. The UDDI Server returned a single <businessList> structure which, in turn, has a single <businessInfos> structure. The <businessInfos> element can have zero or more <businessInfo> elements, based upon the number of businesses that were matched as part of the query. In this case, the server found only one business matching the name Demi Credit in the UDDI registry.

The <businessInfo> element contains several other important pieces of information. First, the businessKey attribute contains the UUID of Demi Credit. The UUID value is needed to do a more detailed information search or an update using the Publisher's API. Second, the <businessInfo> structure has a <description> that contains a textual description of what the company does. Next, the <businessInfo> structure contains a <serviceInfos> structure that contains a collection of all web services registered by this business. Each web service is described by a single <serviceInfo> structure, which contains the web service's UUID as an attribute.

Now that we've seen what the client does and examined the documents it sends and receives, it is time to look at *UDDISoapClient.java* in its entirety:

```java
import java.io.*;
import java.util.*;

public class UDDISoapClient
{
    // Default values used if no command line parameters are set
    private static final String DEFAULT_HOST_URL =
                            "http://localhost:8080/wasp/uddi/inquiry/";
    private static final String DEFAULT_DATA_FILENAME  = "./Default.xml";

    // In the SOAP chapter, we used "urn:oreilly:jaws:samples",
    // but Systinet UDDI requires this to be blank.
    private static final String URI                    = "";
    private String m_hostURL;
    private String m_dataFileName;
```

```java
public UDDISoapClient(String hostURL, String dataFileName) throws Exception
{
    m_hostURL = hostURL;
    m_dataFileName    = dataFileName;

    System.out.println();
    System.out.println("_____");
    System.out.println("Starting UDDISoapClient:");
    System.out.println("    host url        = " + m_hostURL);
    System.out.println("    data file       = " + m_dataFileName);
    System.out.println("_____");
    System.out.println();
}

public void sendSOAPMessage() {
    try {

        // Get soap body to include in the SOAP envelope from FILE
        FileReader fr = new FileReader (m_dataFileName);
        javax.xml.parsers.DocumentBuilder xdb =
            org.apache.soap.util.xml.XMLParserUtils.getXMLDocBuilder();
        org.w3c.dom.Document doc =
            xdb.parse (new org.xml.sax.InputSource (fr));
        if (doc == null) {
            throw new org.apache.soap.SOAPException
                (org.apache.soap.Constants.FAULT_CODE_CLIENT, "parsing error");
        }

        // Create a vector for collecting the body elements
        Vector bodyElements = new Vector();

        // Parse XML element as soap body element
        bodyElements.add(doc.getDocumentElement ());

        // Create the SOAP envelope
        org.apache.soap.Envelope envelope = new org.apache.soap.Envelope();
        envelope.declareNamespace("idoox", "http://idoox.com/uddiface");
        envelope.declareNamespace("ua", "http://idoox.com/uddiface/account");
        envelope.declareNamespace("config",
            "http://idoox.com/uddiface/config");
        envelope.declareNamespace("attr", "http://idoox.com/uddiface/attr");
        envelope.declareNamespace("fxml", "http://idoox.com/uddiface/formxml");
        envelope.declareNamespace("inner", "http://idoox.com/uddiface/inner");
        envelope.declareNamespace("", "http://idoox.com/uddiface/inner");
        envelope.declareNamespace("uddi", "urn:uddi-org:api_v2");

        //
        // NO SOAP HEADER ELEMENT AS SYSTINET WASP DOES NOT REQUIRE IT
        //

        // Create the SOAP body element
        org.apache.soap.Body body = new org.apache.soap.Body();
        body.setBodyEntries(bodyElements);
        envelope.setBody(body);
```

```
        // Build and send the Message.
        org.apache.soap.messaging.Message msg =
            new org.apache.soap.messaging.Message( );
        msg.send (new java.net.URL(m_hostURL), URI, envelope);
        System.out.println("Sent SOAP Message with Apache HTTP SOAP Client.");


        // Receive response from the transport and dump it to the screen
        System.out.println("Waiting for response....");
        org.apache.soap.transport.SOAPTransport st = msg.getSOAPTransport ( );
        BufferedReader br = st.receive ( );

        if(line == null) {
            System.out.println("HTTP POST was unsuccessful. \n");
        } else {
            while (line != null) {
                System.out.println (line);
                line = br.readLine( );
            }
        }

    /////
    // Version in examples has XML pretty printing logic here.
    ////

    } catch(Exception e) {
        e.printStackTrace( );
    }
}

//
// NOTE: the remainder of this deals with reading arguments
//
/** Main program entry point. */
public static void main(String args[]) {

    // Not Relevant


}
}
```

This code is similar to the code presented in the SOAP chapters, with a couple of exceptions. First, Systinet WASP UDDI uses different servlets to implement the inquiry and publisher ports. When Systinet WASP UDDI is first installed, the URL of the inquiry port is *http://localhost:8080/wasp/uddi/inquiry*. In the program, this URL is assigned to the constant DEFAULT_HOST_URL:

```
private static final String DEFAULT_HOST_URL =
        "http://localhost:8080/wasp/uddi/inquiry/";
```

Second, UDDI SOAP messages don't require the use of a SOAP header. Thus, all of the code used to create a SOAP header and fill it with values, such as mustUnderstand, is not needed. Next, UDDI and Systinet WASP UDDI SOAP envelopes require the addition of several different namespaces that they have defined. These namespaces are required at the envelope level of the message, not the SOAP header or body. In the Apache SOAP API, the `Envelope` interface has a method called `declareNamespace( )` that adds these additional namespaces:

```
// Create the SOAP envelope
org.apache.soap.Envelope envelope = new org.apache.soap.Envelope( );

// Add the Systinet namespaces.
envelope.declareNamespace("idoox", "http://idoox.com/uddiface");
envelope.declareNamespace("ua", "http://idoox.com/uddiface/account");
envelope.declareNamespace("config", "http://idoox.com/uddiface/config");
envelope.declareNamespace("attr", "http://idoox.com/uddiface/attr");
envelope.declareNamespace("fxml", "http://idoox.com/uddiface/formxml");
envelope.declareNamespace("inner", "http://idoox.com/uddiface/inner");

// Add the default namespace
envelope.declareNamespace("", "http://idoox.com/uddiface/inner");

// Include the standard UDDI namespace.
// This URN contains all of the UDDI XML data structures and messages.
envelope.declareNamespace("uddi", "urn:uddi-org:api_v2");
```

 Systinet was formally named Idoox. In their documentation, namespaces, and other declarations, you'll often see references to Idoox. When you come across these references, treat them synonymously with Systinet.

Using Systinet's UDDI Java API

The simple SOAP client we've just examined is sufficient to demonstrate a variety of UDDI APIs and data structures. It has some obvious limitations, however:

- SOAP envelope complexities such as namespaces have to be coded manually.
- SOAP Fault messages that are received have to be handled manually.
- The input and output XML documents are weakly typed as XML. A more sophisticated package would have Java interfaces that represent each UDDI data structure, allowing a program to check datatypes at compile time instead of discovering faults at runtime.

To get a feeling for what these limitations mean, we'll implement the same example using Systinet's UDDI Java API. To run this program, compile the file *SystinetFind-Business.java* and execute the following command:

```
java -Dwasp.restrictor.packages=- SystinetFindBusiness
```

Because of a limitation in the way the Systinet UDDI client library operates, you get a series of array typing error messages if you omit the `-Dwasp.restrictor.packages=-` environment variable definition. Don't forget to include the hyphen (-) after the equal sign!

Here's a listing of the Systenet-based client in its entirety:

```java
import org.idoox.uddi.client.api.v2.request.inquiry.*;
import org.idoox.uddi.client.structure.v2.tmodel.*;
import org.idoox.uddi.client.api.v2.response.*;
import org.idoox.uddi.client.structure.v2.base.*;
import org.idoox.uddi.client.structure.v2.business.*;
import org.idoox.uddi.client.api.v2.*;
import org.idoox.uddi.client.*;

/**
 * This is simple example of Systinet's UDDI Java API for accessing
 * a UDDI registry.
 * This program does a find_business call by name.
 */

public class SystinetFindBusiness {

    // Program Entry Point
    public static void main(String args[]) throws Exception
    {
        String company = "Demi Credit";
        findBusinessByName(company);
    }

    public static void findBusinessByName(String name) throws Exception
    {
        System.out.println("Searching for businesses named '" +
                            name + "'...");

        // Create a FindBusiness instance.
        // This creates a SOAP message.
        FindBusiness findBusiness = new FindBusiness();

        // Set the name to use in the query.
        findBusiness.addName(new Name(name));

        // This will limit the number of returned matches.
        // maxRows is an optional attribute.
        findBusiness.setMaxRows(new MaxRows("10"));

        // This will retrieve a stub to the UDDI inquiry port.
        UDDIApiInquiry inquiry =
                UDDILookup.getInquiry("http://localhost:8080/wasp/uddi/inquiry/");

        // Send the message and retrieve the response.
        BusinessList businessList=inquiry.find_business(findBusiness);

        // Show the results
        if (businessList==null) {
            System.err.println("ERROR: Business list is null!");
        }
        else {
```

```
// Business list is holder for results - business infos.
BusinessInfos businessInfos = businessList.getBusinessInfos();
System.out.println("\nFound: " +
                   businessInfos.size() +
                   " businesses.\n");

// Iterate through each company found in the query.
BusinessInfo businessInfo = businessInfos.getFirst();
BusinessKey result;
if (businessInfo != null) {
    result=businessInfo.getBusinessKey();

    while (businessInfo!=null) {
        System.out.println("BusinessEntity name = " +
                   businessInfo.getNames().getFirst().getValue());
        System.out.println("BusinessEntity UUID = " +
                   businessInfo.getBusinessKey());
        System.out.println("***");
        businessInfo = businessInfos.getNext();
    }
  }
 }
}
}
```

The Systinet UDDI client library is spread throughout several different packages. Since the UDDI API and data structures changed from Version 1.0 to Version 2.0 of the specification, Systinet opted to create separate Java packages for each version. This can be problematic for developers, but it is workable. Here are the import statements needed for the current crop of packages:

```
import org.idoox.uddi.client.api.v2.request.inquiry.*;
import org.idoox.uddi.client.structure.v2.tmodel.*;
import org.idoox.uddi.client.api.v2.response.*;
import org.idoox.uddi.client.structure.v2.base.*;
import org.idoox.uddi.client.structure.v2.business.*;
import org.idoox.uddi.client.api.v2.*;
import org.idoox.uddi.client.*;
```

The main( ) method is responsible for declaring the search string for the company and calling findBusinessByName( ), where the bulk of the work is performed:

```
// Program Entry Point
public static void main(String args[]) throws Exception
{
    String company = "Demi Credit";
    findBusinessByName(company);
}
```

Within findBusinessByName( ), the program needs to create a <find_business> message and populate it with the search criteria we established. The Systinet UDDI library has a separate class abstraction representing each UDDI XML message. Therefore, to create a <find_business> structure, you merely need to create an instance of their FindBusiness class. The FindBusiness class has several methods that add elements and attributes to the underlying <find_business> structure. In this example, we'll use addName( ), which adds the company name to search for, and setMaxRows( ), which limits the number of matches returned:

```
// Create a FindBusiness instance.
// This creates a SOAP message.
FindBusiness findBusiness = new FindBusiness();

// Set the name to use in the query.
findBusiness.addName(new Name(name));

// This will limit the number of returned matches.
// maxRows is an optional attribute.
findBusiness.setMaxRows(new MaxRows("10"));
```

Next, the program creates a connection to a UDDI server's inquiry port. The UDDILookup class has static methods that create a dynamic Java proxy object that communicates using SOAP. From the developer's point of view, it looks and feels like an RMI stub, except it doesn't communicate over RMI. The UDDILookup. getInquiry( ) method creates an inquiry connection. This program uses the same inquiry port as the UDDISoapClient program, *http://localhost:8080/wasp/uddi/inquiry/*. An UDDIApiInquiry object is returned and encapsulates an active stub that communicates with the UDDI server:

```
// This will retrieve a stub to the UDDI inquiry port.
UDDIApiInquiry inquiry =
        UDDILookup.getInquiry("http://localhost:8080/wasp/uddi/inquiry/");
```

Finally, the program needs to send the <find_business> document as part of a SOAP message. The UDDIApiInquiry object has a number of methods that create the SOAP envelope and populate it with an XML structure. A separate method exists for each UDDI XML message in the Programmer's API. For our example, the program calls the find_business( ) method on the UDDIApiInquiry object, passing in the FindBusiness object containing the XML structure.

The Systinet API also has matching classes for the response XML structures. Thus, since a <find_business> request yields a <businessList> response structure, the Systinet API has a BusinessList class. We can traverse this class to get to each subelement and attribute that was returned:

```
BusinessList businessList=inquiry.find_business(findBusiness);

// Show the results
if (businessList==null) {
    System.err.println("ERROR: Business list is null!");
}
else {
    // Business list is holder for results - business infos.
    BusinessInfos businessInfos = businessList.getBusinessInfos();
```

```
        System.out.println("\nFound: " +
                           businessInfos.size( ) +
                           " businesses.\n");

        // Iterate through each company found in the query.
        BusinessInfo businessInfo = businessInfos.getFirst( );
        BusinessKey result;
        if (businessInfo != null) {
            result=businessInfo.getBusinessKey( );

            while (businessInfo!=null) {
                System.out.println("BusinessEntity name = " +
                           businessInfo.getNames().getFirst().getValue( ));
                System.out.println("BusinessEntity UUID = " +
                           businessInfo.getBusinessKey( ));
                System.out.println("***");
                businessInfo = businessInfos.getNext( );
            }
        }
    }
```

Using JAXR

Now that we've looked at a simple SOAP client to build a request by hand, and a client that uses a UDDI API to build a request with slightly higher-level tools, let's proceed to the next level of abstraction: the Java API for XML Registries (JAXR). JAXR is a uniform approach to accessing a registry that advertises business information and services in XML. JAXR attempts to provide a single API that can access many different kinds of registries, including ISO 11179, OASIS, eCo Framework, ebXML, and UDDI (although the reference implementation can access only a UDDI registry).

The JAXR reference implementation is unique because it requires Tomcat for the client implementation! This requirement is somewhat odd, but fortunately, it is only a characteristic of the reference implementation. The provider implementations created by vendors will probably be simple libraries that don't require an external server such as Tomcat. You can get JAXR and Systinet WASP UDDI Standard to use the same Tomcat installation; details on how to accomplish this installation are in this chapter's *README.txt* file. When installing and configuring JAXR on your machine, make sure that the *.jaxr.properties* file included with this chapter's examples is placed in your home directory. On a Unix system, this directory is the *~/ directory*; on NT or Windows 2000, the home directory is given by the value of the %USERPROFILE% environment variable. To run the program to search for Demi Credit using JAXR, use this command:

```
java JAXRFindBusiness "Demi Credit"
```

The following output should be seen on the console:

```
Query string is Demi Credit
JAXR Reference Implementation -- logging started
```

```
Org name: Demi Credit
Org description: A smaller demo credit agency used for illustrating UDDI inquiry
.
Org key id: 892ac280-c16b-11d5-85ad-801eef208714
Contact name: David Tarnov
---
```

Since you should now have a better understanding of how these UDDI queries work, this example provides a more thorough parsing of the response message. This program provides a formatted output, rather than simply dumping an XML document to the screen. The code for this client is in the file *JAXRFindBusiness.java.* Here is the source code in its entirety:

```java
import javax.xml.registry.*;
import javax.xml.registry.infomodel.*;
import java.net.*;
import java.util.*;

/*
 * This is the FindBusiness UDDI example implemented using
 * the JAXR libraries and the reference implementation
 * JAXR provider for accessing a UDDI registry.
 */
public class JAXRFindBusiness {

    public JAXRFindBusiness( ) {}

    public static void main(String[] args) {

        if (args.length != 1) {
            System.out.println("Usage: java " +
                "JAXRFindBusiness <query-string>");
            System.exit(1);
        }

        String queryString = new String(args[0]);
        System.out.println("Query string is " + queryString);

        doQuery(queryString);
    }

    public static void doQuery(String qString) {
        Connection conn = null;

        // Define connection configuration properties
        // To query, you need only the query URL
        Properties props = new Properties( );
        props.setProperty("javax.xml.registry.queryManagerURL",
                        "http://localhost:8080/wasp/uddi/inquiry/");
        props.setProperty("javax.xml.registry.factoryClass",
                        "com.sun.xml.registry.uddi.ConnectionFactoryImpl");

        try {
            // Create the connection, passing it the
```

```
// configuration properties
ConnectionFactory factory =
    ConnectionFactory.newInstance( );
factory.setProperties(props);
conn = factory.createConnection( );

// Get registry service and query manager
RegistryService rs = conn.getRegistryService( );
BusinessQueryManager bqm = rs.getBusinessQueryManager( );

// Define find qualifiers and name patterns
Collection qualifiers = new ArrayList( );
qualifiers.add(FindQualifier.SORT_BY_NAME_DESC);
Collection namePatterns = new ArrayList( );
namePatterns.add(qString);

// Find using the name
BulkResponse response =
    bqm.findOrganizations(qualifiers,
        namePatterns, null, null, null, null);
Collection orgs = response.getCollection( );

// Display information about the organizations found
Iterator orgIter = orgs.iterator( );
while (orgIter.hasNext( )) {
    Organization org =
        (Organization) orgIter.next( );
    System.out.println("Org name: " + getName(org));
    System.out.println("Org description: " +
        getDescription(org));
    System.out.println("Org key id: " + getKey(org));

    // Display primary contact information
    User pc = org.getPrimaryContact( );
    if (pc != null) {
        PersonName pcName = pc.getPersonName( );
        System.out.println(" Contact name: " +
            pcName.getFullName( ));
        Collection phNums =
            pc.getTelephoneNumbers(pc.getType( ));
        Iterator phIter = phNums.iterator( );
        while (phIter.hasNext( )) {
            TelephoneNumber num =
                (TelephoneNumber) phIter.next( );
            System.out.println("  Phone number: " +
                num.getNumber( ));
        }
        Collection eAddrs = pc.getEmailAddresses( );
        Iterator eaIter = eAddrs.iterator( );
        while (phIter.hasNext( )) {
            System.out.println("  Email Address: " +
                (EmailAddress) eaIter.next( ));
        }
    }
```

```java
            // Display service and binding information
            Collection services = org.getServices();
            Iterator svcIter = services.iterator();
            while (svcIter.hasNext()) {
                Service svc = (Service) svcIter.next();
                System.out.println(" Service name: " +
                    getName(svc));
                System.out.println(" Service description: " +
                    getDescription(svc));
                Collection serviceBindings =
                    svc.getServiceBindings();
                Iterator sbIter = serviceBindings.iterator();
                while (sbIter.hasNext()) {
                    ServiceBinding sb =
                        (ServiceBinding) sbIter.next();
                    System.out.println("  Binding " +
                        "Description: " +
                        getDescription(sb));
                    System.out.println("  Access URI: " +
                        sb.getAccessURI());
                }
            }
            // Print spacer between organizations
            System.out.println(" --- ");
        }
    } catch (Exception e) {
        e.printStackTrace();
    } finally  {
        // At end, close connection to registry
        if (conn != null) {
            try {
                conn.close();
            } catch (JAXRException je) {}
        }
    }
}

private static String getName(RegistryObject ro) throws JAXRException {
    try {
        return ro.getName().getValue();
    } catch (NullPointerException npe) {
        return "";
    }
}

private static String getDescription(RegistryObject ro) throws JAXRException {
    try {
        return ro.getDescription().getValue();
    } catch (NullPointerException npe) {
        return "";
    }
}
```

```
        private static String getKey(RegistryObject ro) throws JAXRException {
            try {
                return ro.getKey().getId();
            } catch (NullPointerException npe) {
                return "";
            }
        }
    }
}
```

JAXR uses `javax.xml.registry` for the base package name for all of its classes. The `main()` method for this program parses a single parameter, which is the query string to use as the business name in the request:

```
import javax.xml.registry.*;
import javax.xml.registry.infomodel.*;
import java.net.*;
import java.util.*;

/*
 * This is the FindBusiness UDDI example implemented using
 * the JAXR libraries and the reference implementation
 * JAXR provider for accessing a UDDI registry.
 */
public class JAXRFindBusiness {

    public JAXRFindBusiness() {}

    public static void main(String[] args) {

// Parameter parsing, not entirely relevant

        doQuery(queryString);
    }
```

Most work for this program takes place in the `doQuery()` method. A client program first needs to create a connection to the service provider. In our case, the service provider is our local UDDI registry running at *http://localhost:8080/wasp/uddi/inquiry/*. To create the connection, we create a `Properties` object and fill it with relevant information: the `javax.xml.registry.queryManagerURL` value should be the URL of the UDDI registry that you are accessing, while the `javax.xml.registry.factoryClass` is the class that implements a `ConnectionFactory` object. Different JAXR providers provide different values for this property; the JAXR reference implementation uses `com.sun.xml.registry.uddi.ConnectionFactoryImpl`. Finally, the client code creates an instance of the `ConnectionFactory` class, associates the properties with this class, and then creates a `Connection` object using the `createConnection()` method:

```
    public static void doQuery(String qString) {
        Connection conn = null;

        // Define connection configuration properties
        // To query, you need only the query URL
        Properties props = new Properties();
```

```
props.setProperty("javax.xml.registry.queryManagerURL",
                 "http://localhost:8080/wasp/uddi/inquiry/");
props.setProperty("javax.xml.registry.factoryClass",
                 "com.sun.xml.registry.uddi.ConnectionFactoryImpl");

try {
    // Create the connection, passing it the
    // configuration properties
    ConnectionFactory factory =
        ConnectionFactory.newInstance();
    factory.setProperties(props);
    conn = factory.createConnection();
```

Once we have a connection to a service provider, we need to connect to a RegistryService object. Since different registries support different types of services, a RegistryService object tells your program exactly which services the registry supports. For example, some registries allow declarative SQL queries (UDDI does not). The RegistryService interface has methods for telling a program the registry's capabilities and returning manager objects that support a particular type of capability. For business requests, such as the requests that UDDI supports, the BusinessQueryManager interface must be used. To retrieve a reference to a BusinessQueryManager object, call the getBusinessQueryManager() method on a RegistryService object:

```
// Get registry service and query manager
RegistryService rs = conn.getRegistryService();
BusinessQueryManager bqm = rs.getBusinessQueryManager();
```

The BusinessQueryManager interface has a series of findXXX() methods that perform different types of queries. Different methods query for different items; for example, the findOrganizations() method queries a registry for business information, while the findServices() method asks for different services that may or may not be available. Most methods take one or more Collection objects as input; these objects refine the query using qualifiers. The first parameter of the findOrganizations() method takes a Collection of find qualifiers that refines how the query should be performed. Find qualifiers can apply a sort or restrict the number of entries that are returned; in this case, we ask that the responses be sorted by name. The second parameter of the findOrganizations() takes a Collection of name patterns to apply to the search. To populate this Collection, we add the business name that we read from the command line. The other parameters (all set to null in this example) take qualifiers that search for businesses based upon classifications, specifications supported, external identifiers, and external URLs, respectively. The query returns a BulkResponse object that can be checked for exceptions from the server or converted to a Collection:

```
// Define find qualifiers and name patterns
Collection qualifiers = new ArrayList();
qualifiers.add(FindQualifier.SORT_BY_NAME_DESC);
Collection namePatterns = new ArrayList();
namePatterns.add(qString);

// Find using the name
BulkResponse response =
```

```
        bqm.findOrganizations(qualifiers,
            namePatterns, null, null, null, null);
    Collection orgs = response.getCollection( );
```

The rest of the program is responsible for iterating through the output and formatting it for display on the screen. It's a bit wordy, so it's not included again here. A client application would use the information retrieved from the query to perform other queries or to leverage a particular service.

As you undoubtedly noticed, the JAXR API is more complicated than the Systinet API. JAXR does not have class representations for each UDDI XML structure; instead, we have to work with query managers and lists of various qualifiers. Working with the Systinet API is convenient because every class has an XML counterpart with the same name. You pay a price for abstraction, though: the Systenet client is tied to UDDI, while the JAXR client could conceivably make a similar request from a different kind of registry with little or no modification.

Getting More Detail

find_ messages are designed to return basic information about the structures that a UDDI registry manages. Given the UUID to one of the major data structures, you can drill down into the registry to get a full listing of the details stored in that structure. The UDDI inquiry API provides a series of messages that begin with get_ for retrieving information from the registry. Table 6-3 lists these messages.

Table 6-3. XML documents used to get detailed information

Message name	Response document	Brief description
<get_bindingDetail>	<bindingDetail>	Given one or more UUIDs of different <bindingTemplate> documents, this message returns a <bindingDetail> structure containing the complete <bindingTemplate> document for each matching UUID. The specification recommends that a client application caches <bindingTemplate> documents locally so repeated calls to a web service do not require a query on the UDDI server each time. If a call based on cached <bindingDetail> information fails, a new <binding-Detail> structure can be retrieved using this message.
<get_businessDetail>	<businessDetail>	Given one or more UUIDs of different <businessEntity> documents, this message retrieves a <businessDetail> structure that contains <businessEntity> documents for each matching UUID.
<get_serviceDetail>	<serviceDetail>	Given one or more UUIDs of different <businessService> documents, this message returns a <serviceDetail> structure that contains the complete <businessService> document for each matching UUID.
<get_tModelDetail>	<tModelDetail>	Given one or more UUIDs of different <tModel> documents, this message returns a <tModelDetail> structure containing the complete <tModel> document for each matching UUID.

All of these messages are fairly straightforward. As long as you can get a valid UUID for the data structure you are interested in, you can get its details. In the <find_business> example for Demi Credit, the response document indicated that Demi Credit had published a web service named DCAmail with the UUID 860eca90-c16d-11d5-85ad-801eef208714. Let's send a <get_serviceDetail> message to get all of the information about this web service. To get this information, we'll use the UDDISoapClient program from our previous examples to send a handwritten XML document. This document contains a <get_serviceDetail> message using the UUID for the DCAmail web service. Here's a listing of *Ch6_GetServiceDetail.xml*:

```
<uddi:get_serviceDetail generic="2.0">
  <uddi:serviceKey>860eca90-c16d-11d5-85ad-801eef208714</uddi:serviceKey>
</uddi:get_serviceDetail>
```

The <get_serviceDetail> message doesn't have any optional attributes; it has only one subelement, <serviceKey>, which is the UUID of the web service for which you want more detail. The <get_serviceDetail> message can accept one or more <serviceKey> subelements on which to query. Here is the response document returned by the UDDI server:

```
<serviceDetail generic="2.0" operator="SYSTINET" xmlns="urn:uddi-org:api_v2">
  <businessService businessKey="9a26b6e0-c15f-11d5-85a3-801eef208714"
                   serviceKey="860eca90-c16d-11d5-85ad-801eef208714">
    <name xml:lang="en">DCAmail</name>
    <description xml:lang="en">Get credit assessment by email</description>
    <bindingTemplates>
      <bindingTemplate bindingKey="f9274a50-c16f-11d5-85ad-801eef208714"
                       serviceKey="860eca90-c16d-11d5-85ad-801eef208714">
        <description xml:lang="en">The address to which you should send the name
            and address of your credit report target</description>
        <accessPoint URLType="mailto">mailto:DCAmail@democredit.bar</accessPoint>
        <tModelInstanceDetails>
          <tModelInstanceInfo
             tModelKey="uuid:93335d49-3efb-48a0-acea-ea102b60ddc6">
            <description xml:lang="en">The smtp protocol is used when sending
                information</description>
            <instanceDetails>
              <overviewDoc>
                <description xml:lang="en">Describes how to use this
                    service</description>
                <overviewURL>http://www.creditdemo.bar/DCAmail/howto</overviewURL>
              </overviewDoc>
            </instanceDetails>
          </tModelInstanceInfo>
          <tModelInstanceInfo
             tModelKey="uuid:25ddf051-c164-11d5-85a6-801eef208714">
            <description xml:lang="en">The namespace in which our credit numbers
                are used.</description>
          </tModelInstanceInfo>
        </tModelInstanceDetails>
      </bindingTemplate>
    </bindingTemplates>
```

```
<categoryBag>
  <keyedReference keyName="Personal credit agencies"
                  keyValue="841416"
                  tModelKey="uuid:db77450d-9fa8-45d4-a7bc-04411d14e384"/>
  <keyedReference keyName="Credit agencies"
                  keyValue="8414"
                  tModelKey="uuid:db77450d-9fa8-45d4-a7bc-04411d14e384"/>
  <keyedReference keyName="Netherlands"
                  keyValue="NL"
                  tModelKey="uuid:4e49a8d6-d5a2-4fc2-93a0-0411d8d19e88"/>
  <keyedReference keyName="France"
                  keyValue="FR"
                  tModelKey="uuid:4e49a8d6-d5a2-4fc2-93a0-0411d8d19e88"/>
  <keyedReference keyName="Belgium"
                  keyValue="BE"
                  tModelKey="uuid:4e49a8d6-d5a2-4fc2-93a0-0411d8d19e88"/>
  <keyedReference keyName="Business credit agencies"
                  keyValue="841417"
                  tModelKey="uuid:db77450d-9fa8-45d4-a7bc-04411d14e384"/>
  <keyedReference keyName="Luxembourg"
                  keyValue="LU"
                  tModelKey="uuid:4e49a8d6-d5a2-4fc2-93a0-0411d8d19e88"/>
  <keyedReference keyName="Germany, Federal Republic of"
                  keyValue="DE"
                  tModelKey="uuid:4e49a8d6-d5a2-4fc2-93a0-0411d8d19e88"/>
</categoryBag>
      </businessService>
  </serviceDetail>
```

This document contains a <businessService> structure, which is a logical grouping of web services by a business. In the case of Demi Credit, this grouping lists a number of web services that allow you to do a credit check via email. The returned <businessService> has a single <bindingTemplate> that provides technical details of how to access the web service. The <accessPoint> is the web service endpoint URL. In this case, it is a simple email address: *mailto:DCAmail@democredit.bar*.

More importantly, the <bindingTemplate> has two <tModelInstanceInfo> documents that show where to find more information about how this web service runs and the specifications it supports. Each <tModelInstanceInfo> document contains a tModelKey attribute, which is the UUID of a <tModel> structure that contains a particular specification's metadata. The <tModelInstanceInfo> document also contains an <instanceDetails> subelement that contains a description of how to use the web service.

Categorization

Our <businessService> document also contains a <categoryBag> structure. <categoryBag> documents can appear with <businessEntity>, <businessService>, and <tModel> documents.

Categorization of data was an important requirement during the development of UDDI. Categorization allows data in a UDDI registry to be associated with an industry, product, or geographic code set. Some obvious problems come with the use of categories; they should be familiar to anyone who's ever searched for something on the Web. Broad categories, such as manufacturing, can return thousands of matching services and businesses—certainly too many to sift through manually. On the other hand, specific categories, such as "manufacturing in Buffalo," might be too specific to return any results.

It's probably not realistic to expect software to dynamically discover and use new businesses on the fly in the near future. Realistically, human analysts need to browse a UDDI portal that allows customized searches and queries to discover the businesses they are interested in working with. It's more likely that software will contain the logic necessary to locate and integrate with web services for companies that have been predetermined. It's also likely that businesses will set up private UDDI registries that they can share with their approved partners to facilitate B2B integration.

Many categorization systems can be used on data within UDDI. These systems are summarized in Table 6-4. Each taxonomy categorization is registered as a <tModel> structure within UDDI. This registration means that each categorization has a tModel name and UUID that can be used to reference it. The tModel name is the same in all UDDI registries, but the UUID for the tModel may change between operator nodes.

Table 6-4. Supported categorization taxonomies

Taxonomy name	tModel name	Description
NAICS	ntis-gov:naics:1997	The North American Industry Classification system. Hundreds of classifications are in this system, including "Pet supply stores," "Hazardous waste collection," and "Diet and weight reducing centers." More information can be found at *http://www.census.gov/epcd/www/naics.html*.
UNSPSC	unspsc-org:unspsc:3-1	The Universal Standard Products and Services Classification. It is the first system to classify products and services for worldwide use. More information can be found at *http://www.unspsc.org*.
ISO 3166	iso-ch:3166:1999	International standard geographical regions. This taxonomy includes codes for countries and their administrative support staffs. More information can be found at *http://www.din.de/gremien/nas/nabd/iso3166ma*.
Other	uddi-org:general_ keywords	General-purpose associations that a business might want to make. This taxonomy allows operator nodes to promote invalid entries or entries that would otherwise be rejected by another classification system. There is no specification on how this works; it is operator-node specific.

A <categoryBag> structure contains zero or more <keyedReference> structures. Each <keyedReference> structure contains the name and value of a category to which the data element belongs. In the previous <businessService> example, the <categoryBag> had eight <keyedReference> subelements. Three <keyedReference> subelements were for NAICS categorizations; the other five were for ISO 3166 country categorizations.

Determining which categorization a <keyedReference> belongs to can be difficult, but more details can be discovered by looking up the <tModel> document, using the tModelKey attribute that is also part of a <keyedReference>. If you look at the <categoryBag>, you will notice that three of the <keyedReference> elements have the same tModelKey value and the other five attributes have a different tModelKey value. For example, here is one of the ISO 3166 country categorization <keyedReference> elements returned as part of the <categoryBag>:

```
<keyedReference keyName="Netherlands"
                keyValue="NL"
                tModelKey="uuid:4e49a8d6-d5a2-4fc2-93a0-0411d8d19e88"/>
```

The keyName value identifies the categorization. It is also a textual name given to the categorization. The keyValue is the categorization code, as identified by the specification. The categorization code is guaranteed to be unique. The tModelKey value is the UUID of a <tModel> document that provides metadata of the specification that this categorization supports.

Identifiers

An identifier is a type of property or keyword used to uniquely identify a business or specification. Identifiers can be applied to <businessEntity> and <tModel> structures. Identifiers, like categorizations, can be used as part of a search when doing a <find_business> or <find_tModel> request message.

Identifiers and categorizations are implemented similarly. Identifiers are attached to <businessEntity> and <tModel> documents through an <identifierBag> structure. The <identifierBag> structure can have one or more <keyedReference> structures that provide the name, value, and <tModel> UUID reference for locating more information.

At this time, only two general-purpose identifier schemes have been incorporated into all operator nodes, but other schemes can be used as well. Table 6-5 lists the identifier types that are a core part of an operator node.

Table 6-5. Supported identifier types

Identifier name	tModel name	Description
D-U-N-S	dnb-com:D-U-N-S	The Dun & Bradstreet D-U-N-S number is a unique nine-digit identification sequence. This sequence provides unique identifiers for single business entities, while linking corporate family structures. More information can be found at *http://www.d-u-n-s.com*.
Thomas Register	thomasregister-com: supplierID	This scheme provides identifiers for over 150,000 manufacturing and e-commerce companies worldwide. More information can be found at *http://www.thomasregister.com*.

tModel

<tModel> documents provide metadata information about a web service specification, categorization specification, or identifier specification. <tModel> documents are a core data structure in the UDDI specification and represent the most detailed information that a UDDI registry can provide about any specification.

Looking at Demi Credit, we can see that the DCAmail <businessService> has a <bindingTemplate> with two <tModelInstanceInfo> documents. Each <tModelInstanceInfo> document contains a tModelKey attribute that is the UUID of a <tModel> document representing information about the supporting specification. There are also tModelKey attributes for each <keyedReference> structure that was part of the <categoryBag>. We can use the UDDISoapClient to retrieve the <tModel> document for any of these UUIDs. Let's get the <tModel> document for uuid:93335d49-3efb-48a0-acea-ea102b60ddc6, which is a specification implemented by the DCAmail web service. Here is the listing of *Ch6_GetTModelDetail.xml*, which is used as the body of the SOAP request:

```
<uddi:get_tModelDetail generic="2.0">
  <uddi:tModelKey>uuid:93335d49-3efb-48a0-acea-ea102b60ddc6</uddi:tModelKey>
</uddi:get_tModelDetail>
```

The resulting response is saved as *Ch6_GetTModelDetail_OUTPUT.xml*:

```
<tModelDetail generic="2.0" operator="SYSTINET" xmlns="urn:uddi-org:api_v2">
  <tModel authorizedName="admin"
          operator="SYSTINET"
          tModelKey="uuid:93335d49-3efb-48a0-acea-ea102b60ddc6">
    <name>uddi-org:smtp</name>
    <description xml:lang="en">E-mail based web service</description>
    <categoryBag>
      <keyedReference keyName="A transport tModel is a specific type of protocol"
                      keyValue="transport"
                      tModelKey="uuid:c1acf26d-9672-4404-9d70-39b756e62ab4"/>
    </categoryBag>
  </tModel>
</tModelDetail>
```

The authorizedName attribute is the recorded name of the individual who published this <tModel>. The operator attribute is the certified name of the UDDI registry site that owns the master copy of the <tModel> data. The tModelKey is the UUID of this <tModel>; it matches the tModelKey for the request document. The <name> subelement is the recorded name of the <tModel>; it can be used as part of a search when doing a <find_tModel> request. The <description> subelement provides a specification's textual description. A <tModel> can have an optional <categoryBag> or <identifierBag> structure as well. Finally, a <tModel> can contain an optional <overviewDoc> subelement, which contains a URL that points to remote descriptive information.

Publishing to a UDDI Registry

Publishing to a UDDI registry involves any operation that would create, update, or destroy data in a UDDI registry. Here are some key technical differences between publishing and inquiring:

Authenticated access

All publishing messages require authenticated access. The process for authentication is not defined by the UDDI specification and is specific to the operator node. Given authenticated credentials, however, your program can access any publishing message.

Different access point

Publishing message requests use a different access point than do inquiry messages. The HTTP protocol was suitable for inquiry messages, but HTTPS is required for all publishing messages.

Space limits

Operator nodes can impose space and registration restrictions on an individual or company. For example, a site may limit some users to one <businessEntity> structure and prevent them from inserting additional data without special permissions.

Operator node binding

When information is inserted into an operator node, that site becomes the owner of that data's master copy. Any subsequent updates or changes to the data must be performed at the same operator node. UDDI does not have a mechanism for resolving conflicts if duplicate entries are made at another operator node.

The Publisher API messages that require authentication are listed in Table 6-6.

Table 6-6. UDDI Publisher API messages

Message name	Response document	Brief description
<add_publisherAssertions>	<dispositionReport>	Given a valid authentication token and a <publisherAssertion> document, this message adds a <publisherAssertion> to an individual publisher's collection of assertions. A publisher assertion creates an association between two businesses. When the publishers of both businesses have added matching <publisherAssertion> documents to their collection, the relationship becomes publically visible.
<delete_binding>	<dispositionReport>	Given a valid authentication token and the UUID of one or more <bindingTemplate> documents, this message deletes the matching <bindingTemplate> documents from the UDDI registry.

Table 6-6. UDDI Publisher API messages (continued)

Message name	Response document	Brief description
`<delete_business>`	`<dispositionReport>`	Given a valid authentication token and the UUID of one or more `<businessEntity>` documents, this message deletes the matching `<binding-Template>` documents from the UDDI registry. Deleting these documents causes the deletion of any contained `<businessService>` or `<bindingTemplate>` data. Additionally, any `<publisherAssertions>` created with the UUID of this `<businessEntity>` will be deleted.
`<delete_publisherAssertions>`	`<dispositionReport>`	Given a valid authentication token and the UUID of one or more `<publisherAssertion>` documents, this message deletes the matching `<publisherAssertion>` documents from this publisher's collection. If other companies have created similar `<publisherAssertion>` documents, their documents remain part of their collection.
`<delete_service>`	`<dispositionReport>`	Given a valid authentication token and the UUID of one or more `<businessService>` documents, this message deletes the matching `<businessService>` documents from the UDDI registry.
`<delete_tModel>`	`<dispositionReport>`	Given a valid authentication token and the UUID of one or more `<tModel>` documents, this message logically deletes the matching `<tModel>` documents from the UDDI registry by marking them as hidden. The documents are not actually destroyed. Hidden `<tModel>` documents are not returned as part of a result of a `<find_tModel>` message, but are still accessible through `<get_tModelDetail>` and `<get_registeredInfo>` messages. `<tModel>` messages are not permanently destroyed, which allows any organization still using the `<tModel>` to get basic details about it.
`<discard_authToken>`	`<dispositionReport>`	Given a valid authentication token, this message tells an operator node to discard the active authentication session, effectively logging out the client. To perform additional Publishing API operations, a new authentication token must be retrieved from the operator node by using the `<get_authToken>` message.

Table 6-6. UDDI Publisher API messages (continued)

Message name	Response document	Brief description
`<get_assertionStatusReport>`	`<assertionStatusReport>`	Given a valid authentication token, this message returns a report that details all `<publisher-Assertion>` documents that have been created on any `<businessEntity>` documents managed by this publisher. This report returns `<publisherAssertion>` documents that were created by this publisher and other publishers. This query can search for complete or incomplete associations.
`<get_authToken>`	`<authToken>`	Given a username and password, this message retrieves an authentication token from an operator node to be used on other Publisher API messages.
`<get_publisherAssertions>`	`<publisherAssertions>`	Given a valid authentication token, this message returns a complete list of `<publisherAssertion>` documents that have been associated with the authenticated publisher account.
`<get_registeredInfo>`	`<registeredInfo>`	Given a valid authentication token, this message returns a complete list of `<businessEntity>` and `<tModel>` documents that are managed by the individual associated with the authentication credentials.
`<save_binding>`	`<bindingDetail>`	Given an authenticated token and one or more `<bindingTemplate>` documents, this message inserts or updates a UDDI registry with the `<bindingTemplate>` documents passed as input. This message can also update any associations made between a `<businessService>` document and a `<bindingTemplate>` document. This message returns a `<binding-Detail>` message that contains the final results of the call that reflect the information in the UDDI registry.
`<save_business>`	`<businessDetail>`	Given an authenticated token and one or more `<businessEntity>` documents, this message inserts or updates a UDDI registry with the `<businessEntity>` documents passed as input. This message can make sweeping changes to a UDDI registry; the changes may involve inserts, updates, and deletes of subdocuments contained within a `<businessEntity>`. Changes to an existing `<businessEntity>` can impact existing references to `<publisher-Assertion>` documents, `<businessService>` documents, and `<bindingTemplate>` documents. This message returns a `<businessDetail>` message that contains the final results of the call that reflect the UDDI registry information.

Table 6-6. UDDI Publisher API messages (continued)

Message name	Response document	Brief description
`<save_service>`	`<serviceDetail>`	Given an authenticated token and one or more `<businessService>` documents, this message inserts or updates a UDDI registry with the `<businessService>` documents passed as input. This message can modify `<businessService>` data and any references to `<bindingTemplate>` structures. This message returns a `<serviceDetail>` message that contains the final results of the call that reflect the UDDI registry information.
`<save_tModel>`	`<tModelDetail>`	Given an authenticated token and one or more `<tModel>` documents, this message inserts or updates a UDDI registry. If a passed-in `<tModel>` documet refers to a `<tModel>` that was previously deleted (hidden), it will be made visible again. This message returns a `<tModelDetail>` message that contains the final results of the call that reflect the UDDI registry information.
`<set_publisherAssertions>`	`<publisherAssertions>`	Given an authenticated token and one or more `<publisherAssertion>` documents, this message updates a UDDI registry to contain a complete collection of `<publisherAssertion>` documents while deleting documents that are not present as part of the input. This message returns a `<publisherAssertions>` document that contains the current collection of `<publisherAssertions>` as they are stored in the UDDI registry.

Security and Authentication

Authentication with an operator node is typically straightforward. Most operator nodes implement a name/password scheme that allows you to retrieve an authentication token. Operator nodes that support the name/password scheme for authentication expose their authentication interface through the `<get_authToken>` message. Operator nodes do not have to support this scheme for authentication and can provide alternative techniques for allowing a client to get an authentication token. Those techniques are not documented by the UDDI specifications and are specific to the operator node. An operator node also has specific ways of registering new publishers and verifying their information. The only requirement that an operator node has to adhere to is that the authentication token returned must be a text value that can be inserted in subsequent XML messages.

The Systinet WASP UDDI Standard has a preconfigured username (admin) and password (changeit). We can obtain an authentication token by running the

`UDDISoapClient` program with the *Ch6_GetAuthToken.xml* file as input and two command-line modifications:

```
java -Djava.protocol.handler.pkgs=com.sun.net.ssl.internal.www.protocol
    UDDISoapClient
    -url https://localhost:8443/wasp/uddi/publishing/
    -df Ch6_GetAuthToken.xml
```

First, the JDK `java.net.URL` class does not support HTTPS as a standard protocol. The `Message.send( )` method in the Apache SOAP library requires a `URL` object as input, so enabling HTTPS is key. Enabling HTTP is done by including the `–Djava.protocol.handler.pkgs=com.sun.net.ssl.internal.www.protocol` option on the command line. Using this option assumes that you have installed the *jsse.jar* library. This library is installed as part of Systinet WASP UDDI; if you use a different UDDI package, you may have to install JSSE yourself. Second, since we are using the Publishing API, we must access a different URL than the default that is configured for inquiries. The publishing URL for Systinet WASP UDDI is *https://localhost:8443/wasp/uddi/ publishing/*.

Using the JSSE library directly is not for the weak of heart. In addition to setting up JSSE and enabling HTTPS as a valid protocol, SSL requires that your program have a valid client certificate to be used against the server. Fortunately, Systinet WASP UDDI Standard installs a client certificate for your use, but otherwise, you would have to create a new certificate using Java's keytool utility.

The real value of using a custom Java API such as Systinet's is apparent when you look at the difficulty of using the `UDDISoapClient` to generate HTTPS messages. Two complete round-trip SOAP invocations have to be made and you have to go through the rigmarole of configuring SSL appropriately on the client. Systinet's library handles this situation cleanly by providing one method that retrieves your authentication credentials and other methods that use the rest of the Publishing API.

Here is the *Ch6_GetAuthToken.xml* document that we send to the server to request an authentication token:

```
<uddi:get_authToken generic="2.0" userID="admin" cred="changeit" />
```

The `<get_authToken>` element doesn't have any subelements and passes the name and password as the `userID` and `cred` attributes, respectively. Here's the body of the SOAP response:

```
<authToken xmlns="urn:uddi-org:api_v2" generic="2.0" operator="SYSTINET">
    <authInfo>
MIHLMDYbBWFkbWluMB4XDTAxMTIzMDAwNDYzNVoXDTAxMTIzMDAxNDYzNVoEDUFkbWluaXNOcmFOb3IwDQYJK
oZIhvcNAQEEBQADgYEA4Cci/CbDji6RiQFneRt7gVXwX/4TA7qCZNUmTnXFJdVNFIDvp4WV+IW+/
deDCQkOGVAdsub0vkXJX3dqdDGqDsDleXwm7cDN2ENW7K/IeN9ii7/
pfbVryPtKzzbe07ETcWAoRnkcgDteC7I77VpyiqKHUqwmi5+kN10XMRXfkTw=
    </authInfo>
</authToken>
```

The response document contains an <authToken> element that has an <authInfo> subelement. The value of the <authInfo> subelement is a key that will be used as the authentication token on all other publishing messages. To write a program that makes a series of updates on a UDDI registry, you must parse the <get_authToken> response message and store the authentication token as a String object. Your program would then have to create a second SOAP message to perform an insert, an update, or a delete operation.

Errors and <dispositionReport> Documents

Errors can occur on any request message, whether they are part of the inquiry API or the Publishing API. UDDI errors are always returned as SOAP Fault messages. (For more information on SOAP Fault messages and their structure, refer to Chapter 4.) The subelement of a SOAP Fault <detail> message is a UDDI <dispositionReport> document; this document is defined in the UDDI schema. Despite being used for all error code situations, <dispositionReport> documents are also used in some non-error situations as a status indicator. Non-error <dispositionReport> documents are returned as part of a standard SOAP response for any UDDI delete_ message.

UDDI SOAP Faults can be returned for dozens of reasons: expiration of an authentication token, a server that is busy and unable to handle requests, the use of invalid categorization and identifiers, unsupported APIs, etc. A full listing of error codes is contained in Appendix A of the UDDI Programmer's API specification. Here is an error that I received one time when I tried to exceed my limit for <businessEntity> documents while using Systinet's WASP UDDI Standard:

```
<SOAP-ENV:Envelope xmlns:SOAP-ENV="http://schemas.xmlsoap.org/soap/envelope/">
  <SOAP-ENV:Body>
    <ns0:Fault xmlns:ns0="http://schemas.xmlsoap.org/soap/envelope/">
      <faultcode>
        ns0:Client
      </faultcode>
      <faultstring>
        ClientError
      </faultstring>
      <detail>
        <dispositionReport generic="2.0"
                           operator="SYSTINET"
                           xmlns="urn:uddi-org:api_v2">
          <result errno="10160">
            <errInfo errCode="E_accountLimitExceeded">
              An attempt to save more data than allowed.
            </errInfo>
          </result>
        </dispositionReport>
      </detail>
    </ns0:Fault>
  </SOAP-ENV:Body>
</SOAP-ENV:Envelope>
```

A <dispositionReport> has a <result> subelement with an errno attribute. The <result> subelement also has an <errInfo> subelement with an errCode attribute. The value of the errCode attribute must be one of the error codes that are identified in Appendix A of the UDDI Programmer's API specification. In this example, the errCode value is E_accountLimitExceeded. The value of the <errInfo> element is a textual explanation of the error that can be displayed to a user.

When designing a program that interacts with a UDDI registry, your program needs to be prepared to handle SOAP Faults and react appropriately. If you want your program to parse UDDI responses intelligently, use the DOM API to parse a <dispositionReport> structure and then implement specialized actions to handle different errCode situations.

Abstraction APIs, such as the UDDI API provided by Systinet and JAXR, capture SOAP Faults and convert their contents into a specialized exception. This action allows you to write a program that has a familiar try/catch block to handle SOAP Fault scenarios, rather than using the DOM API to parse a <dispositionReport>.

What About the Rest of the Publishing API?

Using the rest of the Publishing API is straightforward. If you have the UUID of one major data structure element, you can use the delete_ messages to destroy data in the registry. If you want to insert or update data in a UDDI registry, construct a valid data structure, such as a <businessEntity>, and then use one of the save_ messages.

Since this chapter has already covered the major talking points of every major UDDI data structure, demonstrating Publishing APIs in full form would be repetitive. At this stage, you have all the necessary tools to work with the UDDI Programmer's and Data Structure specifications.

When working with the Publishing API, keep a couple of points in mind:

- Your program signals the difference between a creation and an update by the value of a document's UUID fields on a save_ message. If a save_ message is used for updating an existing document in a UDDI registry, the value of the existing document's UUID is placed in the input document's UUID field. If a save_ message is used to create a new document in a UDDI registry, the UUID should be left blank. For example, if you wanted to update a <businessEntity> document with a fictional UUID of 43, then you would create a <businessEntity> document, fill it with the contents you want stored in the registry, and then set this document's businessKey attribute to 43. However, if you wanted to insert a new registration into the registry, the businessKey value would be "".

- Be careful when using the delete_ and save_ messages. If the structure you are updating has a number of subelements, such as a <businessEntity>, you can inadvertently destroy them by removing their containment. If you delete a <businessEntity>, it will delete all <businessService> and <bindingTemplate>

elements contained within the ‹businessEntity›. It will not delete a ‹businessService› referenced by the ‹businessEntity›, which would occur only if the ‹businessService› is contained with a different ‹businessEntity›. For example, if you want to update a ‹businessEntity› document using a save_ message, you might accidentally delete ‹businessService› and ‹bindingTemplate› structures in the process. If the existing ‹businessEntity› element stored in a UDDI registry has ‹businessService› or ‹bindingTemplate› structures, but the ‹businessEntity› document used as input to the save_ message does not have those same subelements, the ‹businessService› and ‹bindingTemplate› subelements will be destroyed automatically as part of the update process.

- ‹tModel› documents are never fully destroyed. When you use the ‹delete_ tModel› message, a ‹tModel› element saved in the registry is merely hidden. Hidden documents can be located through ‹get_tModelDetail› and ‹get_ registeredInfo› messages, but will not be displayed by any find_ queries. This behavior ensures that the details associated with any ‹tModel› are still available to anyone who may currently implement the specifications referred by the ‹tModel›. ‹tModel› documents can be unhidden by using the ‹save_tModel› message.

Using WSDL Definitions with UDDI

WSDL is used to describe the interface of a web service. ‹tModel› UDDI documents provide metadata descriptions of a web service and pointers to specifications that describe their implementation. Given this provision, WSDL documents tie into the UDDI data structures in a couple of places:

- A ‹tModel› document should be created for each WSDL document supported by a web service. The ‹tModel› describes the abstract service type, not the service instance; if appropriate, the WSDL file pointed to by the ‹tModel› should not contain the ‹service› and ‹port› elements. Omitting the ‹service› and ‹port› elements allows a WSDL document to describe many web services located in several different places. The WSDL document's URL should be listed as the value of the ‹overviewURL› element. A ‹tModel› that references a WSDL document should have a categorization taxonomy of uddi-org:types; a categorization value of wsdlSpec should be applied to it by using a ‹categoryBag› element.

- A ‹bindingTemplate› structure is created for each unique URL access point used by the web service. The ‹bindingTemplate› document references one or more ‹tModel› documents containing the WSDL definitions supported at this access point.

- A ‹businessService› document is created for each web service. The document contains one ‹bindingTemplate› for each of the access points supported by the web service.

For example, if you implement one web service that has a single access point and is defined by a single WSDL document, you would create a single <tModel>, a single <bindingTemplate>, and a single <businessService>. Also, if you implement one web service that has two separate access points, each defined by a different WSDL document, you would create two <tModel> documents (one for each interface), two <bindingTemplate> documents (one for each access point), and a single <businessService> document. Each <bindingTemplate> document must point to the <tModel> that references its interface.

The Hertz reservation system web service provides a concrete example of how UDDI and WSDL work together. Here is the <tModel> for this web service:

```
<tModel authorizedName="..." operator="..." tModelKey="...">
    <name>HertzReserveService</name>
    <description xml:lang="en">WSDL description of the Hertz reservation service
      interface</description>
    <overviewDoc>
        <description xml:lang="en">WSDL source document.</description>
        <overviewURL>http://mach3.ebphost.net/wsdl/hertz_reserve.wsdl</overviewURL>
    </overviewDoc>
    <categoryBag>
        <keyedReference tModelKey="uuid:C1ACF26D-9672-4404-9D70-39B756E62AB4"
          keyName="uddi-org:types" keyValue="wsdlSpec"/>
    </categoryBag>
</tModel>
```

The WSDL document URL that this web service implements is contained as the value of the <overviewURL>. Additionally, this <tModel> is categorized as a web service by incorporating a <categoryBag>. <categoryBag> has a <keyedReference> that specifies the keyName attribute as uddi-org:types and the keyValue attribute as wsdlSpec.

A <tModel> can further qualify the portion of the WSDL document it refers to. For example, a <tModel> can refer to a specific <binding> element within a WSDL document that has multiple <binding> elements. A pound sign fragment identifier is used between the URL of the WSDL document and the name of the <binding> element that accomplishes this qualification. For example:

```
<overviewURL>http://mach3.ebphost.net/wsdl/hertz_reserve.wsdl#HertzReserveBinding
</overviewURL>
```

An Abstraction API

Writing a Java program that creates a complete web service registration to a UDDI registry requires a lot of effort: an understanding of SOAP, accessing a UDDI registry using the correct SOAP messages, and ensuring that WSDL documents are placed in the correct locations in a UDDI registry. A developer can easily make mistakes when following this model.

It didn't take long for companies to begin developing abstraction APIs that facilitate this process. It is argued that companies and developers will use the UDDI/WSDL/SOAP model more than any other model since it is a worldwide standard and supported by every major technology business. As such, providing an abstraction layer that simplifies publishing documents following this model makes sense.

IBM created an API that does this abstraction very cleanly. This API is called the Service Registry Proxy (SRP) and is contained as part of the UDDI4J project at IBM. This pseudocode demonstrates how to publish a new web service exposed by WSDL into a UDDI registry:

```
// Create an active connection to a UDDI registry
ServiceRegistryProxy srp = new ServiceRegistryProxy(
                "http://localhost:8080/wasp/uddi/inquiry/",
                "https://localhost:8443/wasp/uddi/publishing/",
                "admin",
                "changeit");

// Create a category list for an existing tModel (<categoryBag> document)
CategoryList categoryList = new CategoryList(
            TModelKeyTable.getTModelKey(TMODEL_UUID_VALUE_HERE),
            "uddi-org:types",
            "wsdlSpec");

// Create service provider (<businessService> document)
ServiceProvider serviceProvider = new ServiceProvider(
                "Demi Credit",
                "Financing Company",
                categoryList);

// Publish the service to UDDI
srp.publish(serviceProvider);
```

The ServiceRegistryProxy class creates connections to an inquiry and publishing access point. The program instantiating the proxy passes in all the information needed to create these connections, including the username and password needed to get an authentication token. The CategoryList object creates the equivalent of a <categoryBag> document for a specific <tModel>. Since WSDL <tModel> documents are supposed to have a special categorization, creating a CategoryList instance and passing this instance as an input parameter to the ServiceProvider constructor creates this categorization. A ServiceProvider object is an abstraction of a <businessService> document. Finally, the ServiceProvider object has a series of methods that allow a program to perform such actions as publish, unpublish, and find. All of these actions result in SOAP messages that are sent to the UDDI server.

CHAPTER 7
JAX-RPC and JAXM

The Java API for XML Messaging (JAXM) and the Java API for XML-based RPC (JAX-RPC) are both part of the Java Web Services Developer Pack, Winter 01 release.* These APIs are a key part of Sun's plans to integrate web services interfaces into future versions of the J2EE platform. JAXM provides a common set of Java APIs for creating, consuming, and exchanging SOAP envelopes over various transport mechanisms. It is intended mainly for a document-style exchange of information because it requires the use of low-level APIs to manipulate the SOAP envelope directly. JAX-RPC provides a means for performing RMI-like Remote Procedure Calls over SOAP. In addition, JAX-RPC provides rules for such things as client code generation, SOAP bindings, WSDL-to-Java and Java-to-WSDL mappings, and data mappings between Java and SOAP.

Fundamentally, JAXM supports synchronous communications. In fact, if you don't run your JAXM provider in a J2EE web container (i.e., it is implemented as a message-driven bean or servlet), then it supports only synchronous communications. You don't get asynchronous exchanges unless you use the connection provider. Don't get hung up by the "M" versus "RPC" mislabeling. You can use JAXM to exchange document- or RPC-style SOAP messages, just as you can with JAX-RPC. The real distinction between JAXM and JAX-RPC is that JAXM forces the developer to work directly with the SOAP envelope constructs, and JAX-RPC provides a high-level, WSDL-based framework that hides details of the SOAP envelope from the developer. JAX-RPC uses WSDL to generate your messages and provides an object-oriented (i.e., RMI-like) interface to the developer. JAXM doesn't use WSDL, so the developer must construct messages by hand and send or process them explicitly. You could make an analogy in terms of database access. You can access a database using

---

* Sun remamed the Java XML Pack to the Java Web Services Developer Pack in February 2002. The new name is confusing—the Java XML Pack still exists and remains unchanged; the Web Services Developer Pack is the XML Pack with the addition of Tomcat, Ant, and other tools. We don't know what name Sun is likely to use in the future, so be prepared for some confusion when you go to their web site.

JDBC, in which case the developer must construct SQL queries and work with the details of the database schema. Or, the developer can use JDO, which hides details of the database schema from the developer and allows the developer to work with the data as a set of Java objects.

JAXM defines the `javax.xml.soap` package, which includes the APIs for constructing and deconstructing a SOAP envelope directly, including a MIME-encoded multipart SWA (SOAP with attachments) message. Both JAXM and JAX-RPC share this package. Even if you only care about RPC, you should still go through the JAXM section to understand the SOAP Envelope APIs.

Java API for XML Messaging (JAXM)

JAXM consists of two main areas. The "messaging" capability provides a pattern for sending and receiving SOAP messages, with or without attachments. The SOAP packaging part provides APIs for constructing and deconstructing SOAP and MIME envelopes. Generally, the functionality is separated cleanly between the `javax.xml.messaging` package and `javax.xml.soap` packages.[*]

Where's the Messaging?

The word "messaging" means different things to different people. For some, it refers to instant messaging or email. For others, it means reliable, asynchronous transport of critical business data, such as with Java Message Service (JMS)[†] or ebXML Message Service. In JAXM, the "M" could be any or none of those things. Like a chameleon, JAXM can take on the personality of another existing messaging protocol through the use of profiles.

Don't infer that JAXM doesn't support synchronous request/response interactions. JAXM can do both asynchronous, one-way communication and a synchronous request/response with the `send()` and `call()` methods, respectively. It can even do an RPC call. We will see an RPC call later when we revisit the `GetBookPrice` example using JAXM.

Simple Servlet Deployment

There's that word again—"simple." The bare minimum runtime requirement for JAXM is that it be deployable in a J2SE environment. This requirement means that there is no dependency on anything, except for the ability to send something over HTTP and receive it via a servlet interface, as illustrated in Figure 7-1.

---

[*] We say "generally" because of the subtleties relating to the placement of the `send()` and `call()` methods, which we will cover in a later section.

[†] For more information on JMS, please refer to *Java Message Service*, by Richard Monson-Haefel and David Chappell (O'Reilly).

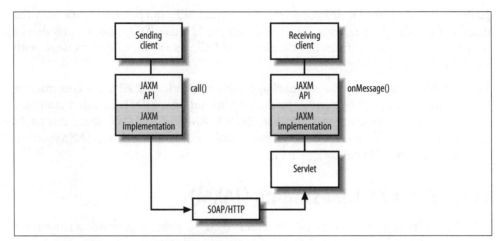

Figure 7-1. JAXM invocation in a servlet-based environment

In this type of environment, one can't rely on having a JNDI store available. Therefore, instead of performing a lookup( ) to obtain a connection, you can get a connection by calling the static newInstance() method on the javax.xml.soap. SOAPConnectionFactory object:

```
SOAPConnectionFactory scf = SOAPConnectionFactory.newInstance( );
SOAPConnection connection = scf.createConnection( );
```

For sending messages in this kind of environment, we use the javax.xml.soap. SOAPConnection.call( ) method. We will encounter this method again later.

Receiving the message is fairly straightforward. To receive a message, the application implements the onMessage( ) method. In a simple servlet environment, JAXMServlet. doPost() delegates the call to onMessage( ). There is no concept of registering a message listener. In the provider situation, the provider may invoke the onMessage( ) method any way it likes, in accordance with its own particular delivery semantics:

```
public class ReceivingServlet extends JAXMServlet implements OnewayListener {
    ...
    public void onMessage(SOAPMessage msg) {
        System.out.println("onMessage( ) called in receiving servlet");
        msg.writeTo(System.out);
}
```

The onMessage( ) method may return void or return a SOAP message, depending on whether it is intended for one-way message processing or two-way request/response. The class that implements the onMessage( ) method must extend either the OnewayListener or ReqRespListener interface to indicate its intent. Remember that you aren't allowed to overload return values; therefore, these two versions of onMessage( ) must be defined in different interfaces.

The SOAP Package

Table 7-1 shows classes and interfaces found in the `javax.xml.soap` package. These items represent the Envelope API, which is shared by both JAXM and JAX-RPC. Collectively, they provide all the functionality you need for constructing and deconstructing a SOAP or a SOAP with Attachments envelope. In Chapter 3, we used Apache SOAP, portions of the `org.w3c.dom.DocumentBuilder` interface, and portions of the JavaMail API to accomplish the same thing.

Table 7-1. The SOAP package

Interface/class	Description
AttachmentPart	A single attachment to a SOAPMessage object
Detail	A container for DetailEntry objects
DetailEntry	The content for a Detail object, giving details for a SOAPFault object
MessageFactory	A factory used to create SOAPMessage objects
MimeHeader	An object that stores a MIME header name and its value
MimeHeaders	A container for MimeHeader objects, which represent the MIME headers present in a MIME part of a message
Name	A representation of an XML name
Node	A representation of a node (element) in a DOM representation of an XML document that provides tree manipulation methods
SOAPBody	An object that represents the contents of the SOAP body element in a SOAP message
SOAPBodyElement	An object that represents the contents in a SOAPBody object
SOAPConnection	A point-to-point connection that a client can use to send messages directly to a remote party (represented by a URL, for instance) without using a messaging provider
SOAPConnectionFactory	A factory used to create SOAPConnection objects
SOAPConstants	The definition of constants pertaining to the SOAP 1.1 protocol (e.g., URI_SOAP_ACTOR_NEXT and URI_NS_SOAP_ENCODING)
SOAPElement	An object representing the contents of a SOAPBody object, the contents of a SOAPHeader object, the content that can follow the SOAPBody object in a SOAPEnvelope object, or what follows the detail element in a SOAPFault object
SOAPElementFactory	A factory for XML fragments that eventually end up in the SOAP part
SOAPEnvelope	The container for the SOAPHeader and SOAPBody portions of a SOAPPart object
SOAPFault	An element in the SOAPBody object that contains error and/or status information
SOAPFaultElement	A representation of the contents in a SOAPFault object
SOAPHeader	A representation of the SOAP header element
SOAPHeaderElement	An object representing the contents in the SOAP header part of the SOAP envelope
SOAPMessage	The root class for all SOAP messages
SOAPPart	The container for the SOAP-specific portion of a SOAPMessage object
Text	A representation of a node whose value is text

Let's see how these classes and interfaces fit together in some working examples.

The JAXM Sender—Request/Reply Client

This example shows how to construct a simple SOAP message and send it to a synchronous request/reply service that is expected to respond back. Let's start by running the sender and looking at the results. Run the following command in a command window:

```
java SimpleJAXMClient
```

This command produces the following output in the sender window:

```
Starting SimpleJAXMClient:
    host url      = http://localhost:8080/examples/servlet/SimpleJAXMReceive
```

```
Sending message to URL: http://localhost:8080/examples/servlet/SimpleJAXMReceive
Received reply from: http://localhost:8080/examples/servlet/SimpleJAXMReceive
Result:
<soap-env:Envelope xmlns:soap-env="http://schemas.xmlsoap.org/soap/envelope/"><soap-
env:Header/><soa
p-env:Body><Response>This is the response</Response></soap-env:Body></soap-env:
Envelope>
```

In the Tomcat servlet engine window, you should see:

```
On message called in receiving servlet
There are: 0 message parts
Here's the message:
<soap-env:Envelope xmlns:soap-env="http://schemas.xmlsoap.org/soap/envelope/"><soap-
env:Header/><soa
p-env:Body><Text>Some Body text</Text></soap-env:Body></soap-env:Envelope>
```

Soon we'll inspect the sending code in detail and look at the receiving code that sends the response. First, here is the sending client in its entirety:

```java
import java.io.*;
import java.util.*;

public class SimpleJAXMClient {

    //Default values used if no command line parameters are set
    private static final String DEFAULT_HOST_URL =
        "http://localhost:8080/examples/servlet/SimpleJAXMReceive";
    private static final String URI = "urn:oreilly-jaws-samples";

    //Member variables
    private String m_hostURL;

    public SimpleJAXMClient(String hostURL) throws Exception
    {
        m_hostURL = hostURL;
```

```java
        System.out.println();
        System.out.println
            ("_____");
        System.out.println("Starting SimpleJAXMClient:");
        System.out.println("    host url        = " + m_hostURL);
        System.out.println
            ("_____");
        System.out.println();
    }

    public void sendJAXMMessage()
    {
        try {
            javax.xml.soap.SOAPConnectionFactory scf =
            javax.xml.soap.SOAPConnectionFactory.newInstance();
            javax.xml.soap.SOAPConnection connection = scf.createConnection();

            // Get an instance of the MessageFactory class
            javax.xml.soap.MessageFactory mf =
            javax.xml.soap.MessageFactory.newInstance();

            // Create a message from the message factory. It already contains
            // a SOAP part
            javax.xml.soap.SOAPMessage message = mf.createMessage();

            // Get the message's SOAP part
            javax.xml.soap.SOAPPart soapPart = message.getSOAPPart();

            // Get the SOAP part envelope.
            javax.xml.soap.SOAPEnvelope envelope = soapPart.getEnvelope();

            // Get the Body from the SOAP envelope
            javax.xml.soap.SOAPBody body = envelope.getBody();

            // Add an element and content to the Body
            javax.xml.soap.Name name = envelope.createName("Text");
            javax.xml.soap.SOAPBodyElement bodyElement =
            body.addBodyElement (name);
            bodyElement.addTextNode ("Some Body text");

            // Send the message
            System.err.println("Sending message to URL: " + m_hostURL);

            // Synchronously send the message to the endpoint and wait for a reply
            javax.xml.soap.SOAPMessage reply =
            connection.call(message,
                new javax.xml.messaging.URLEndpoint (m_hostURL));

            System.out.println("Received reply from: " + m_hostURL);

            // Display the reply received from the endpoint
            boolean displayResult = true;
            if( displayResult ) {
```

```
            // Dump out message response.
            System.out.println("Result:");
            reply.writeTo(System.out);
        }

        connection.close();

    } catch(Throwable e) {
        e.printStackTrace();
    }
  }
}

public static void main(String args[]) {

    ...
  }
}
```

Understanding the Simple JAXM Sender

We'll start our examination of the code with the main( ) method. It's not unlike the main( ) method in the other examples we have covered in the book. This method parses incoming parameters, calls the constructor, and then calls sendJAXMMessage( ) to do the real work:

```
public static void main(String args[]) {

    . . .

        // Start the SimpleJAXMClient
        try
        {
            SimpleJAXMClient jaxmClient = new SimpleJAXMClient(hostURL);
            jaxmClient.sendJAXMMessage();
        }
    . . .
    }
```

sendJAXMMessage( )does all the interesting work; it creates and populates the SOAP envelope. First, we obtain a connection factory and use it to create a connection:

```
public void sendJAXMMessage()
{
    try {
            javax.xml.soap.SOAPConnectionFactory scf =
            javax.xml.soap.SOAPConnectionFactory.newInstance();
            javax.xml.soap.SOAPConnection connection = scf.createConnection();
```

Creating the message

Next, we obtain a message factory and create an instance of a SOAP message. The simple call to MessageFactory.createMessage( ) creates the SOAP envelope with header and body elements already in it.

Here is an example:

```
javax.xml.soap.MessageFactory mf =
    javax.xml.soap.MessageFactory.newInstance( );
javax.xml.soap.SOAPMessage message = mf.createMessage( );
```

If we were to look inside the SOAP message created so far, we would see that it already has the following contents:

```
<soap-env:Envelope xmlns:soap-env="http://schemas.xmlsoap.org/soap/envelope/">
<soap-env:Header/>
<soap-env:Body/>
</soap-env:Envelope>
```

These contents are accessible using the SOAPPart, SOAPEnvelope, SOAPHeader, and SOAPBody objects. In JAXM, a message is accessible using parts: either a SOAPPart or an AttachmentPart. The SOAPPart is the portion of the message that contains the envelope. The envelope contains the SOAPHeader and the SOAPBody:

```
// Get the message's SOAP part
javax.xml.soap.SOAPPart soapPart = message.getSOAPPart( );

// Get the SOAP envelope.
javax.xml.soap.SOAPEnvelope envelope = soapPart.getEnvelope( );

// Get the Body from the SOAP envelope
javax.xml.soap.SOAPBody body = envelope.getBody( );
```

Adding content to the message

The pieces of the message to which we add content are SOAPHeader and SOAPBody; we can also add content indirectly by adding attachments to the message using the AttachmentPart object. In a later example, we will show how to add attachments. For now, we'll add some simple content to our Body. To do so, we must use the addBodyElement( ) method of the Body object. Each body element or header element must be associated with a Name object, which you obtain from the SOAPEnvelope using the createName( ) method. This method has two signatures: one takes a simple String argument, and the other requires a String, a prefix designation, and a URI designation. The latter approach is intended to create an element in a specific namespace.

After creating the Name object and using it to create a Body element, we add content by calling addTextNode( ) on the body element we just created:

```
// Add an element and content to the Body
javax.xml.soap.Name name = envelope.createName("Text");
javax.xml.soap.SOAPBodyElement bodyElement = body.addBodyElement (name);
bodyElement.addTextNode ("Some Body text");
```

Making the call

To execute the call, we use `SOAPConnection.call( )`, passing it the message we created and a `URLEndpoint`. The `URLEndpoint` object, which inherits from `Endpoint`, specifies an absolute URL as a destination. The call blocks until a response is received:

```
// Send the message
System.err.println("Sending message to URL: " + m_hostURL);

// Synchronously send the message to the endpoint and wait for a reply
javax.xml.soap.SOAPMessage reply =
    connection.call(message,
        new javax.xml.messaging.URLEndpoint (m_hostURL));

System.out.println("Received reply from: " + m_hostURL);
```

To dump the SOAP response from the called service, we use a convenience method that JAXM provides: `writeTo( )`. This method sends the raw SOAP message to the specified output stream. This method even handles attachments correctly, as we'll see later. When complete, we free resources by closing the connection explicitly:

```
// Display the reply received from the endpoint
boolean displayResult = true;
if( displayResult ) {
    // Dump out message response.
    System.out.println("Result:");
    reply.writeTo(System.out);
}
connection.close( );
```

Understanding the JAXM Receiver

The JAXM Receiver used in these examples is a simple request/reply servlet. There's nothing profound here that we haven't already covered. The servlet receives the SOAP message from the sender and responds with a SOAP message. The servlet code in the following listing creates a message factory during its initialization phase:

```
import java.io.*;
import java.util.*;

public class SimpleJAXMReceive
    extends javax.xml.messaging.JAXMServlet
    implements javax.xml.messaging.ReqRespListener {

    static javax.xml.soap.MessageFactory fac = null;

    static {
        try {
            fac = javax.xml.soap.MessageFactory.newInstance( );
        } catch (Exception ex) {
            ex.printStackTrace( );
        }
    }
```

```
public void init(javax.servlet.ServletConfig servletConfig)
    throws javax.servlet.ServletException {
    super.init(servletConfig);
}
```

Next, onMessage() dumps the contents of the message to the console by using writeTo(); then it constructs a new message to return to the sender. Later, we will see how this same receiver and method can handle multipart messages with attachments:

```
// This is the application code for handling the message. We simply display
// the message and create and send a response.

public javax.xml.soap.SOAPMessage onMessage
        (javax.xml.soap.SOAPMessage message) {

    System.out.println("On message called in receiving servlet");
    try {

        int count = message.countAttachments();
        System.out.println("There are: " + count + " message parts");

        /// Dump the raw message out
        System.out.println("Here's the message: ");
        message.writeTo(System.out);

        /// Construct and send SOAP message response
        javax.xml.soap.SOAPMessage msg = fac.createMessage();
        javax.xml.soap.SOAPPart part = msg.getSOAPPart();
        javax.xml.soap.SOAPEnvelope env = part.getEnvelope();
        javax.xml.soap.SOAPBody body = env.getBody();
        javax.xml.soap.Name name = env.createName("Response");
         javax.xml.soap.SOAPBodyElement bodyElement =
        body.addBodyElement (name);
        bodyElement.addTextNode ("This is the response");

        return msg;

    } catch(Exception e) {
        System.out.println("Error in processing or replying to a message");
        return null;
    }
  }
}
```

Using JAXM for SOAP with Attachments

We will now show how to modify our sending client to use the JAXM API to add attachments and headers. To see the behavior and output of this new client, execute the following command:

```
java GenericJAXMSWAClient
```

This client assumes that files named *PO.xml* and *attachment.txt* are in the current directory. You should see the following output from the sending client:

```
Starting GenericJAXMSWAClient:
    host url        = http://localhost:8080/examples/servlet/SimpleJAXMReceive
    data file       = PO.xml
    attachment      = Attachment.txt


Sending message to URL: http://localhost:8080/examples/servlet/SimpleJAXMReceive

Received reply from: http://localhost:8080/examples/servlet/SimpleJAXMReceive
Result:
<?xml version="1.0" encoding="UTF-8"?>
<soap-env:Envelope xmlns:soap-env="http://schemas.xmlsoap.org/soap/envelope/"><s
oap-env:Header/><soap-env:Body><Response>This is the response</Response></soap-e
nv:Body></soap-env:Envelope>
```

The sender's output is similar to the output from the previous example. The real difference is what is seen in the Tomcat console window. The same receiver we used before generates much different results because we're now sending a multipart message. Note the MIME boundaries that separate the message's parts. The first part of the message is the SOAP envelope; the next two parts are the added attachments:

```
On message called in receiving servlet
There are: 2 attachment parts
Here's the message:
--2023334682.1010158929328.JavaMail.chappell.nbchappell3
Content-Type: text/xml

<soap-env:Envelope xmlns:soap-env="http://schemas.xmlsoap.org/soap/envelope/"><s
oap-env:Header/><soap-env:Body><PurchaseOrder><shipTo country="US"><name>Joe Smi
th</name><street>14 Oak Park</street><city>Bedford</city><state>MA</state><zip>0
1730</zip></shipTo><items><item partNum="872-AA"><productName>Candy Canes</produ
ctName><quantity>444</quantity><price>1.68</price><comment>I want candy!</commen
t></item></items></PurchaseOrder></soap-env:Body></soap-env:Envelope>
--2023334682.1010158929328.JavaMail.chappell.nbchappell3
Content-Type: text/plain

This is an attachment.
--2023334682.1010158929328.JavaMail.chappell.nbchappell3
Content-Type: text/plain; charset=ISO-8859-1

Another Part
--2023334682.1010158929328.JavaMail.chappell.nbchappell3--
```

Understanding the SwA Sender

Here's the code for the new sender, GenericJAXMSWAClient. We will break it down and walk through the new parts in a moment.

First, however, look at the whole thing:

```java
import java.io.*;
import java.util.*;

public class GenericJAXMSWAClient {

    //Default values used if no command line parameters are set
    private static final String DEFAULT_DATA_FILENAME   = "PO.xml";
    private static final String DEFAULT_HOST_URL
        = "http://localhost:8080/examples/servlet/SimpleJAXMReceive";
    private static final String URI = "urn:oreilly-jaws-samples";
    private static final String DEFAULT_ATTACHMENT_FILENAME
        = "Attachment.txt";

    //Member variables
    private String m_hostURL;
    private String m_dataFileName;
    private String m_attachment;

    public GenericJAXMSWAClient(String hostURL, String dataFileName,
                                          String attachment) throws Exception
    {
        m_hostURL = hostURL;
        m_dataFileName      = dataFileName;
        m_attachment = attachment;

        System.out.println();
        System.out.println("_____");
        System.out.println("Starting GenericJAXMSWAClient:");
        System.out.println("    host url       = " + m_hostURL);
        System.out.println("    data file      = " + m_dataFileName);
        System.out.println("    attachment     = " + m_attachment);
        System.out.println("_____");
        System.out.println();
    }

    public void sendJAXMMessage()
    {
        try {

            // for doing JAXP transformations
            javax.xml.transform.TransformerFactory tFact
                = javax.xml.transform.TransformerFactory.newInstance();
            javax.xml.transform.Transformer transformer
                = tFact.newTransformer();

            // Create an specific URLEndpoint
            javax.xml.messaging.URLEndpoint endpoint
                = new javax.xml.messaging.URLEndpoint(m_hostURL);

            // Create a connection
            javax.xml.soap.SOAPConnectionFactory scf
                = javax.xml.soap.SOAPConnectionFactory.newInstance();
            javax.xml.soap.SOAPConnection connection = scf.createConnection();
```

```java
// Get an instance of the MessageFactory class
javax.xml.soap.MessageFactory mf
    = javax.xml.soap.MessageFactory.newInstance( );

// Create a message from the message factory.
// It already contains a SOAP part
javax.xml.soap.SOAPMessage message = mf.createMessage( );

// Get the message's SOAP part
javax.xml.soap.SOAPPart soapPart = message.getSOAPPart( );

// Get the SOAP envelope from the SOAP part of the message.
javax.xml.soap.SOAPEnvelope envelope = soapPart.getEnvelope( );

// Read in the XML that will become the body in the SOAP envelope
javax.xml.parsers.DocumentBuilderFactory dbf =
    javax.xml.parsers.DocumentBuilderFactory.newInstance( );
javax.xml.parsers.DocumentBuilder db = dbf.newDocumentBuilder( );
org.w3c.dom.Document poDoc = db.parse(m_dataFileName);

// Get the empty SOAP envelope as a generic Source
// and put it into a DOMResult
javax.xml.transform.Source spSrc = soapPart.getContent( );
javax.xml.transform.dom.DOMResult domResultEnv
        = new javax.xml.transform.dom.DOMResult( );
transformer.transform(spSrc, domResultEnv);

// Now that we have the empty SOAP envelope in a DOMSource, we
// need to put it together with the DOM we just built from the
// input file.
// Get the document
org.w3c.dom.Node envelopeRoot = domResultEnv.getNode( );
if (envelopeRoot.getNodeType( ) == org.w3c.dom.Node.DOCUMENT_NODE)
{
    // Get the root element of the document.
    org.w3c.dom.Element docEl
        = ((org.w3c.dom.Document)envelopeRoot).getDocumentElement( );

    // Find the <SOAP-ENV:Body> tag using the envelope namespace
    org.w3c.dom.NodeList nList
        = docEl.getElementsByTagNameNS(
            javax.xml.soap.SOAPConstants.URI_NS_SOAP_ENVELOPE,"Body");
    if (nList.getLength( ) > 0)
    {
        // Found our <PurchaseOrder> element.  Plug it in
        org.w3c.dom.Node bodyNode = nList.item(0);
        org.w3c.dom.Node poRoot = poDoc.getDocumentElement( );

        // Import the node into this document.
        org.w3c.dom.Node importedNode
            = ((org.w3c.dom.Document)envelopeRoot).importNode(poRoot,
                    true);
        bodyNode.appendChild(importedNode);
```

```java
                // Now shove it all back into the envelope.
                javax.xml.transform.dom.DOMSource domSource
                    = new javax.xml.transform.dom.DOMSource(envelopeRoot);
                soapPart.setContent(domSource);
            }
        }
        else if (envelopeRoot.getNodeType( ) == org.w3c.dom.Node.ELEMENT_NODE)
            System.out.println("ElementNode");
        else
            System.out.println("Unknown Node type");


        // Get the Header from the SOAP envelope
        javax.xml.soap.SOAPHeader header = envelope.getHeader( );

        // Add an element and content to the Header
        javax.xml.soap.Name name
            = envelope.createName("MessageHeader",
                "jaxm","urn:oreilly-jaws-samples");
        javax.xml.soap.SOAPHeaderElement headerElement
            = header.addHeaderElement(name);

        // Add an element and content to the Header
        name = envelope.createName("From");
        javax.xml.soap.SOAPElement childElement
            = headerElement.addChildElement (name);
        childElement.addTextNode ("Me");

        // Add an element and content to the Header
        name = envelope.createName("To");
        childElement = headerElement.addChildElement(name);
        childElement.addTextNode ("You");

        // Add additional Parts to the message
        javax.activation.FileDataSource fds
            = new javax.activation.FileDataSource(m_attachment);
        javax.activation.DataHandler dh
            = new   javax.activation.DataHandler(fds);
        javax.xml.soap.AttachmentPart ap1
            = message.createAttachmentPart(dh);
        message.addAttachmentPart(ap1);

        javax.xml.soap.AttachmentPart ap2
            = message.createAttachmentPart("Another Part",
                "text/plain; charset=ISO-8859-1");
        message.addAttachmentPart(ap2);

        // Save the changes made to the message
        message.saveChanges( );

        System.err.println("Sending message to URL: "+ endpoint.getURL( ));

        // Send the message to the endpoint and wait for a reply
        javax.xml.soap.SOAPMessage reply
            = connection.call(message, endpoint);
```

```
            System.out.println("Received reply from: " + endpoint);

            // Display the reply received from the endpoint
            boolean displayResult = true;

            if( displayResult ) {
                // Document source, do a transform.
                System.out.println("Result:");
                javax.xml.soap.SOAPPart replyPart = reply.getSOAPPart();
                javax.xml.transform.Source src = replyPart.getContent();
                javax.xml.transform.stream.StreamResult result
                    = new javax.xml.transform.stream.StreamResult( System.out );
                transformer.transform(src, result);
                System.out.println();
            }
            connection.close();

        } catch(Throwable e) {
            e.printStackTrace();
        }
    }


    //
    // NOTE: the remainder of this deals with reading arguments
    //
    /** Main program entry point. */

    public static void main(String args[]) {

        // Process command line, etc
    ...
        // Start the GenericJAXMSWAClient
        try
        {
            GenericJAXMSWAClient jaxmClient =
                new GenericJAXMSWAClient(hostURL, dataFileName, attachment);
            jaxmClient.sendJAXMMessage();

        }
        catch(Exception e)
        {
            System.out.println(e.getMessage());
        }
    }
    ...
}
```

Attaching an XML fragment to the SOAP envelope

Much of the code in this chapter deals with attaching *PO.xml* to the SOAP envelope. When trying to port our Apache SOAP example from the previous chapter, we ran into a bit of a gotcha. Attaching an existing XML document to a SOAP envelope is reasonable—but you can't do it, at least not simply. This flaw is by far the biggest we have encountered in the API. The MessageFactory creates an envelope with empty `<Header>` and `<Body>` elements. APIs exist for creating and manipulating elements individually, but nothing lets you take a whole document and attach it. A SOAPPart. setContent( ) method takes a document source and attaches it as the SOAP part of the message, but the document that you give it must have the envelope structure in place already. This sort of defeats the purpose. If we had corporate data that was already packaged in full SOAP envelopes, we wouldn't need an API at all, would we?

Evidence suggests that this package was created solely for the purpose of providing an API for connecting to an ebXML infrastructure. In ebXML, the body of the envelope is intended to be a manifest and the actual payload of the message is intended to be an attachment. What if you don't want to use it in that way?

Enough of the soapbox. Our solution converts both the envelope and the XML document into DOM trees, plugs them together, and assigns the whole thing back into the envelope. To help do this, we use a JAXP Transformer object. The javax.xml. transform package is an API in JAXP, which is mainly intended for transforming documents using XSLT stylesheets. We use it as a utility to convert the envelope and the XML document between a DOM tree representation and the javax.xml.transform. Stream datatype that is required by some JAXM envelope methods we will use:

```
// for doing JAXP transformations
javax.xml.transform.TransformerFactory tFact
    = javax.xml.transform.TransformerFactory.newInstance( );
javax.xml.transform.Transformer transformer
    = tFact.newTransformer( );
```

First, read in the XML document (*PO.xml*) from a disk and put it into a document:

```
// Read in the XML that will become the body in the SOAP envelope
javax.xml.parsers.DocumentBuilderFactory dbf =
    javax.xml.parsers.DocumentBuilderFactory.newInstance( );
javax.xml.parsers.DocumentBuilder db = dbf.newDocumentBuilder( );
org.w3c.dom.Document poDoc = db.parse(m_dataFileName);
```

After creating the message and getting its SOAPPart, getContent( ) retrieves the envelope as a generic javax.xml.transform.Source object. The Source object is the superclass of either DOMSource, SAXSource, or StreamSource. Likewise, the Result object is the superclass of DOMResult, SAXResult, and StreamResult. The transformer can take any Source object and do the right thing automatically, regardless of its subtype, and convert it to the desired Result, as shown in the following listing:

```
// Get the empty SOAP Envelope as a generic Source
// and put it into a DOMResult
javax.xml.transform.Source spSrc = soapPart.getContent( );
javax.xml.transform.dom.DOMResult domResultEnv
        = new javax.xml.transform.dom.DOMResult( );
transformer.transform(spSrc, domResultEnv);
```

Now that we have the envelope as a DOMResult, retrieve the Document and its root element:

```
org.w3c.dom.Node envelopeRoot = domResultEnv.getNode( );
if (envelopeRoot.getNodeType( ) == org.w3c.dom.Node.DOCUMENT_NODE)
{
    // Get the root element of the document.
    org.w3c.dom.Element docEl
        = ((org.w3c.dom.Document)envelopeRoot).getDocumentElement( );
```

Next, find the `<SOAP-ENV:Body>` tag using the namespace of the envelope and plug in the purchaseOrder document:

```
// Find the <SOAP-ENV:Body> tag using the envelope namespace
org.w3c.dom.NodeList nList
    = docEl.getElementsByTagNameNS(
        javax.xml.soap.SOAPConstants.URI_NS_SOAP_ENVELOPE,"Body");
if (nList.getLength( ) > 0)
{
    // Found our <PurchaseOrder> element.  Plug it in
    org.w3c.dom.Node bodyNode = nList.item(0);
    org.w3c.dom.Node poRoot = poDoc.getDocumentElement( );
```

Now we have the two elements that need to be attached to one another: the SOAP Body element and the PurchaseOrder element. However, you can't just reparent a Node from one document to another; doing so causes an error. Each element keeps track of its owning Document, which is checked by the individual routines that insert elements. Move a Node into another document properly by importing the Node and its subelements into the Document first. This operation performs a copy. The second parameter to import( ) is a Boolean that indicates whether this is a deep copy of all subnodes or just the current one. Once the nodes are imported into the Document that represents the envelope, we can simply attach the root Node as the immediate child of the `<Body>` element:

```
org.w3c.dom.Node importedNode
    = ((org.w3c.dom.Document)envelopeRoot).importNode(poRoot,
        true);
bodyNode.appendChild(importedNode);
```

 If you use DOM level 3, there is an alternative to doing a copy. An experimental adoptNode( ) method reassigns an actual instance of a Node from one Document to another.

Now that the envelope is joined to the PO document, we take the root Node, convert it to a DOMSource, and place the whole thing into the messages's SOAPPart:

```
javax.xml.transform.dom.DOMSource domSource
    = new javax.xml.transform.dom.DOMSource(envelopeRoot);
soapPart.setContent(domSource);
```

Adding a header dynamically

You will encounter no surprises here. This code is symmetric to the Body APIs that we saw at the beginning of this section:

```
// Add an element and content to the Header
javax.xml.soap.Name name
    = envelope.createName("MessageHeader",
        "jaxm","urn:oreilly-jaws-samples");
javax.xml.soap.SOAPHeaderElement headerElement
    = header.addHeaderElement(name);

// Add an element and content to the Header
name = envelope.createName("From");
javax.xml.soap.SOAPElement childElement
    = headerElement.addChildElement (name);
childElement.addTextNode ("Me");

// Add an element and content to the Header
name = envelope.createName("To");
childElement = headerElement.addChildElement(name);
childElement.addTextNode ("You");
```

Adding MIME attachments

Next, let's look at two (of many) ways to add attachments to our SOAP message. The simple sender uses both methods. No matter how you add an attachment, though, it requires two steps: call createAttachmentPart( ) with the appropriate content to get an attachment and addAttachmentPart( ) to add the attachment to the message.

The first method is arguably more complex; we use it to insert an external file (in this case, a purchase order, formatted as XML) as an attachment. First, we use the Activation Framework to create a FileDataSource that points at our external purchase order. We then convert the FileDataSource to a DataHandler; in turn, we use the DataHandler to create our first attachment, ap1, by calling createAttachmentPart( ). Finally, we call addAttachmentPart( ) to add the attachment to the message.

Note that we don't need to specify the content type anywhere; the content type is provided automatically by the DataHandler object:

```
// Add additional Parts to the message
javax.activation.FileDataSource fds
    = new javax.activation.FileDataSource(m_attachment);
javax.activation.DataHandler dh
    = new  javax.activation.DataHandler(fds);
javax.xml.soap.AttachmentPart ap1
    = message.createAttachmentPart(dh);
message.addAttachmentPart(ap1);
```

Perhaps a more intuitive way to create an attachment is to call createAttachmentPart( ) with the content and content type as arguments, as we've done here in the attachment ap2:

```
javax.xml.soap.AttachmentPart ap2
    = message.createAttachmentPart("Another Part",
        "text/plain; charset=ISO-8859-1");
message.addAttachmentPart(ap2);
```

JAXM Profiles

JAXM is capable of morphing itself into an API that frontends any number of SOAP-based messaging frameworks through the use of "profiles." A key part of a message profile is the ability to automate the creation of message headers and body elements that may be specific to Framework. We will describe this concept in more detail in a moment. In the 1.0 reference implementation, an ebXML MS profile and a SOAP-RP profile are provided as examples.

A profile consists of a ProviderConnectionFactory, a ProviderMetaData object that provides a list of profiles via a getSupportedProfiles( ) method, and a custom MessageFactory used to create messages specific to the profile being used. Let's look at how these are used.

ProviderConnectionFactory

ProviderConnectionFactory allows a JAXM client to obtain a ProviderConnection to a messaging provider, such as an ebXML Message Service, or a JMS provider that supports SOAP over JMS. A ProviderConnectionFactory can be configured administratively and retrieved via a JNDI lookup( ). From there, a ProviderConnection is established:

```
ctx = new InitialContext();
ProviderConnectionFactory pcf =
    (ProviderConnectionFactory)ctx.lookup("GuaranteedMessaging");
ProviderConnection pc = pcf.createConnection();
```

Obtaining the profile via ProviderMetaData

Once the ProviderConnection is instantiated, the ProviderMetaData class can be queried to discover whether this connection supports a desired profile. The getSupportedProfiles( ) returns an array of Strings that lists the profiles that the ProviderConnection supports. For example, if ebXML is supported, the array will contain the string "ebXML":

```
ProviderMetaData pMetaData = pc.getMetaData();
String[] supportedProfiles = pMetaData.getSupportedProfiles();
String desiredProfile = null;

for(int i=0; i < supportedProfiles.length; i++) {
    if(supportedProfiles[i].equalsIgnoreCase("ebxml")) {
```

```
            desiredProfile = supportedProfiles[i];
            break;
        }
    }
```

Using the custom MessageFactory to create profile-specific messages

It is possible to plug in a custom `MessageFactory` that creates a message in the form expected by the transport being used. For example, a `MessageFactory` for an ebXML profile might create a message with a SOAP envelope, which is prepopulated with the `<MessageHeader>` element in the SOAP header. In the following code, the `EbXMLMessageImpl` is a custom extension of the `javax.xml.soap.SOAPMessage`:

```
MessageFactory mf = pc.createMessageFactory(desiredProfile);
EbXMLMessageImpl ebxmlMsg = (EbXMLMessageImpl)mf.createMessage();
```

Sending the message

You can send a message with JAXM in two ways. One way uses the `ProviderConnection.send()` method. The other uses `SOAPConnection.call()`. The two methods have different purposes and different semantics. Since we are on the subject of `ProviderConnection`, we will talk about `send()` first and defer `SOAPConnection.call()` to the section "Simple Servlet Deployment."

The `ProviderConnection.send()` method assumes that one-way asynchronous sending can occur. Whether the `send()` method blocks and waits for the operation to occur depends on the provider's underlying message delivery semantics.

If you look at the API document for `ProviderConnection.send()`, you may notice that there is no way to specify a destination as part of the method signature. It assumes that the destination is established and somehow already associated with the SOAP message. There are a number of reasons for this design:

- The JAXM API is intended to be agnostic with regard to the underlying workings of the provider. The API is designed to work with many different providers, and specifying the destination as a parameter to `send()` may not always be appropriate.

- Whether the destination is a URI, URN, or an absolute URL is a function of the underlying infrastructure to which the JAXM API is attached. For instance, the messaging provider may provide an administration piece that maps generic URIs to specific destinations such as a URL or a JMS Topic or Queue.

- The SOAP header element stores the destination (or destinations). The SOAP header is constructed using the Envelope APIs (just like any other part of the message).

To facilitate setting the destination, JAXM provides an `Endpoint` class that specifies a URI as a destination. The following code assumes that the profile-specific message has defined additional setFrom( ) and setTo( ) methods, and that the underlying infrastructure knows how to interpret the URI string used to construct the Endpoint object:

```
ebxmlMsg.setFrom(new Endpoint(from));
ebxmlMsg.setTo(new Endpoint(to));
pc.send(ebxmlMsg);
```

A strange inconsistency seems to exist in the API here: the code one would use to connect and send SOAP messages depends on how the client is deployed. When using a ProviderConnection, you send a message using the java.xml.messaging. ProviderConnection.send( ) method. Otherwise, you send the message using the javax.xml.soap.SOAPConnection.call( ) method. One could argue that the two scenarios are sufficiently different and don't warrant consistent APIs. If you write an application that is intended to connect to a larger framework, which implies using the ProviderConnection approach, many things specific to that framework have to be coded into the application (beyond just the connect and send operations).

JAX-RPC

JAX-RPC is a specification that is developing through the Java Community Process (JCP). It aims to provide a JCP-sanctioned standard set of Java APIs for both a client-side and server-side programming model.

These APIs leverage interoperable communications within Java applications with a protocol design center based on, but not limited to, SOAP. It covers the following areas:

- A Java code generation model for client-side stubs and server-side tie classes, based on a set of conventions for mapping WSDL to Java and Java to WSDL.
- An API for dynamic SOAP-RPC and a Call interface that is conceptually similar to Apache SOAP. Call semantics include synchronous invoke and synchronous invoke/one-way. JAX-RPC does not address asynchronous invocation in its 1.0 rendition. A true asynchronous model would require callbacks (onMessage, etc). The one-way invocation model defined in the API is considered synchronous.
- A model for defining a service, registering it, and invoking it within the J2EE and J2SE environments. This model covers typical J2EE/J2SE deployment issues such as creating deployment descriptors and packaging Web Application Archive (WAR) files.
- A binding to SOAP, including SOAP Fault handling through Java exceptions and HeaderFault processing.
- Type mappings between Java and XML datatypes.
- A service-side invocation handler mechanism used to chain together service method invocations.

- A reference implementation (RI) that provides a runtime implementation and a code generation tool, *xrpcc*.
- A serialization framework for marshalling and unmarshalling data between Java and XML based on soap-encoding rules. The RI from Sun includes an implementation of this framework.

JAX-RPC is a funny kind of animal. Finding the right kinds of things to write about it in the context of this book was a challenge. At the time of writing, the specification was still evolving. This chapter is based on a Version 0.6 snapshot of the specification's first public draft, issued as part of the Winter 01 Java Web Services Developer Pack. There are no known implementations, except for the RI (which is evolving with the specification) and the Apache Axis project (which is in alpha stage and based on Version 0.5 of the specification). Therefore, many examples in this section are repurposed directly from the specification. Several areas in the specification are in flux, need more definition, and are extremely likely to change before it hits a 1.0 status. Currently, the specification is 152 pages long and has enough information in it to comprise a whole book when it's finally finished.

In spite of its al dente status, the JAX-RPC specification has a brief working tutorial (as do all JAX products) that walks you through installation and setup and guides you through building a simple "Hello World" example. The RI runtime requires Tomcat; its installation, code generation tool, and deployment tool are based on Ant.

Most of the specification iterates over details and rules for mapping things between Java, XML, SOAP, and WSDL—not only for infrastructure provider runtime interactions, but also to provide directives and guidelines for code generation tools. If you are building a code generation tool, you will need more than we are presenting in this book.

Considering these factors, we still chose to write about JAX-RPC because it is a significant piece of functionality that is slated for J2EE 1.4. Therefore, its "baketime" will have to be short. We'll focus on the things that are baked and concentrate on the things that are exposed to the application developer. As the specification progresses, we will update our examples and provide new examples to go with them. Check this book's home page on the O'Reilly web site (*http://www.oreilly.com/catalog/javawebserv*) occasionally to see what we have placed there.

Stubs and Tie Classes

The concepts of "stub" and "tie" are not unique to JAX-RPC. The terms have been used in many other distributed-computing technologies, such as RMI, CORBA, and DCE RPC. Some of you may also be familiar with the terminology "stubs and skeletons." To understand stubs and ties, it is important to understand what's so exciting about remote procedure calls in the first place. The idea behind a remote procedure call is that an application makes a call to a method on an object, and the actual implementation of that object exists in another process space. The processes are typically located on different machines separated by a network connection. The application making the method call (the client) does not need to know that it actually makes a call to a remote object (the service), nor does it need to worry about the details of how that happens.

The client application has a local object, the "stub," that acts as a proxy for the remote object. The stub object has the same methods as the remote object, but does not implement the business logic. Instead, the stub represents an interface to an underlying infrastructure that is responsible for packaging the method name and its parameters into an agreed-upon wire format. This operation is sometimes referred to as *marshalling* or *encoding*. Upon reaching its destination, the skeleton or tie class is responsible for unmarshalling the wire format and reconstructing the data into a form that is recognizable by the server application. In the case of a remote procedure call, this means invoking the actual method with the expected parameters and datatypes, then marshalling return values back to the sender.

An assumption here is that a tool generates the stub and tie code, isolating the developer from the details of the marshalling and the transport protocol. In other distributed-computing technologies, in which both sides of the conversation are under the domain of a single vendor, a tool typically generates the stub and the skeleton at the same time, based on a generic description of an interface. With SOAP and web services, we break tradition because we can't assume that the invoking client and the receiving service are part of the same software infrastructure. It is likely that each end of the conversation is built upon different software platforms. The one constant in the picture is that each side needs to interact with the same interface definition defined in WSDL and speak the same interoperable protocol, such as SOAP, which is also specified in WSDL as a binding.

Stub generation by a tool is only one option in JAX-RPC. We will discuss other options in the "JAX-RPC Client Invocation Models" section.

WSDL to Java, Java to WSDL

JAX-RPC defines a mapping of datatypes between WSDL and Java. The mappings cover simple datatypes, such as short, int, long, float, and double. It also has some fairly dry and boring rules about the mapping of arrays, structs and complex types, and enumerations. The good news is that this part of the specification is intended for vendors who build code generation tools that hide all these details behind a stub class.

You should also be familiar with definitions of parameter-passing modes. Some highlights that we will cover include remote references, pass-by-copy, and Holder classes.

Remote references

The generally accepted definition of a remote reference is an instance of a proxy that represents a particular instance of a remote object or service that can be transferred from one client to another. Remember that JAX-RPC doesn't support remote references in its pre-1.0 rendition, largely because SOAP doesn't have a model for remote references, either. A JAX-RPC client or server must be able to support any arbitrary SOAP message to or from a non-JAX-RPC entity.

Pass-by-copy and Holder classes

In a WSDL operation, a message part can be specified to appear within the input message only. This message part is considered an In parameter. A WSDL message part appearing only within an operation's output message can be thought of as an out parameter. Message parts appearing in both input and output messages within a WSDL operation can be called inout parameters.

A parameter marked as in indicates that the sending client has no further concern with what that remote procedure does with it once it is sent over the wire. This concept is commonly referred to as *pass-by-value* or *pass-by-copy*. An out parameter is a return value. An inout parameter is expected to be modified by the remote procedure, causing the calling client to see the modified value after the method invocation returns.

Generally speaking, you can support inout parameters in two ways: with pass-by-reference and Holder classes. In distributed-computing environments that support pass-by-reference, an object reference is a specific datatype that can be passed as a parameter to a remote object. It can be treated as the handle to an actual instance of the parameter. Once the remote method call is complete, it may be dereferenced by the client program to obtain the newly modified value. The underlying infrastructure marshalls the data over the wire to get the right result.

Java doesn't support pass-by-reference natively for primitive types. Instead, JAX-RPC uses Holder classes, which are classes used by the underlying infrastructure to act as a place to hold the values. A stub uses a Holder to store the modified values after the method invocation so the calling client can then access them. Here's an example illustrating the use of Holders:

```
public interface StockQuoteProvider extends java.rmi.Remote {
// Method returns last trade price
float getStockQuote(String tickerSymbol,
    javax.xml.rpc.holders.IntHolder volume,
    javax.xml.rpc.holders.FloatHolder bid,
    javax.xml.rpc.holders.FloatHolder ask)
  throws java.rmi.RemoteException;
}

//Java
package javax.xml.rpc.holders;
public final class IntHolder {
    public int value;
    public IntHolder() { }
    public IntHolder(int value) {
    this.value = value;
    }
}
```

Holders are also used to represent complex data structures as parameters. The java.xml.rpc Holders package defines Holders for all the built-in Java primitives. Beyond that, the code generation tool is responsible for creating Holders for the parameters. In either case—whether using the supplied Holder classes or the custom generated ones—the code generation tool is also responsible for creating the code that serializes and deserializes data sent across the wire.

Generated service interface

JAX-RPC allows a code generation tool to create an implementation class for the Service interface based on an existing WSDL document. While the implementation details of the generated class are vendor-specific, the generated interface is required to adhere to the following design pattern:

```
public interface <ServiceName> extends javax.xml.rpc.Service {
    public <ServiceDefInterface> get<Name of the wsdl:port>( )
        throws JAXRPCException;
    ...
}
```

In the previous listing, the *<ServiceName>* of the generated service interface is mapped from the name attribute of the corresponding wsdl:service definition. The *<ServiceDefInterface>* name is mapped from the portType, and the get*<Name of the wsdl:port>*( ) method is mapped from the—you guessed it—wsdl:port definition's name attribute. For example, given the following WSDL definition:

```
<service name="StockQuoteService">
    <port name="StockQuoteProviderPort" binding="tns:somebinding">
        <http:address location="http://example.com/"/>
    </port>
</service>

<portType name="StockQuoteProvider">
    <operation name="GetLastTradePrice"
        parameterOrder="tickerSymbol">
    ...
    </operation>
</portType>
```

a JAX-RPC implementation creates the following Java interface; the get method returns an instance of a stub class that implements the *<ServiceDefInterface>*:

```
package com.example;
    public interface StockQuoteService extends javax.xml.rpc.Service {
    public StockQuoteProvider getStockQuoteProviderPort( )
        throws JAXRPCException;
    ...
}
```

Value types

Value types are specific to the generation of WSDL from a Java class. A value type is a special form of serializable class, containing data values that are capable of being marshaled between a client and a service. It must implement `Serializable`, but does not follow the standard rules for Java serialization. Only public, nontransient data members are mapped to the WSDL. A value type may also be a JavaBean, in which case, the WSDL generation may use bean introspection to identify the properties and map them to the WSDL. The methods in the value class are not mapped to the WSDL; it is strictly for data. Whether a value type should use the `Serializable` marker interface or whether a different interface should be defined is still undecided.

SOAPElement API

JAX-RPC also allows the use of a `javax.xml.soap.SOAPElement` object as a parameter value for a remote method. This object is intended for when you want to bypass an existing datatype mapping or when a mapping doesn't exist for the data you are using. You can also use it if you just want to plug in the element by hand. Regardless of the reasons, whatever you place in the `SOAPElement` parameter becomes the request envelope's body.

If you recall the JAXM section, we used the `SOAPElement` like this:

```
// Add an element and content to the Header
name = envelope.createName("From");
javax.xml.soap.SOAPElement childElement
    = headerElement.addChildElement (name);
childElement.addTextNode ("Me");
```

In this code, we create the element as a side effect of appending the name to the `headerElement`. A more direct way to create an element uses the `SOAPElementFactory` to create an element and populate its contents. To create a `SOAPElementFactory`, call its static method `newInstance( )`:

```
javax.xml.soap.SOAPElementFactory sef
    = javax.xml.soap.SOAPElementFactory.newInstance( );
javax.xml.soap.SOAPElement sel = sef.createElement(...);
```

The interface for the `SOAPElementFactory` is:

```
package javax.xml.soap;
public abstract class SOAPElementFactory {
  public abstract SOAPElement create(Name name)
    throws SOAPException;
  public abstract SOAPElement create(String localName)
    throws SOAPException;
  public abstract SOAPElement create(String localName, String prefix,String uri)
    throws SOAPException;
  public static SOAPElementFactory newInstance( )
    throws SOAPException;
}
```

The first public draft of the JAX-RPC specification identifies some problems with this approach, which may mean that it's likely to change in a future draft. One problem is that the Name object is created using the Envelope object, which is not available to the JAX-RPC programmer. "Not available" means that nothing exposed in the JAX-RPC client interface lets you peek at the envelope that will eventually be sent. The lack of a factory for a Name is not that big of an issue in itself. The Name interface contains a local name, a namespace prefix, and a URI. An alternate method signature lets you create the SOAPElement with the desired result. More significant issues are probably also behind this problem.

JAX-RPC Client Invocation Models

JAX-RPC defines three different client models used to invoke a remote method: one static model and two dynamic models. The statically defined stub model is typically based on a code generation tool. The dynamic proxy invocation model is based on building a proxy object dynamically using the reflection APIs (java.lang.reflect). The Dynamic Invocation Interface (DII) is based on a Call object similar to the Apache SOAP Call interface we saw in Chapter 5.

Statically Generated Stubs

A tool can generate a class that implements the javax.xml.rpc.stub interface, which contains the following methods:

```
package javax.xml.rpc;
public interface Stub {
    public void _setProperty(String name, Object value);
    public Object _getProperty(String name);
    public java.util.Iterator _getPropertyNames();
}
```

In addition to implementing these methods, the generated stub would have a method that matches the name of the actual service method, such as getLastTradePrice( ). The underlying implementation of this method can be anything the tool and the infrastructure agree upon. It is not required to be transport-independent; in fact, stubs are usually bound directly to a transport. The methods in the Stub interface exist to allow dynamic capabilities in the static stub.

Table 7-2 lists the handful of predefined properties that can be set on the Stub class. These properties are expected to be set prior to making a method call, based on the assumption that the underlying transport or infrastructure might need the information contained in these properties to reach the service successfully.

Table 7-2. Stub properties

Property name	Value	Description
http.auth.username	java.lang.String	Username for the HTTP Basic authentication.
http.auth.password	java.lang.String	Password for the HTTP Basic authentication.
javax.xml.rpc.service. endpoint.address	java.lang.String	Target service endpoint address. The URI scheme for the end-point address specification must correspond to the protocol/transport binding for this stub class.

By convention, the fully qualified package name should be part of any property name. Vendor-specific properties should follow the same naming convention, using the vendor's package-naming style.

As of JAX-RPC 1.0 Public Draft, whether there should be a standard set of accessor methods for these standard properties was an issue under discussion.

Dynamic Invocation Using the Service Interface

The javax.xml.rpc.Service interface encapsulates two flavors of dynamic invocation that do not require any generated code. These methods are dynamic proxy invocation via the getPort( ) method and the DII using the Call interface. Here is the Service interface definition:

```
package javax.xml.rpc;
public interface Service {
    public Call createCall( )
            throws JAXRPCException;
    public Call createCall(QName portName)
            throws JAXRPCException;
    public Call createCall(QName portName, java.lang.String operationName)
            throws JAXRPCException;
    public java.rmi.Remote getPort(QName portName,
                                    java.lang.Class serviceDefInterface)
            throws JAXRPCException;
    public java.util.Iterator getPorts( );
    public Qname getServiceName( );
    public TypeMappingRegistry getTypeMappingRegistry( )
            throws JAXRPCException;
    public java.net.URL getWSDLDocumentLocation( );
    public void setTypeMappingRegistry(TypeMappingRegistry registry)
            throws JAXRPCException;
}
```

The dynamic proxy approach doesn't require any generated code. javax.xml.rpc. Service.getPort( ) returns a dynamic proxy for the object being operated on. Only a QName to identify the port and a compiled interface definition class are required:

```
com.example.StockQuoteProvider sqp =
    (com.example.StockQuoteProvider)service.getPort(portName,
        StockQuoteProvider.class);

float price = sqp.getLastTradePrice("ACME");
```

In this code, the getPort( ) method is passed in an interface definition that will be used as a template for building a runtime instance of a dynamic proxy. Thus, the returned object is not the same as the passed-in object. A typical dynamic proxy implementation uses the java.lang.reflect.Proxy object to build a table of method objects, which are dispatched using java.lang.reflect.InvocationHandler.invoke( ). In the context of JAX-RPC, that validation would result in constructing the appropriate SOAP envelope and sending it on its way. getPort( ) may choose to validate the interface and the port name against its WSDL if it likes, but this is not required by the specification.

For more information on dynamic proxies, refer to the J2SE documentation for java. lang.reflect.Proxy and java.lang.reflect.InvocationHandler, found at *http://java. sun.com/j2se/1.3/docs/guide/reflection/*.

Dynamic Invocation Interface (DII)

DII is based on a Call object. To get a Call object, use the javax.xml.rpc.Service. createCall( ) method. There are three overloaded versions of createCall( ):

```
package javax.xml.rpc;
public interface Service {
  public Call createCall( ) throws JAXRPCException;
  public Call createCall(QName portName) throws JAXRPCException;
  public Call createCall(QName portName, String operationName)
    throws JAXRPCException;
  ...
}
```

When the Call object is created, it has little or no information about the invocation that needs to be made. The information required to execute the call (parameters, types, etc.) is constructed using its set methods. Here's the definition of the Call interface; note that the methods that are not highlighted are listed in the specification, but are not yet implemented in the reference implementation or listed in the javadoc:

```
public interface Call {
  public boolean isParameterAndReturnSpecRequired( );

  // Parameter passing and return type handling
  public void addParameter(String paramName,
            QName xmlType, ParameterMode parameterMode)
    throws JAXRPCException;
  public QName getParameterTypeByName(String paramName);
  public void setReturnType(QName xmlType)
    throws JAXRPCException;
  public QName getReturnType( );
  public void removeAllParameters( );

  // WSDL operation
  public QName getOperationName( );
  public void setOperationName(QName operationName);
```

```
// WSDL portType
public QName getPortTypeName( );
public void setPortTypeName(QName portType);

// WSDL endpoint
public String getTargetEndpointAddress( );
public void setTargetEndpointAddress(String address);

// properties
public void setProperty(String name, Object value)
    throws JAXRPCException;
public Object getProperty(String name);
public void removeProperty(String name);
public java.util.Iterator getPropertyNames( );

// Remote Method Invocation methods
public Object invoke(QName operationName, Object[] inputParams)
    throws java.rmi.RemoteException, JAXRPCException;
public Object invoke(Object[] inputParams)
    throws java.rmi.RemoteException, JAXRPCException;
public void invokeOneWay(Object[] inputParams)
    throws javax.xml.rpc.JAXRPCException;
public java.util.Map getOutputParams( )
    throws javax.xml.rpc.JAXRPCException;
}
```

The Call object in JAX-RPC differs from the Apache SOAP Call object; it encapsulates both message-style invocation and RPC-style invocation in a single interface. Unlike ApacheSOAP, Call.invoke( ) and Message.send( ) operations aren't separate.

Building the method signature

When using a Call object, you can build parameters dynamically by using the addParameter( ) method. Two modes of invocation are available: synchronous request/response (using the invoke( ) method) and asynchronous fire-and-forget (using invokeOneWay( )). The addParameter( ) method has the following signature:

```
public void addParameter(String paramName,
              QName xmlType, ParameterMode parameterMode)
```

The ParameterMode class evaluates to one of three possible values: in, out, or inout. The definition of the class is:

```
// Typesafe Enumeration for ParameterMode
public class ParameterMode {
    private final String mode;
    private ParameterMode(String mode) {
        this.mode = mode;
    }
    public String toString( ) { return mode; }
    public static final ParameterMode PARAM_MODE_IN =
        new ParameterMode("PARAM_MODE_IN");
    public static final ParameterMode PARAM_MODE_OUT =
        new ParameterMode("PARAM_MODE_OUT");
```

```
    public static final ParameterMode PARAM_MODE_INOUT =
        new ParameterMode("PARAM_MODE_INOUT");
}
```

The Call implementation is required to validate the parameters and the return type. It can do so by relying on the client code to call the addParameter() and setReturnType() methods.

Notice that addParameter() doesn't take a value. It is not building a parameter list; it is simply building the method signature. In JAX-RPC, the values for the parameters are passed as an array of Objects to invoke() or invokeOneway(). The invoke() implementation is responsible for validating the parameters with the signature that is built. An implementation that requires you to build the parameter list must explicitly return true from the isParameterAndReturnSpecRequired() method.

Alternatively, an implementation may support the definition of a method signature through a type mapping registry or through another means that matches a signature with its corresponding WSDL definition. In this case, the client code is not required to call addParameter() and setReturnType(). If the implementation doesn't require or support the addParameter()/setReturnType() approach, it must throw a JAXRPCException if the client code attempts to call these methods. Furthermore, the isParameterAndReturnSpecRequired() method must return false.

Setting the properties

Like the Stub class, the Call class has several predefined properties that are listed in Table 7-3. These properties are expected to be set prior to making the actual method call, based on the assumption that the underlying transport or infrastructure might need this kind of information to reach the service successfully.

Table 7-3. Call properties

Property name	Property type	Description
javax.xml.rpc.security .auth.username	java.lang.String	Username for Authentication.
javax.xml.rpc.security .auth.password	java.lang.String	Password for Authentication.
javax.xml.rpc.soap .operation.style	java.lang.String	"rpc" if the operation style is rpc; "document" if the operation style is document. Note that a Call implementation may choose not to allow the setting of this property. In this case, the setProperty method throws JAXRPCException.
javax.xml.rpc.soap.http .soapaction.use	java.lang.Boolean	Indicates whether SOAPAction will be used.
javax.xml.rpc.soap.http .soapaction.uri	java.lang.String	Indicates the SOAPAction URI if the javax.xml. rpc.soap.http.soapaction.use property is set to true.
javax.xml.rpc.encodingstyle .namespace.uri	java.lang.String	Encoding style specified as a namespace URI. The default value is the SOAP 1.1 encoding.

Making the call and retrieving the results

Regardless of how the method signature is created, the invoke( ) and invokeOneWay( ) methods are responsible for matching up the parameters and return types with the supplied signature. They are required to generate a JAXRPCException if an error occurs until the client has delivered its payload onto the wire. Examples of errors that can occur include signature/parameter mismatch, or specifying an out or inout parameter and calling invokeOneWay( ). The invoke( ) method must continue to block until the remote service receives the method call and returns either a response or a remote exception. The invokeOneWay( ) method is not allowed to propagate a remote exception—another subtle difference between JAX-RPC and Apache SOAP.

Once the invocation has taken place, you can obtain the out and inout parameters by calling the getOutputParams( ) method:

```
// create the call object.
javax.xml.rpc.Call call = service.createCall(portName, "<operationName>");

// build the method signature.
call.addParameter("param1", <xsd:string>, ParameterMode.PARAM_MODE_IN);
call.addParameter("param2", <xsd:string>, ParameterMode.PARAM_MODE_OUT);
call.setReturnType(<xsd:int>);

// build the parameter list itself.
Object[] inParams = new Object[] {"<SomeString>"};

// invoke the remote method
Integer ret = (Integer) call.invoke(inParams);

// get the output parameters
Map outParams = call.getOutputParams( );
String outValue = (String)outParams.get("param2");
```

Note that the number of calls to addParameter( ) does not necessarily match the number of parameters placed on the parameter list. This mismatch is not obvious at first. The reason for the discrepancy is that some parameters are purely output parameters, as specified by the ParameterMode.PARAM_MODE_OUT.

Service Context Propagation and SOAP Message Handlers

Remember the discussion we had about SOAP headers in Chapter 3? A typical use for a header element would be to pass around a transaction ID; that is one example of propagating conversational or contextual information between service clients and service implementations. In JAX-RPC, this contextual information is referred to as a *Service Context*. A Service Context is implementation-dependent and may include such things as a transaction ID, a security token, or some sort of conversation ID.

A Service Context may be handled explicitly or implicitly by the JAX-RPC runtime environment. Those of you familiar with CORBA OTS or JTA should be familiar with the notions of implicit and explicit propagation. For implicit propagation, the generated client stub code may transparently propagate a security token by marshalling it into the SOAP header when it generates the envelope. In the explicit case, the generated stub code has additional parameters appended to the end of each method signature. For example:

```
public interface StockQuoteProvider extends java.rmi.Remote {
    // Method returns last trade price
    float getStockQuote(String tickerSymbol, StringHolder context)
        throws java.rmi.RemoteException;
}
```

The SOAP Message Handler APIs provide a way to expose implicit context propagation to the application developer. The Handler interface is basically a way to plug your own interceptors into the runtime infrastructure for both the client-side stub implementation or the server-side invocation. Simply write a class that extends the javax.xml.rpc.handler.Handler interface and plug it into a Handler chain. At runtime, your Handler.handle( ) method is invoked and is passed a SOAPMessageContext object. The SOAPMessageContext gives you full access to the SOAP envelope, to do with what you wish.

CHAPTER 8

J2EE and Web Services

This book has discussed in detail how Java and web services fit together. Web services use standards-based frameworks to extend an application's reach. However, a web service isn't the application itself. The web service must still be implemented on a proven application infrastructure—one that supports reliability, availability, serviceability, transactions, security, and other critical enterprise needs. Ultimately, J2EE tries to define just such an infrastructure. Thus, if web services and Java can fit together, and J2EE is the Java form of application infrastructure, the question of how web services fit together with J2EE comes straight to the forefront.

This chapter discusses different approaches of integrating J2EE and web services. How does a web service map into an EJB, a servlet, or J2EE Connector Architecture (CA) adapter? This chapter discusses these topics, looks at some existing standards initiatives, and speculates on what might happen over the next few years.

The SOAP-J2EE Way

Since SOAP is the cornerstone of interoperability and web services, understanding how J2EE and web services work together comes down to analyzing how SOAP and J2EE can work together. SOAP is a wire protocol that can be layered upon other wire protocols such as HTTP, FTP, and SMTP. J2EE supports these Internet protocols through servlets. Therefore, it makes sense that servlets and JSP technology will become the entry point into a J2EE framework for web services. Let's look at how this occurs.

Within J2EE, servlets, JSPs, EJBs, JMS resources, JDBC drivers, and J2EE CA adapters provide access to the business logic and enterprise resources that a web service needs. Servlets and JSPs are designed to encapsulate page-based flow and logic and can also work with numerous Internet protocols. It makes sense that servlets will become the entry point for web services and an automatic bridge between a web service message and the other J2EE services contained within an application server (see Figure 8-1).

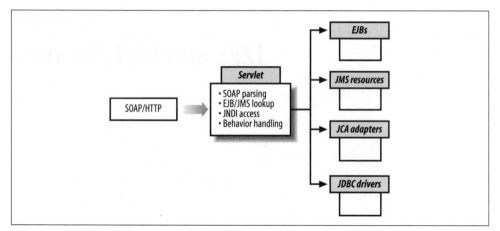

Figure 8-1. SOAP servlet integration

Even though Figure 8-1 presents a simplistic view of SOAP and J2EE integration, a servlet must work hard to make this integration possible. Let's look at some of the issues involved.

SOAP Parsing

First, servlets are responsible for extracting the SOAP contents from another wire packet. The SOAP contents must then be parsed so the servlet can acquire access to the elements and attributes contained within the SOAP document. A servlet must contain the logic for:

Envelope parsing
> The servlet must gain access to the SOAP envelope. The servlet must be able to extract the SOAP header and body portions of the envelope separately.

Parsing attachments
> SOAP messages may use attachments to transport payload information. Therefore, the servlet must be able to access all attachments.

Validating message format
> If the servlet is the entry point for an endpoint represented by another WSDL file, it must confirm that the format of the SOAP message conforms to the abstract message defined in the corresponding WSDL file. If the incoming message does not conform to the constraints as defined in the corresponding WSDL file, the servlet must create a SOAP Fault message and deliver it to the client.

Validating XML
> The SOAP message is in XML format and may be bound to an external XML Schema. The servlet must determine the different namespaces for the elements contained in the SOAP packet and validate the contents of the XML payload against those namespace schema definitions.

Rapid XML parsing

An XML parser that does full validation of elements, attributes, and datatypes won't be the fastest parser on the market. Since many J2EE applications are designed for performance, a servlet has a responsibility to find unique ways to parse the XML payload rapidly. For example, a vendor could implement a parser that specializes in small XML packets if it expects that most SOAP messages will be tiny. Or, if the servlet is invoked by SOAP clients that are trusted to deliver prevalidated messages, the servlet may have a SOAP parser that does only partial validation

XML-Java binding

After an XML packet is parsed and its elements are understood, some data contained within the SOAP payload may need to be converted to a Java object. This conversion might be necessary if the SOAP message is an RPC-style message that requires invocation of an EJB method. EJB interfaces are entirely in Java, so any SOAP payload information that must be delivered as an input parameter needs to be converted to a Java object. The XML-Java binding can be custom binding from an application server provider, or it can take a standards-based approach such as one proposed by JAXB.

Payload conversion

If the SOAP message is a message-style invocation, the XML data contained within the SOAP packet is placed into a JMS destination. The XML data contained within the SOAP message must be converted to a message type that is valid to JMS. This message type could simply be a `BytesMessage`, `TextMessage`, or `ObjectMessage`—or it could be a specialized extended type designed to handle XML and SOAP with Attachments payloads.

Explicit versus implicit servlet processing

The mapping and translation between a SOAP-over-HTTP message and a backend J2EE component such as an EJB or JMS destination may not be exposed explicitly in the servlet layer. Higher-level layering may implicitly hide that information from the programmer. Or, the servlet API may actually be extended across an RMI or JMS infrastructure and exposed to the service at the ultimate remote destination. We will refer to the servlet layer abstractly, mainly because that layer is easily identifiable in the J2EE architecture diagrams.

Behavior Handling

Based upon how WSDL, JAXM, and JAX-RPC eventually define the behavior of web services, four fundamental types of messages can be transported over SOAP:

- Request/response
- Solicit/response

- One-way
- Notification

The format and behavior of these transmission primitives are described in more detail in Chapter 5. These primitives provide an intriguing technical challenge for application server architects, however, since servlets were primarily designed to handle client-invoked, request-response behavior. A servlet that supports web services obviously needs to support familiar request-response behavior; however, it must also support server-invoked, solicit-response behavior and other server-initiated invocations.

This topic is technically challenging because a servlet must be engineered to receive asynchronous notifications from other resources located in the same application server. Servlets are invoked synchronously by a wire protocol, but to support asynchronous web services, they need to be engineered to receive asynchronous messages while they execute for inclusion on any outgoing response. Additionally, a servlet is generally thought of as something that reacts to inbound requests passively. It must now also be able to actively generate an outbound SOAP-over-HTTP solicitation. Your SOAP provider is responsible for implementing this servlet behavior. Vendor offerings such as BEA WebLogic Server, SonicXQ, CapeClear Studio, and Systinet WASP all provide these implementations to developers transparently.

Figuring Out What to Invoke

After a servlet parses the SOAP message, it needs to either do an RPC-style invocation or deliver the XML message to another resource, such as a JMS destination. Before the servlet can pass processing on to the next resource, though, it must determine what that resource is. How does it do this? A servlet has some options for determining the next step in the process:

SOAPAction header field
> The SOAPAction header field value can contain information that indicates which JMS destination or EJB needs to be invoked. Or, the value of this field can contain the information needed to perform a lookup in a web services routing table that an application server supports.

Determine through WSDL
> If the application server knows which WSDL file the incoming message belongs to, it may contain an internal mapping indicating how EJBs and JMS destinations map to SOAP messages. An application server can provide tools for mapping message definitions in a WSDL file to the resources available within an application server.

Contained within the SOAP message
> The SOAP header and body may contain proprietary information that helps the servlet determine how to route the message. However, any vendor that decides to use custom tags for routing probably makes its service nonportable as a result.

Mapping of header information

Converting HTTP header information or SOAP Header elements into JMS properties for server-side filtering may be desirable, particularly if a response to a request will be handled asynchronously or at a later time.

One of the interesting problems posed by this scenario is how an application server should handle conversational web services. SOAP, in its basic form, does not have a standardized way to track session tokens. Session tokens are needed to associate a message with an established conversation. For servlets, conversations are associated with a `sessionID` variable that accompanies every HTTP request. SOAP messages can carry these session tokens, but since no standardized way exists for them to be incorporated into the message, any session enablement of a SOAP message is nonportable. Despite this factor, conversational web services are very important and many vendors are building the extensions needed to support them.

If web services are going to be conversational, then the servlet SOAP handler needs to handle conversations, too. This means that a servlet implementation must figure out whether a message is part of a conversation, where that conversation is managed, and whether any special routing needs to occur as a result of the conversational dynamics.

RPC-Style Invocations

Mapping web service invocations to EJBs is important because EJBs provide the component framework necessary for implementations of reliable and highly available business logic. EJBs have access to a range of enterprise technologies and provide a portable way to encapsulate the business logic necessary to interact with them. Mapping SOAP to EJBs is important because it allows application developers to continue to develop portal logic solutions for their systems while leveraging the benefits offered by web services. Figure 8-2 depicts the steps involved in generating an EJB invocation from a SOAP message:

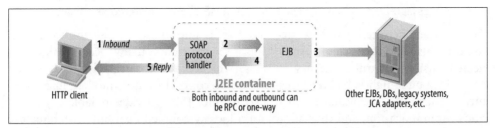

Figure 8-2. SOAP-EJB invocation model

1. An inbound SOAP message arrives at a SOAP protocol handler. The SOAP protocol handler parses the message and determines which EJB instance needs to be invoked. This process may or may not involve a JNDI lookup. The reference to the EJB may already be cached within the handler.

2. The SOAP handler invokes the EJB with the appropriate input parameters. The EJB can be a stateless session, a stateful session, or an entity EJB. If the EJB is a stateful session or an entity EJB, the SOAP message must have some way to maintain the session token or primary key of the entity EJB.

3. The EJB can invoke any number of backend resources, including other EJBs, databases, J2EE CA adapters, or JMS destinations. The EJB should contain the meat of the web service implementation.

4. The EJB sends its response to the SOAP handler. The SOAP handler must convert the response from the EJB to XML to be part of the SOAP response payload. If the EJB throws a system exception, then the SOAP handler needs to create a SOAP Fault for delivery to the client.

5. The SOAP handler creates the SOAP envelope for the response and delivers the message to the client.

This process is pretty straightforward. It's so simple, in fact, that most vendors now have toolkits that, given an EJB, perform most of these steps automatically. If you have a stateless session EJB, a SOAP handler generator creates the servlet that serves as the SOAP handler, creates the necessary deployment descriptors, and generates any WSDL necessary to map SOAP messages to an EJB. The code generator also creates any Java-XML binding that needs to occur. This process allows EJB developers to develop EJBs to implement their business logic without having to worry about the semantics of SOAP development. It provides a seamless transition from one paradigm to the other. In the next section, we provide pseudocode that shows how a servlet might integrate SOAP and JMS. That pseudocode can be extended to do the same for integrating SOAP and EJBs.

Message-Style Invocations

A very important notion for B2B, workflow, and system connectivity is the idea of mapping a WSDL endpoint to a JMS Topic or Queue. The Topic or Queue may have either a Message-Driven Bean or a standalone JMS client registered as a listener.

The interface between a web service and JMS is important because the world out there is "usually connected." An organization may have many occasionally connected business partners. Legacy systems, which may be designed to move data around via bulk nightly batch processes, need to connect to more modern infrastructures designed to communicate in near-real time. JMS provides reliable asynchronous communication, and thus allows for a loosely coupled distributed architecture in which all parts of a distributed system don't have to run constantly for the whole system to remain healthy. If you recall, one of the defining characteristics of web services is that they are also loosely coupled. Therefore, mapping web services to JMS is natural and important. Figure 8-3 shows the steps required to receive a SOAP message and, as a result, send a JMS message to a JMS destination.

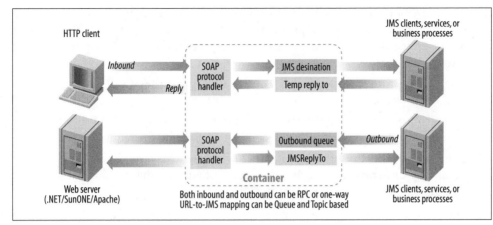

Figure 8-3. SOAP-JMS invocation model

In Figure 8-3, the SOAP-JMS invocation can begin in two ways. First, a SOAP message sent by a client starts a request/response scenario or a one-way invocation that causes a JMS message to be placed onto a destination. In the second model, a message is placed onto a JMS destination monitored by an outbound SOAP handler. Any messages initiated by a JMS client are converted into SOAP messages and delivered using a solicit-response model.

1. An inbound SOAP message arrives at a SOAP protocol handler. The SOAP protocol handler parses the message and determines which JMS destination the message should be delivered to. This step may or may not involve a JNDI lookup.

2. The XML payload is converted to a JMS message and placed onto the appropriate JMS destination. This destination can be a JMS Topic or Queue. The conversion may be a thorough deep mapping into a natively supported JMS message type such as BytesMessage, TextMessage, or ObjectMessage. Alternatively, it may use a vendor-supplied extension that allows the SOAP envelope to be retained in its natural form and dealt with as SOAP throughout its lifespan in the system. HTTP header fields and SOAP header elements need to be preserved as part of the mapping in the event that the message response, or a related descendant of it, is eventually reconstructed as an outbound SOAP-over-HTTP message.

3. A JMS consumer consumes the JMS message and performs any related business logic. Depending on what type of mapping is used to create the message, the consumer may use either JMS APIs directly or API extensions that allow a DOM interface, JAXM APIs, or Apache SOAP APIs.

4. If the SOAP invocation is a one-way, asynchronous invocation, the Message-Driven Bean does not need to deliver a response. However, if the transmission behavior is request-response, the JMS client needs to place the response message onto the JMS destination indicated by the ReplyTo field of the original JMS request message.

5. The SOAP protocol handler acts as a message consumer on the response JMS destination. It waits for a response message. When the response is delivered, the SOAP protocol handler converts the JMS response into a SOAP response or fault message.

6. The SOAP protocol handler delivers the message to the SOAP client that initiated the process.

7. If an error occurs during the request/response processing, a SOAP Fault may be generated and sent back to the SOAP client originating the request.

8. If an error occurs during the processing of an asynchronous invocation, a SOAP Fault may be generated and sent to a known Fault destination that is monitored administratively and dealt with at the application level.

The same process occurs for the solicit-response model, except that it is initiated by a backend resource that places a JMS message onto a queue monitored by a SOAP protocol handler. The protocol handler must then wait for responses from the clients to which the SOAP message is delivered. In the case of a one-way or notification model, no response is necessary—the rest of the steps are identical. In fact, a truly asynchronous environment may consist entirely of one-way and notification operations.

A Simple Example

To demonstrate how integration between web services and J2EE works in practice, we have provided pseudocode that shows how an application server or JMS vendor might create a servlet that receives SOAP messages, parses their content, creates a JMS message, and places that message onto a JMS destination. Since most vendors provide this type of implementation, you will never have to write this code yourself. We provide it to show how things work internally and to give you a better understanding of how web services and J2EE interact:

```
// JAVA PSEUDO-CODE FOR INTEGRATING A SERVLET WITH SOAP & JMS
// This code is designed to receive a SOAP message and then
// to parse the message and to place that message onto a JMS Queue
//
// NOTE: This class is not compilable and does not have proper
//       Exception handling.  It is just pseudo-code to demonstrate
//       how Servlet / JMS / SOAP can work together.
//
// This servlet is NOT responsible for receiving JMS messages.
// Web Services are loosely coupled, so a separate servlet is
// responsible for checking to see if a response message has been
// delivered onto the response queue.  That receive servlet has to
// be invoked separately to check for the correct contents.
// If the vendor supports asynchronous outbound notifications,
// then polling the servlet for response is not necessary.
//
import javax.jms.*;
import com.vendor.specific.SOAPMessage;
import com.vendor.specific.SOAPMessageFactory;
```

```java
public class SoapJMSSendServlet extends HttpServlet {

    static String SEND_QUEUE_NAME = "SomeQueueName";
    static String QUEUE_CONNECTION_FACTORY = "SomeConnectionFactoryName";
    static String SOAP_MESSAGE_FACTORY = "SomeSoapMessageFactoryName";
    private Destination destination;
    private ConnectionFactory factory;
    private QueueConnection qConnect;
    private QueueSession qSession;
    private QueueSender qSender;

    private SOAPMessageFactory smf;
    private SOAPMessage soapMessage, responseMessage;
    private long requestTimeout = 180000; // 30 seconds

    public void doPost(HttpServletRequest httpRequest,
        HttpServletResponse httpResponse) throws ServletException {

        // Parse SOAP input from HTTP Stream.
        org.w3c.dom.Document doc
            = SOAPParser.getDocument(
                new InputSource(httpRequest.getInputStream()));

        // This representative "SOAPMessage"
        // could be a JAXM-based message, and ApacheSoap kind of message, or an
        // Axis message.  The important thing to note is that it contains a SOAP
        // envelope along with any other runtime-specific information that allows
        // it to be routed appropriately.  The runtime-specific information could
        // be derived from HTTP headers, from SOAP headers, WSDL, or deployment
        // descriptors
        soapMessage = smf.createSOAPMessage(doc, request);

        if (soapMessage.isRPC())
            responseMessage = callEJB(soapMessage);
        else if (soapMessage.isJMSSender())
            responseMessage = sendToQueue(soapMessage);

        // We have to send a SOAP response to the client informing them
        // of the success.
        if (responseMessage != null)
            responseMessage.write(httpResponse.getOutputStream());
    }

    // this method converts the SOAPMessage into a JMS message and places it onto
    // a JMS queue.  If the message is supposed to be participating in a
    // synchronous request/reply, then it blocks and waits for the reply
    // to be received, or a timer expires - whatever comes first.
    private SOAPMessage sendToQueue(SOAPMessage soapMessage)
                    throws ServletException  {
        SOAPMessage responseMessage = null;

        // This hypothetical SOAPMessage knows how to marshall itself
        // into a JMS Message
        qSender.send(soapMessage.createJMSMessage());
```

```
                // This could be a request/response
                if (soapMessage.needsReply( )){
                    // receive blocks until either a message is received,
                    // or timeout occurs.  If timeout occurs, msg is null
                    javax.jms.Message msg = qReceiver.receive(requestTimeout);

                    if (msg == null)
                        // generate fault.  This hypothetical SOAPMessage has a
                        // static method for doing that
                        responseMessage
                            = SOAPMessage.createSOAPFault("Request Timed out");
                    else
                        // The SOAPMessage can also create a SOAP envelope
                        // from a JMS message
                        responseMessage = SOAPMessage.createSOAPMessage(msg);
                }
                else
                    responseMessage
                        = SOAPMessage.createSOAPMessage("Message Delivered");
                return responseMessage;
        }

        public void init( ) throws ServletException {
            // Set up Queue -- only needs to occur once.
            InitialContext ctx = new InitialContext( );
            factory
                = (ConnectionFactory)ctx.lookup(QUEUE_CONNECTION_FACTORY);
            destination = (Destination)ctx.lookup(SEND_QUEUE_NAME);
            smf = (SoapMessageFactory)ctx.lookup(SOAP_MESSAGE_FACTORY);
            qConnect = factory.createQueueConnection(username, passwd);
            qSession
                = qConnect.createQueueSession(false,
                        javax.jms.Session.AUTO_ACKNOWLEDGE);
            qSender = qs.createSender(destination);
        }
    }
```

The code provided here is a standard servlet that acts as a JMS message producer.
We'll look at a few of the more interesting pieces in detail. Since SOAP over HTTP
has just the SOAP payload as part of the HTTP request, the servlet accesses the
SOAP envelope by using the HttpServletRequest object and the InputStream by using
the getInputStream( ) method. The contents of this method are then passed into a
SOAP parser. In this example, a SOAPParser object represents the SOAP parser:

```
            // Parse SOAP input from HTTP Stream.
            org.w3c.dom.Document doc
                = SOAPParser.getDocument(
                    new InputSource(httpRequest.getInputStream( )));
            soapMessage = smf.createSOAPMessage(doc, request);
```

This representative SOAP message could be based on JAXM, JAX-RPC, Apache
SOAP, or Axis. The important thing to note is that it contains a SOAP envelope
along with any other runtime-specific information that allows it to be routed appropriately. Since the XML in the SOAP message could represent a message that will be

placed on the JMS queue or topic, an RPC invocation, or something else, our hypothetical SOAP message has an isRPC( ) and an isJMSSender( ) method for determining how to dispatch the message. The dispatching information could be derived from
HTTP headers, SOAP headers, WSDL, or deployment descriptors.

```
if (soapMessage.isRPC())
    responseMessage = callEJB(soapMessage);
else if (soapMessage.isJMSSender())
    responseMessage = sendToQueue(soapMessage);
```

The callEJB( ) method simply deserializes the method name and its parameters,
invokes the appropriate EJB, and then sends the response back. In J2EE 1.4, this
method will be based on the rules defined by JAX-RPC.

The sendToQueue( ) method needs more explanation since it is a bit more complicated. It can send the message and optionally wait for a synchronous reply. We will
see the JMS replier side in a moment. For the purpose of our pseudocode example,
let's assume that the createJMSMessage( ) creates a JMS message and marshals the
SOAP content into it. It doesn't matter what the type is, as long as sufficient APIs are
on either side (for accessing the message by using JMS APIs and accessing the XML
content by using JAXP or SOAP Envelope APIs). The JMS message is created and
sent to its destination:

```
private SOAPMessage sendToQueue(SOAPMessage soapMessage)
                    throws ServletException  {
    SOAPMessage responseMessage = null;

    // This fictitous SOAPMessage knows how to marshall itself
    // into a JMS Message
    qSender.send(soapMessage.createJMSMessage());
```

Next, the SOAP message also knows enough about itself to determine whether it
should be an asynchronous send( ) or a synchronous request/reply operation. If a reply
is expected, the QueueReceiver.receive( ) blocks until a message is returned or a timeout occurs. The timeout is important because we must satisfy the HTTP request with
either a response message or a Fault message before the HTTP request itself times out:

```
    // This could be a request/response
    if (soapMessage.needsReply()){
        // receive blocks until either a message is received,
        // or timeout occurs.  If timeout occurs, msg is null
        javax.jms.Message msg = qReceiver.receive(requestTimeout);

        if (msg == null)
            // generate fault.  This hypothetical SOAPMessage has a
            // static method for doing that
            responseMessage
                = SOAPMessage.createSOAPFault("Request Timed out");
        else
            // The SOAPMessage can also create a SOAP envelope
            // from a JMS message
            responseMessage = SOAPMessage.createSOAPMessage(msg);
    }
```

```
    else
        responseMessage
            = SOAPMessage.createSOAPMessage("Message Delivered");
    return responseMessage;
}
```

In JMS, an asynchronous response might result from this message. However, the "response" may not happen immediately. It may occur hours or days after the request, or the "response" may be just another message delivered to a new destination that is not related to the SOAP client that initiated the request. This servlet is responsible only for retrieving any JMS response messages that might be created for an immediate synchronous response. To handle the other situations, there are other possibilities:

- A separate servlet could be established to act as a holding mechanism for responses. In this scenario, a SOAP client sends to one servlet and queries another servlet at a later point to pick up any responses.

- If the vendor supports asynchronous outbound notifications, then polling the servlet for response messages is not necessary. The responses are converted to SOAP-over-HTTP messages as they are created, and delivered in real time to the receiving party.

The JMS replier

The JMS replier also uses our hypothetical SOAP message.[*] It first looks to see if the message contains an attachment. If so, it uses JavaMail Multipart API's to get at the first part of the message, which is the SOAP envelope:

```
public class PsuedoJMSSoapReplier
    implements javax.jms.MessageListener
{
// ...
    public void onMessage( javax.jms.Message aMessage)
    {
        if (aMessage instanceof SOAPMessage)
        {
            SOAPMessage sMsg = (SOAPMessage)aMessage;

            int partCount = sMsg.getPartCount();
            //Display number of parts in multipart message
            System.out.println("MultipartMessage received with : "
                + partCount + " parts");

            Part part = null;
            for(int i = 0; i < partCount; i++)
            {
```

---

[*] This example is derived from Sonic Software's SonicXQ. The original code is included with the online example archive and is available with the SonicXQ product.

```
                part = sMsg.getPart(i);
                System.out.println("Multipart message part(" + i
                    + ") has content type: "
                    +  part.getHeader().getContentType());
                System.out.println("Multipart message part(" + i
                    + ") has size: "
                    + part.getContentBytes().length + " bytes");
            }
            org.w3c.dom.Document doc
                = SOAPParser.getDocument(
                    new InputSource(sMsg.getPart(0).getInputStream()));

            if (doc == null)
            {
                throw new org.apache.soap.SOAPException (
                    org.apache.soap.Constants.FAULT_CODE_CLIENT, "parsing error");
            }

            //Validate the XMLMessage content using Apache SOAP
            org.apache.soap.Envelope msgEnv =
                org.apache.soap.Envelope.unmarshall (doc.getDocumentElement());

            //... Do SOAP Envelope things....

            System.out.println("Successfully processed MultipartMessage");
        }
```

The destination could be either a response or another destination where one could
forward the message. Any number of mechanisms can be used—the JMSReplyTo
destination, for example, or a WSDL endpoint—to determine which destination to
go to next.

```
            // Check for a ReplyTo Queue and send one if necessary
            javax.jms.Queue replyQueue = (javax.jms.Queue) aMessage.getJMSReplyTo();
            if (replyQueue != null){
                // create reply message and send it.
            }else{
                // create a new SOAP message to go to another destination
                String urlEndpoint = sMsg.getNextURLEndpoint();
                ...
            }
        }
    }
```

Content-Based Routing, Data Transformation, and the J2EE Connector Architecture

In an enterprise environment, the processing of SOAP requests often doesn't fit a
simple request/response model involving a simple servlet interaction; the servlet
model doesn't necessarily work well for a multistep workflow web service. In this
section, we will describe how J2EE technologies such as servlets, JMS, and EJB can

be used together with XML-related technologies to orchestrate a multistep complex business process that supports the implementation of a web service.

Consider a company that exposes its business interface to its customers as a web service. It regularly receives purchase orders for its goods from any number of prospective buyers. Figure 8-4 shows the complex chain of events that occurs when a purchase order is received. The purchase order may come into the system as a SOAP message over the HTTP protocol. Upon arriving at the servlet or the SOAP processor, the message may be sent immediately to a routing service that uses an XPATH expression such as /PurchaseOrder/Items to identify that it is indeed a purchase order. If the routing service uses a parser that supports JavaScript extensions, then additional logic may be plugged into the routing service to do some real-time expression evaluation.

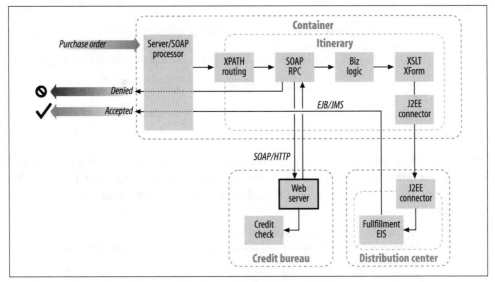

Figure 8-4. Content-based routing, XSLT transformation, and J2EE connectors

The routing service may then determine that this purchase order is valid and needs to proceed to the next step in the process—performing a credit authorization. It sends the purchase order on to the next step by placing a message onto a JMS queue. The credit authorization service listening on that queue may run some business logic and choose to delegate its credit checking responsibility to another external web service. To accomplish this delegation, it may make a direct SOAP call over an HTTP connection or choose to create a new JMS message and place it on a queue destination that is mapped to an outbound SOAP-over-HTTP handler. If that request for credit approval is denied, then a "credit denied" message is sent back to the sender, either synchronously or asynchronously, depending on how the whole service is described in WSDL.

If the credit check is successful, the next step may be to execute some business logic by invoking an EJB—directly as a synchronous call or asynchronously by sending a message to a message-driven bean listening on a queue. The business logic might break the purchase order into its respective line items and send each item to the legacy fulfillment application (EIS) that resides at the remote warehouse. In the process, several things need to happen: the purchase order's line items must be broken into separate requests, the data must be converted from XML into the proprietary format that is used by the EIS, and the logic must communicate with the EIS in a standardized way.

The breaking of <Items> into multiple entries and the transformation from XML into the legacy format required by the EIS are both accomplished by routing the purchase order to a special XSLT-based translation service. Given the appropriate style sheet, we can rely on the parser to do most of the work.

The next step, communicating with the EIS, is accomplished by using a connector, as defined by the J2EE Connector Architecture. In Figure 8-4, the implementation of the connector may reside in the local container, at the remote location, or it may be spread across both places. After the processing is complete, a final SOAP response message may be generated to travel back to the sender, using similar processes.

JSR109: Industry in Flux

Unfortunately, although integration between J2EE and web services has matured among many of the providers, the Java Community Process (JCP) has not yet standardized it. JSR109, "Implementing Enterprise Web Services," is intended to provide a standardized approach for J2EE/web services integration. Unfortunately, as of early 2002, JSR109 has stalled, and may not be delivered to the public until the middle of 2002. This means that any vendor implementations following the standard probably won't be fully realized until 2003 or 2004. That is a very long time, given the pace at which technology tends to mature.

One positive, note, however, is the expectation that the contents of JSR109 will be incorporated into J2EE 1.4, forcing application server vendors to provide a standardized level of web services support by 2003.

JSR109 is expected to cover several things. Everything is in flux at this point, but some of the highlights appear to be:

Mapping rules
> The main portion of the specification will focus on rules for mapping SOAP and WSDL onto J2EE 1.3 components such as EJBs and JMS destinations.

JNDI lookup rules
> The specification will highlight how J2EE services bound into a JNDI tree map to services described via WSDL. This process will allow a SOAP protocol handler that has the WSDL of a web service and access to a J2EE JNDI directory to connect SOAP messages with J2EE services.

WSDL binding extensions for JMS and EJB

Given a JMS destination or an EJB (and a WSDL file describing abstract messages), how should those messages be mapped onto the interfaces of J2EE components? For example, if a WSDL file has a `DeliverMe` message, is it supposed to map to a `deliverMe()` method on an EJB's remote interface, local interface, or the `DeliverMe` JMS destination?

WSDL generation rules

Given the deployment descriptor of an EJB, what policies should be followed for the automatic generation of WSDL from the deployment descriptor?

JAX API integration

The charter of the JSR should eventually have the specification define the official role of JAX-RPC, JAXR, and JAXM with J2EE.

Service publication

What services developed with the J2EE framework will be published to a UDDI registry, and how will a J2EE framework automate the publication process?

Security, transactions, and management

How do the web services standards that are trying to add security, transaction contexts, and management get mapped to the equivalent services offered in an application server? For example, if a SOAP message has a transaction context associated with it, what are the semantics for associating the SOAP message with an existing J2EE transaction or for starting a new J2EE transaction?

The Java Web Service (JWS) Standard

Not to be confused with the topic of this book, a newly proposed standard called the Java web service (JWS) standard is currently in development. It is spearheaded by BEA Systems, which also has a reference implementation.

The JWS is a format designed to integrate non-Java developers with J2EE. Sounds ambitious, doesn't it? BEA has actually designed a technology that might work. At the core of the JWS specification is the idea that developers don't create J2EE components. Rather, developers create a web service, and a single Java class represents web service implementation. The Java class then has a number of simple, predefined JavaDoc tags that indicate different behavioral implementations of the web service. Based on the values of the JavaDoc tags inserted into the Java class, a behind-the-scenes code generator then creates all necessary J2EE components required to implement the web service.

The JWS JavaDoc system has tags representing a full range of web service behaviors, including stateless methods, stateful methods, and asynchronous invocations. The challenge left to JWS implementations is to take the definition of the JavaDoc tags and generate J2EE components that implement this behavior in a reliable and available manner.

The JWS proposal is appealing because tool vendors can support BEA's prototype implementation quickly. It comes with a nice IDE that ties together design, coding, and testing. The concept of deployment is completely hidden from the developer. The goal is to have a framework for developing web services with J2EE that is similar to working in Visual Basic.

Let's look at an example. The following listing, *HelloWorld.jws*, shows all of the code necessary to create a complete web service:

```
import com.bea.jws.*;
import com.bea.jws.control.*;

/**
 * A simple web service that returns a string.
 */
public class HelloWorld extends Service
{
    /**
     * @operation
     * @conversation stateless
     */
    public String getHellowWorld( )
    {
        return "Hello World";
    }
}
```

That's it. A JWS file is simply a Java class that implements the Service interface. The methods of the class implement the web service; the JavaDoc extensions tell the behind-the-scenes code generator what type of web service to produce. The methods in the Java class may not be exposed as part of the WSDL of the web service. If the method you create should be part of the external WSDL, then the @operation tag should be placed in the JavaDoc before the method. This tag causes the code generator to create necessary definitions in the WSDL file.

The @conversation tag defines the behavior of this method as part of the web service. The @conversation tag takes a single parameter that can be stateless, start, continue, or finish. The stateless parameter means that this method supports only the request/response paradigm. If the @conversation parameter is start, continue, or finish, then the underlying generated infrastructure is responsible for associating incoming messages with a conversation handler for each client. If the start parameter is used, the infrastructure needs to create a new session when the method is invoked. If the continue parameter is used, the infrastructure needs to determine which existing session this client belongs to and make sure the method invocation occurs in that context. Finally, if the finish parameter is used, the infrastructure executes the method in the appropriate session context and ends the session afterwards.

JWS can be slightly more complicated. JWS has JavaDoc tags for defining different aspects of parameters, methods, and the class itself. These parameters include:

Asynchronicity
> A method can be made asynchronous with a simple JavaDoc tag. Clients can implement a polling model to get a result or the web service can do a notification.

Buffering
> If the `@buffer` tag is used on any method, a JMS destination is inserted between any SOAP messages and the web service implementation. Buffering the messages in JMS provides better scalability and is transparent to the developer.

Controls
> The JWS specification has a simple way to represent EJBs, JMS destinations, J2EE CA adapters, databases, and other web services through a simple Java interface, called a Java Web Interface (JWI) file. An enterprise developer who creates one of these resources is expected to provide a JWI file that is merely a Java interface with JavaDoc tags. JWS implementations can then access any resource exposed through JWI either visually or via a straightforward Java invocation. JWI files allow tools to hide all J2EE semantics from developers and expose these components and services as simple Java interfaces. Given this factor, any developer with a cursory knowledge of Java can reuse complex services.

XML maps
> JWS provides an extension to ECMAScript that maps the fields of Java objects to XML (and vice versa). A developer with a cursory understanding of JavaScript or VBScript can take the XML format of parameters and map them into the fields of the Java objects used as input parameters on the web service without knowing the details of how the Java objects are structured.

The simplicity of the JWS standard enables a large body of developers to use J2EE, including many who do not have enough experience with Java or J2EE to be successful on their own terms. The number of companies that choose to adopt the standard will certainly factor into the success of JWS. However, this standard doesn't necessarily have to be adopted by an application server vendor. A JWS code engine must create J2EE-compliant code, so the generated web service can operate in any J2EE-certified application server. Adoption of JWS will probably occur at the tool level and will be driven by whether other tool vendors support the standard or add extensions to it.

CHAPTER 9

Web Services Interoperability

The Concept of Interoperability

Much of the promise of web services is its potential for seamless interoperability across heterogeneous systems, platforms, applications, and programming languages. Interoperability is a primary goal of web services. However, it is not a given. Web services standards facilitate interoperability, but do not ensure it. Many considerations and issues need to be resolved to achieve full interoperability. As the number of specifications expands to address gaps, so do the interoperability challenges.

A web service has many potential clients, and this array of clients can use a variety of libraries and providers to connect. Services can, in turn, become clients of other services. Ensuring that clients based on different implementations of the standards can interoperate with the service is critical to the service's success.

This chapter points out many issues that currently prohibit interoperability. It also focuses on the positive aspects of web services, including community efforts such as the SOAPBuilders Interoperability Labs, an organization chartered with identifying interoperability problems, fixing them through consensus, and creating compliance tests. Their goal is to provide a community environment in which anyone can test for interoperability with other web services infrastructures.

The Good, Bad, and Ugly of Interoperability

The primary considerations for achieving interoperability are:

Using the same version or compatible versions of the specifications. Not all specifications are backward compatible. For example, SOAP 1.2 as proposed in its latest draft form is not totally backward compatible with SOAP 1.1 or SOAP 1.0. For instance, according to the 1.2 draft specification, a node complying with SOAP 1.1 generates a SOAP Fault indicating version mismatch if it receives a SOAP Version 1.2 message. A 1.2 node has the option of processing a 1.1

message or generating a SOAP Fault. The W3C XML Protocol Working Group (XMLP) has used a different namespace for each version to give implementations a way to distinguish different versions of the specification.

Using the same version of the web service. Like any software, web services change over time. New versions are released that may not be compatible with earlier versions. It's not clear how the standards for web services will support versioning—that is, how a client will find out what versions of a particular service are available.

Sharing semantics. The semantics must be understood and agreed upon in advance by the parties through some mechanism.

Beyond these general considerations, interoperability can depend on interpretations or misunderstandings of specifications, support for optional features within a particular web services standard, the addition of proprietary extensions, or the lack of a standard.

Interoperability problems can occur at a number of levels:

Service development
> The use of a WSDL or not, differing service definition methodologies, incompatible tools, etc.

Service discovery
> The use of different registry mechanisms, service definition and representative syntax, etc.

Service deployment
> Different security mechanisms, wire-level compatibilities (encoding, serialization, SOAP header extensions and how they're applied through such efforts as BizTalk and ebXML)

As both authors represent companies that provide web services infrastructure, we have experienced some of these problems firsthand, either directly or indirectly through colleagues. As an added exercise, we scoured newsgroups and mailing list archives, including standards bodies and user discussion threads, to find out what others considered important issues. We also ran a few of our own tests. What follows represents a broad overview of the types of interoperability issues that can be encountered and some specific problems and scenarios.

SOAP

Initial SOAP interoperability problems were largely the result of specification ambiguities and varying interpretations. Implementations that conformed to the specification could still prove incompatible. In April 2000, Tony Hong from XMethods compiled a detailed list of interoperability issues between implementations (*http://www.xmethods.net/soapbuilders/interop.html*). This list gives an idea of how extensive interoperability problems were.

SOAP interoperability has improved substantially since then. Much of this improvement can be attributed to the SOAPBuilders community interoperability test labs and discussion forum. Many other efforts have helped. A turning point was the development of "A Busy Developer's Guide to SOAP 1.1" (BDG), developed by Dave Winer (one of the original SOAP authors) and Jake Savin from UserLand in March 2001 (*http://www.soapware.org/bdg*). It was a first attempt to define a common subset for implementations of the specification, something like a base implementation that developers could agree upon. It also started a dialogue that helped identify interoperability issues. One outcome of the BDG was the evolution of using a SOAP Fault to handle a problem in a well-defined way. This provided a way to handle failures between implementations in a predictable and understandable fashion.

In its draft set of specificationss for Version 1.2, XMLP addressed the interoperability issues that were identified for Version 1.1, so many problems should be eliminated or at least be less problematic with SOAP 1.2. XMLP also plans to provide a non-normative Primer (SOAP Version 1.2 Part 0: Primer), a tutorial on how to use SOAP 1.2. In addition, they are developing a conformance test suite, which is discussed in more detail in the following section. The Primer and test suite should help reduce confusion and differences of interpretation. However, since 1.1 is the currently implemented version and the only one that's considered a standard, let's look at some areas of interoperability problems in that specification.

Encoding

In Chapter 3, we talked about the two models for using SOAP: the document exchange model and RPC. In Chapter 4, we introduced SOAP encoding, which defines a serialization mechanism for exchanging application data. Encoding and how it is used in each model are some of the biggest challenges to interoperability.

In SOAP 1.1, the RPC model requires the SOAP server to map data from a given native type into the XML encoding for that type and convert the encoding back from the XML encoding to the native type. RPC method calls are also encoded into XML, with method names mapped to the SOAP body child tags and arguments to child tags of the method name. Mapping between a number of type systems and XML is a difficult challenge, and not all languages can be mapped equally well. Toolkits may map to and from any given programming language's type system differently.

There is no default encoding in SOAP. SOAP 1.1 defines a SOAP encoding style, often called Section 5 encoding (since it appears in Section 5), specifying how to express complex programming language types in XML. Section 5 encoding provides simple (scalar) and compound (composed of multiple parts) type categories and a set of rules for serialization. The specification also allows other encoding styles through the encodingStyle attribute, which can be used with "any element, and is scoped to that element's contents and all child elements not themselves containing such an attribute, much as an XML namespace declaration is scoped" (Section 4.1.1). The encodingStyle attribute identifies serialization rules. Serialization is discussed in more detail in the "SOAPBuilders Interoperability" section later in this chapter.

SOAP 1.1 provides an optional encoding mechanism called literal encoding. With literal encoding, an XML document is sent as the payload. In contrast, with the standard encoding style, application data such as primitive types, methods, and objects, are serialized to XML. In this case, the XML payload is not really a document. The distinction between literal and encoded SOAP bindings in 1.1 is another source of problems. For example, Apache SOAP defaults to Section 5 encoding, while ASP.NET uses literal encoding. To get them to interoperate, one side must specify the encoding explicitly rather than use its default. ASP.NET can be forced to use Section 5 encoding by applying the SoapRpcService attribute to the class containing the web methods. To force Apache SOAP to use literal encoding, you must specify that the method takes a single parameter of type org.w3c.dom.Element as an argument and returns a response of the same type. You must then create an XML tree for the input parameter and modify the XML tree for the response.

In contrast with RPC, the document exchange model does not inherently require encoding. With the XML Schema Recommendation, a native XML type system can be used as well, so Section 5 encoding or another specialized encoding is not required.

In summary, there are four common combinations of style and encoding. Both ends must agree on a particular combination. For example, a server that supports only document exchange using the literal encoding won't be able to communicate with a client that wants to use RPC with Section 5 encoding. Here's a summary of the possible combinations:

- Document/literal
- Document/encoded (Section 5)
- RPC/literal
- RPC/encoded (Section 5)

xsi:type

SOAP 1.1 defines a way to type each value explicitly through the xsi:type attribute. The xsi:type attribute is optional and generally not required if the type being used is made known through the use of a schema, WSDL, or another form of metadata exchange. The specification states:

> For each element containing a value, the type of the value MUST be represented by at least one of the following conditions: (a) the containing element instance contains an xsi:type attribute, (b) the containing element instance is itself contained within an element containing a (possibly defaulted) SOAP-ENC:arrayType attribute or (c) or the name of the element bears a definite relation to the type, that type then determinable from a schema. (Section 5.1).

If one implementation expects type information, it probably won't be able to process a message from an implementation that doesn't include it. For example, earlier versions of Apache SOAP required explicit declaration of element datatypes. Because they did not use an external data typing mechanism (such as WSDL), the early Apache releases required explicit typing to determine how to map into native datatype representations.

While Apache tools required explicit typing of RPC parameters, earlier Microsoft implementations didn't support it at all. They relied on WSDL, which created a significant interoperability problem. As of Apache 2.1, a workaround for this problem has been provided. To deserialize a parameter in a SOAP-RPC, the SOAP engine requires notification of the type for each parameter (since no metadata is available to the SOAP engine). Because Apache does not support WSDL, if explicit typing (the xsi:type attribute) is not used, explicit mapping is an option. The element name of the parameter can be used as the schema type, so the engine can associate a Java type for mapping. This association requires the user to tell Apache SOAP what the deserializer is for each type. We will talk about custom types and serialization when we get to the "SOAPBuilders Interoperability" section.

Microsoft's BizTalk Framework 2.0 specification now supports the xsi:type attribute.

Proprietary datatypes

Implementations often define proprietary datatypes beyond the primitive types specified by SOAP. An implementation that uses only the SOAP-defined types has much greater interoperability potential.

Serialization

SOAP 1.1 does not specify an order for data serialization. Implementations can choose the order, which can cause problems between implementations.

SOAPAction

The SOAP 1.1 specification leaves the use of this element open for interpretation. For example, it is defined in the context of the HTTP header as a URI identifying the "intent of the message." This definition could be interpreted as the intended target for the message or the name of the target service. Another interpretation extends SOAPAction to accommodate different versions of the service. Service versioning is an interoperability issue in its own right, which we'll discuss in the context of WSDL later in this chapter. The fact is that there are currently several different interpretations of how SOAPAction should be used.

In addition, the use of SOAPAction for transports other than HTTP, or between transports, is not specified in SOAP 1.1. Providing equivalent functionality for other protocols is up to the implementation, regardless of which interpretation is applied. As a rule, if another protocol is used, interoperability issues are likely to arise until standards are defined that explicitly specify bindings to other protocols.

The functionality that SOAPAction provides is useful. Being able to identify, route, or dispatch requests without having to parse XML is a good idea. The problem is in the implementation. In retrospect, it was probably not a good idea to overload the Action verb in HTTP. If SOAP is truly designed to be layered upon multiple protocols, then what's needed is some sort of metadata that provides SOAPAction-like functionality. Then the binding to a particular protocol can map this metadata to whatever headers it likes: SOAPAction, SOAPRouting, SOAPDispatch, SOAPMethod, etc. To extend the scope of bindings for SOAP 1.2, the XMLP group defines a Transport Binding Framework. This framework defines a convention that describes binding property and feature types, a Message Exchange Pattern (MEP), and an HTTP binding based on the description convention and the MEP.

Even if HTTP is the protocol of choice, there is additional confusion about how SOAPAction works. Section 6.1.1 states:

> The presence and content of the SOAPAction header field can be used by servers such as firewalls to appropriately filter SOAP request messages in HTTP. The header field value of empty string ("") means that the HTTP Request-URI provides the intent of the SOAP message. No value means that there is no indication of the intent of the message.

In essence, the specification allows two ways to declare the intent (whatever "intent" is interpreted to mean) of a message: through SOAPAction or through the HTTP Request-URI. To add to the confusion surrounding SOAPAction, if a SOAP server requires a null value, HTTP clients that cannot set a null HTTP header value will have problems. Also, no distinction is made between an empty string ("") and a null value, so both interpretations can be valid. SOAPAction is definitely a can of worms for interoperability.

The XMLP group has debated whether to keep SOAPAction in 1.2 or deprecate it. The current wording in the SOAP 1.2 draft Part 2, Adjuncts, Section 8.5.5 is:

> Use of the SOAP Action feature is OPTIONAL. SOAP Receivers MAY use it as a hint to optimise processing, but SHOULD NOT require its presence in order to operate. Support for SOAPAction is OPTIONAL in implementations. Implementations SHOULD NOT generate or require SOAPAction UNLESS they have a particular purpose for doing so (e.g., a SOAP Receivers specifies its use).

This wording does not guarantee full interoperability between implementations without prior negotiation, but does improve the current state of affairs.

Multireference (id/href)

Not all SOAP implementations support multireference values. Nonetheless, some implementations, including Microsoft's .NET Framework, do employ them. The .NET Framework uses multireference values to represent every element of an array.

Processing order

The SOAP 1.1 specification does not define the order in which either SOAP headers or the SOAP body should be processed. Currently, each SOAP processor determines the processing order. This determination can lead to interoperability issues in scenarios involving intermediaries, in areas such as error processing, or in consistent, predictable service behavior across SOAP processors.

Header extensions

SOAP is designed to be extensible through the definition of additional headers. While extensibility is good, it also opens up the potential for abuse. Mandatory headers can be defined that can turn on or off the processing of other headers. Parties can define headers that are not standardized or widely supported. For example, BizTalk Server defines proprietary headers. The BizTalk Framework 2.0 specification defines Biz-Tags, a set of XML tags used to indicate document handling. BizTags can be mandatory or optional; they are used to create SOAP headers in an XML BizTalk business document. BizTalk Framework 2.0 compliant servers, or BFC Servers, must be able to process headers composed of BizTags. However, SOAP servers that are not BFC-aware are not likely to understand BizTags or BizTalk-defined header extensions.

Section 7 of the BizTalk Framework specification defines five BizTag header extensions used to specify document routing, identification and other document properties, requested delivery services, a catalog of document contents and attachments, and tracking of the full business process context to which the document belongs. Each extension is comprised of BizTag elements and attributes (such as to or from, which are used in the endpoints header extension). These header extensions include:

- endpoints (mandatory—document source and destination)
- properties (mandatory—identify and other properties)
- services (optional—reliable delivery services)
- manifest (optional—document catalog information)
- process (optional—process management information)

Processing and understanding these header extensions is mandatory for a BFC server, and most, when present, require mustUnderstand="1". The exception is the manifest extension, which becomes mandatory when the document is part of a compound package. In this case, it must be present and mustUnderstand="1" is required. If the manifest header is used only to verify package integrity or catalog what is contained in the document, processing its contents is not required.

The following example, extracted from the BizTalk Framework 2.0 specification, illustrates the endpoints header extension:

```
<SOAP-ENV:Header>
  <eps:endpoints SOAP-ENV:mustUnderstand="1"
      xmlns:eps="http://schemas.biztalk.org/btf-2-0/endpoints"
```

```
              xmlns:agr="http://www.trading-agreements.org/types/">
        <eps:to>
          <eps:address xsi:type="agr:department">Book Orders</eps:address>
        </eps:to>
        <eps:from>
          <eps:address xsi:type="agr:organization">Book Lovers</eps:address>
        </eps:from>
      </eps:endpoints>
    </SOAP-ENV:Header>
```

Services incorporating such proprietary header definitions are not fully interoperable with clients or other servers that don't understand them. While they'll probably be able to fail in a predictable and understandable fashion through the SOAP Fault, they won't get past that level.

Content type

SOAP 1.1 specifies a content type of text/xml in the HTTP header. This type designation is problematic, though. MIME user agents that do not support text/xml explicitly treat it as text/plain, displaying the XML MIME part as plain text. This plain text display is not appropriate for casual users (not programmers) who can't be expected to take interest in the contents of a SOAP document. The XMLP group has agreed that text/xml should not be used. One proposal is to use a media type of application/soap, for which application is the MIME media type name and soap is the MIME subtype name. An extension mechanism may be provided; for example, application/soap+xml could be used to describe SOAP1.2 messages serialized as XML. Because SOAP 1.2 is based on the XML Infoset, alternate serializations of messages are permitted. The application/soap+xml content type would identify SOAP messages using XML 1.0 serialization.

Whatever the outcome of the XMLP discussions, text/xml will not be supported in SOAP 1.2.

mustUnderstand

SOAP 1.1 defines a mustUnderstand attribute, which we discussed in Chapter 4. Apache SOAP does not support the mustUnderstand attribute. It offers a workaround; an attribute in the deployment descriptor tells the runtime (per-service) whether to fault if any mustUnderstand headers are present. This workaround is supported only for RPC-style SOAP.

SOAP 1.1 defines values for the mustUnderstand attribute as 0 (false) or 1 (true). Some implementations have used the values false or true. The SOAP 1.2 draft indicates that true or 1 may be used (and because the value is defined as Boolean, one would assume 0 or false are also valid). This definition may present a problem with backward compatibility for some implementations. The use of unique namespaces for each version of SOAP should prevent most interoperability problems in this regard, however.

There have been some differences in the interpretation of how a given actor should verify that it understands all headers with mustUnderstand equal to 1 or true. One interpretation is that all mustUnderstand headers should be checked prior to processing. A second interpretation is that mustUnderstand headers can be checked and processed individually. The outcome from these varying approaches can also differ. XMLP has proposed the following change to clarify this processing order:

> A SOAP node's processing of the MU checks needs to 'appear' to be done before any processing occurs. This is to guarantee that no undesirable side-effects will occur as a result of noticing an unknown MU header too late.

SOAP actor

In SOAP 1.1, the actor attribute provides a targeting capability. An actor is of the type anyURI and can have more than one URI identifier. The target, or final recipient, can be designated in two ways: explicitly as the next actor or by the absence of an actor. Providing multiple ways to identify the targeted destination can result in confusion and interoperability between implementations.

There is semantic confusion about SOAP 1.1's definitions for the designated roles of actors. The terms (default actor, anonymous actor, ultimate recipient, and endpoint) are not commonly understood and are often used interchangeably. For example, the lack of consensus about what the term "endpoint" means is a problem: does it designate a final destination, or can an intermediary be considered an endpoint? This lack of semantic consensus has resulted in misunderstandings between implementations.

WSDL

Two camps represent very different views on the value of WSDL. One camp, including Dave Winer from UserLand, believes that WSDL and UDDI are impediments to interoperability because they are too complicated; are less open than HTTP, XML, or SOAP; and encourage vendor lock-in. They claim that the net effect is limited opportunities for smaller, independent players. Another camp, which includes vendors such as Microsoft and IBM, argues that WSDL enhances interoperability and facilitates development and implementation of web services across platforms and tools through better standardized definition and documentation of services. Some articles and interviews that discuss these issues are listed in the "Resources" section at the end of this chapter.

Contrary to some opinions, WSDL is not required for web services interoperability. It may be very useful in some scenarios, but in others, it may not be necessary or beneficial. For example, it may be more convenient in some scenerios to exchange service information via email or configure applications to offer or consume a service through existing tools and documentation processes.

Dynamic languages

WSDL works well with Java and the .NET programming languages, but does not work as well with dynamic languages such as Python or Perl. This may be because participants from these development environments were not involved in the initial development of the WSDL specification. WSDL has since been submitted to the W3C, so it will hopefully be modified to become a more useful standard across environments.

Documentation

WSDL allows `<wsdl:documentation>` elements to occur at numerous places in a WSDL document. Depending on how a toolkit works, it may map WSDL documentation in various ways. For example, Systinet's WASP maps WSDL to Java by generating a Java interface from the WSDL `portType`, so the `portType` documentation element is used for the interface's javadoc. Methods are generated from `portType` and its operations, so the corresponding documentation element is the documentation used for a method's javadoc.

Because this behavior is not standardized, toolkits may map documentation elements differently.

Tool and library variances

Web services tools generate WSDL based on nonstandardized language mappings. The way a SOAP/XML schema library reads a WSDL document and matches return values can vary based on the implementation. Furthermore, not all toolkits support the same set of options in the WSDL standard.

A WSDL file may require some minor customization to function on a specific platform or with a specific toolkit, depending on the implementation. For example, Microsoft SOAP Toolkit 2.0 used a namespace of `wsdlns` when generating a WSDL. The proxy generator tool in IBM's Web Services Toolkit did not recognize this namespace. To make the tool work, `wsdlns` had to be deleted in the tool's local copy of the WSDL.

Initially, incompatibilities existed between the SOAP::Lite WSDL reader for Perl and the .NET WSDL generator. The SOAP::Lite reader expected all XSD type information to be contained in a namespace `xsd`. A .NET-generated WSDL file required modification to change the XML namespace from:

```
xmlns:s=http://www.w3.org/2001/XMLSchema
```

to:

```
xmlns:xsd=http://www.w3.org/2001/XMLSchema
```

The XSD namespace version of this declaration can also be problematic and may require modification in the local copy of the WSDL. For example, if the tool uses the 1999 XSD, it will not understand the 2001 XSD. We'll go into more detail about XSD versions later.

Although you would think otherwise, you can't assume that tools from the same vendor will always interoperate. Problems have been reported when reading a WSDL document between .NET Beta 2 and the SOAP Toolkit Version 2.

Toolkits may add value by hiding interoperability problems from the developer. To do this, they must map between the vendor-specific features and misfeatures of different web service platforms. Hiding interoperability problems isn't as good as eliminating them, but it's still a valuable service.

Versioning

Versioning of WSDL (and of web services in general) is not well understood and there isn't much agreement about how it should work. Currently, WSDL supports implicit versioning through unique namespaces.

One opinion is that WSDL, similar to a CORBA IDL, represents an immutable contract, and a new web service requires a new WSDL document, not just a new version of an existing WSDL. Others feel that a WSDL document can be versioned to support the enhancement of a web service, allowing one document to support multiple versions of the web service. Depending on how support is implemented, interoperability can be impacted severely. Migration to newer versions of web services can also cause problems, creating registry and implementation interoperability issues.

Endpoints

Endpoints are defined through portTypes and operations. However, WSDL does not provide a standard way to pass this information over the wire. For example, the Biz-Talk Framework 2.0 defines endpoints in a BizTalk header extension, explained in more detail in the SOAP section of this chapter. Implementations that do not support BizTalk will not understand endpoints defined through this mechanism.

UDDI

To facilitate UDDI interoperability, services must be registered consistently and unambiguously so that registered services can be recognized within and across registries. There is currently no interoperability test for UDDI registries similar to those available for SOAP and WSDL. As adoption of UDDI expands and the number of public and private registries grows, UDDI interoperability may become more of an issue.

ebXML has also defined a registry. The latest draft of Version 2.0 can be found at *http://www.oasis-open.org/committees/regrep/documents/2.0/specs/ebrs.pdf*. The specification outlines a scenario in which a client discovers an ebXML registry in a public UDDI registry. While the interoperation between ebXML and UDDI registries has gotten some attention, how successfully these two specifications can interact and work together remains unclear.

XML Schema

The three versions of the XSD namespace are 1999, 2000/10, and 2001. Using different XML Schema versions can cause namespace problems or problems with serialization and deserialization. Several datatypes changed names in the 2001 specification; for example, timeInstant became dateTime.

Most tools have been modified to accept the 2001 XSD declaration. At this point, 2001 is probably the safest for new development. However, a number of implementations still rely on earlier versions. When we get to the examples, we will show how to use a different version of the XSD namespace with Apache SOAP. The Microsoft SOAP Toolkit 2.0 supported all three versions, as long as the namespace in the messages matched what was specified in the WSDL file.

The character set may be specified; if not, it defaults to US-ASCII. UTF-8 and UTF-16 are also acceptable. UTF-8 has the widest acceptance and is the recommendation for interoperability. UTF-16 requires a byte order mark (BOM), and some implementations can't process a BOM.

Intermediaries

The draft SOAP 1.2 glossary defines a SOAP intermediary as follows:

> A SOAP intermediary is both a SOAP receiver and a SOAP sender, targetable from within a SOAP message. It processes a defined set of blocks in a SOAP message along a SOAP message path. It acts in order to forward the SOAP message towards the ultimate SOAP receiver.

A web services scenario may include one or more intermediaries. The role of intermediaries can vary. An intermediary's role can include:

- Value-add or brokering
- Routing or switching

Each role presents interoperability considerations. An intermediary may have or require a priori knowledge of other nodes, contracts, or trading partner agreements. A lack of this knowledge can present opportunities for a service to break down in unpredictable ways as messages traverse the paths between nodes. Interoperability problems can arise even if an intermediary just relays a message. For example, the intermediary's SOAP processor may modify SOAP headers when parsing a message to its XML canonical form. The intermediary may modify a mustUnderstand value of 1 to a value of true. Such actions may have unexpected results.

If the intermediary role includes processing, the way in which the node repackages the SOAP message could be different from the original packaging. The ultimate destination might not be able to process this subsequent packaging successfully.

Transactions

Currently, the coordination or orchestration of transactions in a web services model is not standardized. Requirements to handle transaction failure within a web services scenario can extend beyond the X/Open two-phase commit model for distributed transactions. Aggregate web services may need coordination when backing out a transaction or when processing errors. Intermediaries add further complications, depending on their role. Currently, transaction interoperability can be accomplished only through agreements between parties and customized or proprietary solutions. However, although no standards currently facilitate interoperability, several efforts, such as the OASIS Business Transaction Technical Committee (*http://www.oasis-open.org/committees/business-transactions/*), are underway.

Integration

Backend integration of applications presents another challenge. The J2EE Connector Architecture aims to solve this problem for J2EE platforms, and .NET provides integration capabilities through .NET servers (e.g., BizTalk). However, no standard across platforms and applications that ensures interoperability at this level exists.

.NET and J2EE

Whenever the topic of web services interoperability comes up, interoperability between the .NET and J2EE platforms is usually part of the discussion. While the web services model is based on communication and interoperability across heterogeneous platforms, languages, etc., there seems to be a great deal of skepticism as to how well web services can truly bridge .NET and J2EE technologies.

Given the relative immaturity of the open standards, bridging J2EE and .NET actually seems to work pretty well, as we will see when we discuss the SOAPBuilders Interoperability project. Extensions to the core web services standards, such as BizTalk and ebXML, present a greater challenge to interoperability.

The differences in approach between .NET and J2EE and the technical challenges accompanying them are sometimes significant. However, efforts such as the SOAPBuilders interoperability test labs have helped broker a high level of interoperability.

The following list details some key differences between .NET and J2EE:

- J2EE is a set of open standards, not a product. .NET, on the other hand, is a product suite, with some offerings built on standards and others that extend standards in proprietary ways.
- .NET provides runtime support for SOAP and UDDI as native .NET protocols.
- Integrated support is provided in .NET to build and debug XML-based web services. J2EE vendors must provide integration between their J2EE-based products and an IDE offering; requirements for doing so are not part of the standard.

- .NET provides business process management and e-commerce capabilities. These capabilities may be provided in a J2EE implementation, but are not part of the standard.

- J2EE is focused on application portability and connectivity between platforms supporting Java. .NET claims to target application integration between platforms using XML. The layer of abstraction has been raised in this model. J2EE 1.4 will include parts of the Java Web Services Developer Pack and web services support.

- Application and backend integration approaches differ. J2EE includes the Connector Architecture and the Java Message Service (JMS). The Connector Architecture provides a mechanism for plugging in resource adapters to connect to specific systems and applications. These resource adapters can be used in any container that supports the J2EE Connector Architecture. Communication across disparate applications and platforms is supported through JMS and the Java APIs for XML.

- .NET supports integration through several mechanisms: the Host Integration Server 2000, COM Transaction Integrator (COM TI), Microsoft Message Queue (MSMQ), and BizTalk Server 2000. Each solution fits a specific integration space (collaboration transactions across mainframe systems, integrating with legacy systems, integrating with systems based on protocols such as EDI, etc.).

Unique IDs

There is currently no general agreement about how to represent business entities and business domains consistently across web services standards. This deficiency presents a large hurdle to interoperability. Identifier schemes for business entities include Dun & Bradstreet's DUNS numbers, the International Telecommunication Union (ITU), the Object Identifier scheme (OID), vertical domain administered schemes such as the International Air Transport Association (IATA) airline codes, etc. However, there is currently no ubiquitous standard for web services.

For protocols that include the concept of a "from" and "to" party, the lack of identifiers can present an interoperability problem. The ebXML Message Service Specification Draft Version 2.0 contains a PartyID element with a type attribute. The type attribute indicates the domain of names used for the PartyID (such as DUNS). The PartyID is used in the From and To elements. However, a common notation or naming convention is not specified. Parties must agree on the naming convention to interoperate.

Similarly, the BizTalk Framework 2.0 states (Section 7.1):

> The source and destination are specified as names of business entities in the element marked by the <address> BizTag, and these names in general reflect business-related namespaces (such as DUNS numbers) rather than transport endpoints.

WSDL defines endpoints through ports, which specify a single address for a service binding, rather than using a business naming convention.

Potential Interoperability Issues

There are certainly enough interoperability issues to worry about in the present. Unfortunately, they aren't the entire story. A number of other issues are poised to become a problem as web services standards continue to develop.

Layering Decisions

Several extensions, such as security and reliability, are necessary to complete the web services picture. However, standards bodies have not yet decided where these extensions belong. IBM has proposed HTTPR (reliable HTTP), while other participants in web services standards development disagree about whether reliability belongs at the transport protocol level. ebXML has added reliability in their message protocol standard. The same issue exists for security (some of these issues are discussed in Chapter 10) and quality of service (QoS).

Standards Development and Proliferation

Currently, the W3C and other standards bodies are trying to identify which gaps in the web services standards most need to be filled. Reliability and security are mentioned most often, but beyond that, there is no consensus about which missing standards are most critical or what the list should even include. Standards groups are not coordinated as they try to address these gaps, so a proliferation of competing standards often duplicates or overlaps. This proliferation will undoubtedly cause additional interoperability issues to surface. To add to the confusion, vertical markets often create their own standards to expedite business exchange within (or between) markets.

The result is that the most widely implemented standard usually wins, whether or not it represents the best solution. However, until the dust settles, interoperability will become more of a nightmare as web services implementations increasingly require a level of sophistication beyond the existing ubiquitous standards such as SOAP, XML, and HTTP. Here is is an overview of some of the developing standards that could have an effect on the interoperability challenge:

W3C

In April 2001, the W3C held a Web Services Workshop, during which a number of presentations proposed work items for the W3C. The following working groups were identified (in order of priority):

- New Wire working group XML protocol extensions (QoS, reliable messaging, attachments, messaging models, routing, and publish/subscribe)
- Definition language (conversation, QoS, security, representation for business process and state changes, contracts, and negotiation)

- Orchestration (conversations, work flow, and business process)
- Discovery/Registration (generic query language and expression of vocabularies/terminologies)
- Management
- Architecture Group (security and QoS)
- Coordination Group (including external groups)

ebXML

The ebXML effort, initiated jointly by OASIS and UN/CEFACT, is developing standards in a number of areas, including:

- Messaging (based on SOAP with reliability, intermediaries, and some security)
- Business process
- Collaboration party profiles and party agreements

OASIS

OASIS efforts include:

- Security Assertion Markup Language (SAML)
- Business Transaction Processing (BTP)
- Universal Business Language (UBL—business process)
- Web Services for Interactive Applications (WSIA—previously the Web Services Component Model [WSCM])

Conformance and interoperability standards

There has been some call for standardized interoperability. This standard would include definitions of interoperability requirements between deployment environments and strong conformance statements as part of the standards.*

Another proposed idea is that layers of SOAP interoperability should be defined with a minimal SOAP implementation and several extended implementations scoped above the minimum (for example, base SOAP plus reliability). The ebXML Message Specification has taken this approach in their latest draft (2.0). One argument against this approach is that the goal is to encourage open communication among implementations; defining optional subsets increases the risk of interoperability problems.

---

* As we go to press, BEA, IBM, and Microsoft are forming the Web Service Interoperability Organization, which will address some of these issues. Given the existence of the SOAPBuilders Ineteroperability Labs, the formation of this group raises the spectre of interoperability between different interoperability groups.

SOAPBuilders Interoperability

If you are depressed and skeptical by now, read on. A lot of great work is being developed that is producing positive results.

The SOAPBuilders group was created to promote interoperability as the SOAP specification matures. The SOAPBuilders discussion group provides a forum for SOAP implementers to discuss issues related to interoperability and the various specifications. It has existed since January 2001. The group has a community of over 750 members and is highly active.

Through SOAPBuilders, two labs for interoperability testing against SOAP 1.1 have been developed. The test labs provide test suites that can be used by SOAP implementations to test interoperability. The SOAPBuilders test suite was initially based on tests created to improve interoperability between Apache SOAP and SOAP::Lite. The tests are a collection of SOAP-RPC echo invocations. WSDL documents and browser-based clients for using the service are provided for all test suites. A directory of endpoints for each implementation is maintained on the lab site.

XMethods (*http://www.xmethods.net/ilab/*) maintained Round 1, conducted in June 2001. The SOAPBuilders interoperability activity is now in Round 2, maintained by Bob Cunnings of White Mesa (*http://www.whitemesa.com/interop.htm*). For each round, XMethods and White Mesa provide lists of implementations and WSDL documents that have been tested and document the test results. Based on this information, you can determine the state of interoperability for a specific implementation.

Most implementations listed for Round 1 and many listed for initial testing during Round 2 have released updates to correct identified interoperability issues. Many listed Round 1 services are no longer available for testing. The Round 2 tests are better maintained, but don't support Apache SOAP 2.2 clients because that tool generates an older schema reference in the SOAP envelope. We will show how to fix this problem later in this chapter; Axis (the next generation of Apache SOAP) does not have this problem.

The Round 1 Interoperability Lab included specifications for a Service test suite and a Service via SOAP Intermediary test suite.

Round 2

The Standard Round 2 Interoperability Lab has been expanded to include specifications for a Base test suite, a Group B test suite, an echo Header or Group C test suite, a Service via SOAP Intermediary test suite (which duplicates the methods from the Base suite), Digest Authentication Implementation, Web Services Routing Protocol (for intermediary nodes as well), and Document/Literal SOAP Operations.

The *Base* test suite includes methods to test types (string, string array, integer, integer array, float, float array, struct, and struct array). Each method accepts the specific type and echoes it back to the client. Explicit typing information can be carried on the wire, but should not be required on incoming messages. For example, here is the echoString method client request (with sample envelopes). It accepts a string as an argument:

```
POST /interop HTTP/1.0
Host: www.whitemesa.net
User-Agent: White Mesa SOAP Interop Client/1.0
Content-Type: text/xml; charset="utf-8"
Content-Length: 502
SOAPAction: "http://soapinterop.org/"

<?xml version="1.0" encoding="UTF-8"?>

<SOAP-ENV:Envelope
  SOAP-ENV:encodingStyle="http://schemas.xmlsoap.org/soap/encoding/"
    xmlns:SOAP-ENC="http://schemas.xmlsoap.org/soap/encoding/"
    xmlns:SOAP-ENV="http://schemas.xmlsoap.org/soap/envelope/"
    xmlns:xsd="http://www.w3.org/2001/XMLSchema"
    xmlns:xsi="http://www.w3.org/2001/XMLSchema-instance">
  <SOAP-ENV:Body>
    <m:echoString xmlns:m="http://soapinterop.org/">
      <inputString>hello world</inputString>
    </m:echoString>
  </SOAP-ENV:Body>
</SOAP-ENV:Envelope>
```

Here is a successful server response; as you'd expect, it returns the same string:

```
HTTP/1.0 200 OK
Date: Wed, 20 Jun 2001 02:44:16 GMT
Server: WhiteMesa SOAP Server/2.3
Content-Type: text/xml; charset="utf-8"
Content-Length: 508

<?xml version="1.0" encoding="UTF-8"?>

<SOAP-ENV:Envelope
  SOAP-ENV:encodingStyle="http://schemas.xmlsoap.org/soap/encoding/"
    xmlns:SOAP-ENC="http://schemas.xmlsoap.org/soap/encoding/"
    xmlns:SOAP-ENV="http://schemas.xmlsoap.org/soap/envelope/"
    xmlns:xsd="http://www.w3.org/2001/XMLSchema"
    xmlns:xsi="http://www.w3.org/2001/XMLSchema-instance">
  <SOAP-ENV:Body>
    <m:echoStringResponse xmlns:m="http://soapinterop.org/">
      <return>hello world</return>
    </m:echoStringResponse>
  </SOAP-ENV:Body>
</SOAP-ENV:Envelope>
```

Similar echoing methods are provided for:

echoVoid
> Accepts no arguments and returns no arguments

echoBase64
> Accepts a binary object and echoes it back

echoHexBinary
> Accepts a hex-encoded object and echoes it back

echoDate
> Accepts a Date/Time and echoes it back

echoDecimal
> Accepts a decimal and echoes it back

echoBoolean
> Accepts a Boolean and echoes it back

The *Group B* test suite includes methods with more complex serialization requirements. It includes these echo methods:

echoStructAsSimpleTypes
> Accepts a single struct and echoes it (decomposed into three output parameters)

echoSimpleTypesAsStruct
> Accepts three input parameters and echoes them integrated into a single struct

echo2DStringArray
> Accepts a single two-dimensional array of type xsd:string and echoes it

echoNestedStruct
> Accepts a single struct with a nested struct type member and echoes it

echoNestedArray
> Accepts a single struct with a nested array type member and echoes it back

The *echoHeader* or *Group C* test suite offers standard headers used to test header processing. The SOAP body contains an echoVoid method call. The message recipient is the default actor, and the mustUnderstand element value can be either 0 or 1 to test conformance to the SOAP 1.1 specification. The following header entries are provided:

echoMeStringRequest
> Contains a string that is echoed in a corresponding response header entry (echoMeStringResponse)

echoMeStructRequest
> Contains a single, echoed struct (echoMeStructResponse)

Unknown
> Any header that is not understood by the server. If a server cannot process the header and mustUnderstand is set to true (1), the server must issue a SOAP Fault if it is the target of the header entry, based on the value of the actor attribute. If

the target is another server, the server can ignore the header entry. If a server cannot process the header, and mustUnderstand is set to false (0), the server can ignore the header entry and is not required to fault (regardless of whether it is the targeted server).

Polymorphic type methods are also available. They include: echoPolyMorph, echoPolyMorphArray, and echoPolyMorphStruct.

Round 3

Round 3 of interoperability testing, scheduled for the end of February 2002, is co-hosted by IONA and Microsoft and will focus on WSDL interoperability. A formal plan is not yet finalized, but proposed testing includes the following success criteria:

- Tools can generate WSDL documents correctly for designated scenarios and consume WSDLs generated by other tools.
- Tools can consume and reuse WSDL documents.

Discussion topics that have been most active on the SOAPBuilders list will be included in the tests:

- Import (schema import)
- Document/literal services with multiple schema
- SOAP binding interoperability issues

Understanding the Echo Test

Let's examine the EchoTestClient that comes with Apache SOAP 2.2. We picked Apache SOAP because we already explained its underpinnings in earlier chapters and wanted to focus on the test itself. The workings of the test, the interoperability issues, and the concepts of encoding and serialization are generic enough to apply to any SOAP infrastructure you may use. The EchoTestClient represents a Java implementation of the SOAPBuilders Interoperability Labs "Round 1" test and can also be used for the "Round 2: Base" interoperability tests. It can be found in the *soap-2.2\ samples\interop* directory, or as part of the examples available on this book's web site (*http://www.oreilly.com/catalog/javawebserv*).

We also verified some of the test results using the Apache Axis version of the same test and used other third-party visual interfaces. These interfaces will be shown later.

Running the EchoTestClient

To see how these tests work, we need an Internet connection. Let's run the Apache SOAP 2.2 EchoTestClient against the Iona XMLBus echo test service, which Iona has hosted as part of their participation in the SB Round 2 effort:

```
java samples.interop.EchoTestClient http://interop.xmlbus.com:7002/xmlbus/container/
InteropTest/BaseService/BasePort
```

The command must be typed on a single line. If you use the `EchoTestClient` straight from the Apache SOAP distribution, you should see the following errors as output:

```
echoInteger generated fault:
  Fault Code   = SOAP-ENV:Server
  Fault String = xsi:type doesn't match.  Expected http://www.w3.org/2001/
XMLSchema:int but found http://www.w3.org/1999/XMLSchema:int
echoFloat generated fault:
  Fault Code   = SOAP-ENV:Server
  Fault String = xsi:type doesn't match.  Expected http://www.w3.org/2001/
XMLSchema:float but found http://www.w3.org/1999/XMLSchema:float
soapAction: http://soapinterop.org/
echoString generated fault:
  Fault Code   = SOAP-ENV:Server
  Fault String = xsi:type doesn't match.  Expected http://www.w3.org/2001/
XMLSchema:string but found http://www.w3.org/1999/XMLSchema:string
soapAction: http://soapinterop.org/
...
```

This result illustrates one of the most basic interoperability problems. The receiving service expected the schema definition *http://www.w3.org/2001/XMLSchema*, but the sending client generated a SOAP envelope based on *http://www.w3.org/1999/XMLSchema*. We will show how simple it is to fix this problem in a moment, when we get to the code. In the meantime, when the EchoTestClient works correctly, its output looks like this:

```
echoInteger      OK
echoFloat        OK
echoString       OK
echoStruct       OK
echoIntegerArray OK
echoFloatArray   OK
echoStringArray  OK
echoStructArray  OK
```

This test may look simple, but quite a bit is going on internally. At the highest level, this test makes eight RPC calls,[*] each with its own unique datatype as a parameter. The receiving method simply takes that parameter and returns it as the method's return value. The sending client then compares the returned data with the sent data to verify that it is the same. If the data are equal, we know that:

- The sending client successfully packaged the method invocation and its parameters and correctly marshalled it onto the wire as a valid SOAP request.
- The receiving SOAP processor received the request, identified that there was enough correct information in the SOAP request, and dispatched it to the appropriate service method.
- The receiving SOAP processor also (optionally) validated the request against the WSDL that described the service.

---

[*] The scope of the test has grown to include other datatypes. This version of the test exercises eight of them.

- The service method was invoked with the correct data and returned the data intended for the caller as the return value.
- The server implementation correctly marshaled the return values onto the wire as a response envelope.
- The sending client's runtime infrastructure successfully unmarshaled the SOAP response envelope into the appropriate Java object.
- The sent and returned data are equivalent.

The next exercise directs the EchoTestClient at our simple servlet from Chapter 3:

```
java samples.interop.EchoTestClient http://localhost:8080/examples/servlet/
SimpleHTTPReceive
```

You will see several errors in the sending client's console because the simple servlet is not set up to accommodate RPC calls—but that's not important for this discussion. What's important is that you should see the following output in the Tomcat console window. The raw SOAP envelopes that were generated by the EchoTestClient are shown here:

```
Received request.
----------------------
  SOAPAction = "http://soapinterop.org/"
  Host = localhost
  Content-Type = text/xml; charset=utf-8
  Content-Length = 469
----------------------
<?xml version='1.0' encoding='UTF-8'?>
<SOAP-ENV:Envelope xmlns:SOAP-ENV="http://schemas.xmlsoap.org/soap/envelope/"
xmlns:xsi="http://www.w3.org/2001/XMLSchema-instance"
xmlns:xsd="http://www.w3.org/2001/XMLSchema">
<SOAP-ENV:Body>
<ns1:echoInteger xmlns:ns1="http://soapinterop.org/"
SOAP-ENV:encodingStyle="http://schemas.xmlsoap.org/soap/encoding/">
<inputInteger xsi:type="xsd:int">5</inputInteger>
</ns1:echoInteger>
</SOAP-ENV:Body>
</SOAP-ENV:Envelope>


Received request.
----------------------
  SOAPAction = "http://soapinterop.org/"
  Host = localhost
  Content-Type = text/xml; charset=utf-8
  Content-Length = 466
----------------------
<?xml version='1.0' encoding='UTF-8'?>
<SOAP-ENV:Envelope xmlns:SOAP-ENV="http://schemas.xmlsoap.org/soap/envelope/"
xmlns:xsi="http://www.w3.org/2001/XMLSchema-instance"
xmlns:xsd="http://www.w3.org/2001/XMLSchema">
<SOAP-ENV:Body>
```

```
<ns1:echoFloat xmlns:ns1="http://soapinterop.org/"
SOAP-ENV:encodingStyle="http://schemas.xmlsoap.org/soap/encoding/">
<inputFloat xsi:type="xsd:float">55.5</inputFloat>
</ns1:echoFloat>
</SOAP-ENV:Body>
</SOAP-ENV:Envelope>
```

Received request.
```
-----------------------
  SOAPAction = "http://soapinterop.org/"
  Host = localhost
  Content-Type = text/xml; charset=utf-8
  Content-Length = 476
-----------------------
<?xml version='1.0' encoding='UTF-8'?>
<SOAP-ENV:Envelope xmlns:SOAP-ENV="http://schemas.xmlsoap.org/soap/envelope/"
xmlns:xsi="http://www.w3.org/2001/XMLSchema-instance"
xmlns:xsd="http://www.w3.org/2001/XMLSchema">
<SOAP-ENV:Body>
<ns1:echoString xmlns:ns1="http://soapinterop.org/"
SOAP-ENV:encodingStyle="http://schemas.xmlsoap.org/soap/encoding/">
<inputString xsi:type="xsd:string">Hi there!</inputString>
</ns1:echoString>
</SOAP-ENV:Body>
</SOAP-ENV:Envelope>
```

Received request.
```
-----------------------
  SOAPAction = "http://soapinterop.org/"
  Host = localhost
  Content-Type = text/xml; charset=utf-8
  Content-Length = 656
-----------------------
<?xml version='1.0' encoding='UTF-8'?>
<SOAP-ENV:Envelope xmlns:SOAP-ENV="http://schemas.xmlsoap.org/soap/envelope/"
xmlns:xsi="http://www.w3.org/2001/XMLSchema-instance"
xmlns:xsd="http://www.w3.org/2001/XMLSchema">
<SOAP-ENV:Body>
<ns1:echoStruct xmlns:ns1="http://soapinterop.org/"
SOAP-ENV:encodingStyle="http://schemas.xmlsoap.org/soap/encoding/">
<inputStruct xmlns:ns2="http://soapinterop.org/xsd" xsi:type="ns2:SOAPStruct">
<varInt xsi:type="xsd:int">5</varInt>
<varFloat xsi:type="xsd:float">10.0</varFloat>
<varString xsi:type="xsd:string">Hola, baby</varString>
</inputStruct>
</ns1:echoStruct>
</SOAP-ENV:Body>
</SOAP-ENV:Envelope>
```

```
Received request.
-----------------------
  SOAPAction = "http://soapinterop.org/"
  Host = localhost
  Content-Type = text/xml; charset=utf-8
  Content-Length = 748
-----------------------
<?xml version='1.0' encoding='UTF-8'?>
<SOAP-ENV:Envelope xmlns:SOAP-ENV="http://schemas.xmlsoap.org/soap/envelope/"
xmlns:xsi="http://www.w3.org/2001/XMLSchema-instance"
xmlns:xsd="http://www.w3.org/2001/XMLSchema">
<SOAP-ENV:Body>
<ns1:echoIntegerArray xmlns:ns1="http://soapinterop.org/"
SOAP-ENV:encodingStyle="http://schemas.xmlsoap.org/soap/encoding/">
<inputIntegerArray xmlns:ns2="http://schemas.xmlsoap.org/soap/encoding/"
xsi:type="ns2:Array" ns2:arrayType="xsd:int[5]">
<item xsi:type="xsd:int">5</item>
<item xsi:type="xsd:int">4</item>
<item xsi:type="xsd:int">3</item>
<item xsi:type="xsd:int">2</item>
<item xsi:type="xsd:int">1</item>
</inputIntegerArray>
</ns1:echoIntegerArray>
</SOAP-ENV:Body>
</SOAP-ENV:Envelope>
```

```
Received request.
-----------------------
  SOAPAction = "http://soapinterop.org/"
  Host = localhost
  Content-Type = text/xml; charset=utf-8
  Content-Length = 762
-----------------------
<?xml version='1.0' encoding='UTF-8'?>
<SOAP-ENV:Envelope xmlns:SOAP-ENV="http://schemas.xmlsoap.org/soap/envelope/"
xmlns:xsi="http://www.w3.org/2001/XMLSchema-instance"
xmlns:xsd="http://www.w3.org/2001/XMLSchema">
<SOAP-ENV:Body>
<ns1:echoFloatArray xmlns:ns1="http://soapinterop.org/"
SOAP-ENV:encodingStyle="http://schemas.xmlsoap.org/soap/encoding/">
<inputFloatArray xmlns:ns2="http://schemas.xmlsoap.org/soap/encoding/"
xsi:type="ns2:Array" ns2:arrayType="xsd:float[5]">
<item xsi:type="xsd:float">5.5</item>
<item xsi:type="xsd:float">4.4</item>
<item xsi:type="xsd:float">3.3</item>
<item xsi:type="xsd:float">2.2</item>
<item xsi:type="xsd:float">1.1</item>
</inputFloatArray>
</ns1:echoFloatArray>
</SOAP-ENV:Body>
</SOAP-ENV:Envelope>
```

```
Received request.
----------------------
  SOAPAction = "http://soapinterop.org/"
  Host = localhost
  Content-Type = text/xml; charset=utf-8
  Content-Length = 801
----------------------
<?xml version='1.0' encoding='UTF-8'?>
<SOAP-ENV:Envelope xmlns:SOAP-ENV="http://schemas.xmlsoap.org/soap/envelope/"
xmlns:xsi="http://www.w3.org/2001/XMLSchema-instance"
xmlns:xsd="http://www.w3.org/2001/XMLSchema">
<SOAP-ENV:Body>
<ns1:echoStringArray xmlns:ns1="http://soapinterop.org/"
SOAP-ENV:encodingStyle="http://schemas.xmlsoap.org/soap/encoding/">
<inputStringArray xmlns:ns2="http://schemas.xmlsoap.org/soap/encoding/"
xsi:type="ns2:Array" ns2:arrayType="xsd:string[5]">
<item xsi:type="xsd:string">First</item>
<item xsi:type="xsd:string">Second</item>
<item xsi:type="xsd:string">Fifth (just kidding :))</item>
<item xsi:type="xsd:string">Fourth</item>
<item xsi:type="xsd:string">Last</item>
</inputStringArray>
</ns1:echoStringArray>
</SOAP-ENV:Body>
</SOAP-ENV:Envelope>


Received request.
----------------------
  SOAPAction = "http://soapinterop.org/"
  Host = localhost
  Content-Type = text/xml; charset=utf-8
  Content-Length = 1527
----------------------
<?xml version='1.0' encoding='UTF-8'?>
<SOAP-ENV:Envelope xmlns:SOAP-ENV="http://schemas.xmlsoap.org/soap/envelope/"
xmlns:xsi="http://www.w3.org/2001/XMLSchema-instance"
xmlns:xsd="http://www.w3.org/2001/XMLSchema">
<SOAP-ENV:Body>
<ns1:echoStructArray xmlns:ns1="http://soapinterop.org/"
SOAP-ENV:encodingStyle="http://schemas.xmlsoap.org/soap/encoding/">
<inputStructArray xmlns:ns2="http://schemas.xmlsoap.org/soap/encoding/"
xsi:type="ns2:Array" xmlns:ns3="http://soapinterop.org/xsd"
ns2:arrayType="ns3:SOAPStruct[5]"><item xsi:type="ns3:SOAPStruct">
<varInt xsi:type="xsd:int">5</varInt>
<varFloat xsi:type="xsd:float">5.55555</varFloat>
<varString xsi:type="xsd:string">cinqo</varString>
</item>
<item xsi:type="ns3:SOAPStruct">
<varInt xsi:type="xsd:int">4</varInt>
<varFloat xsi:type="xsd:float">4.4444</varFloat>
<varString xsi:type="xsd:string">quattro</varString>
</item>
<item xsi:type="ns3:SOAPStruct">
```

```
<varInt xsi:type="xsd:int">3</varInt>
<varFloat xsi:type="xsd:float">3.333</varFloat>
<varString xsi:type="xsd:string">tres</varString>
</item>
<item xsi:type="ns3:SOAPStruct">
<varInt xsi:type="xsd:int">2</varInt>
<varFloat xsi:type="xsd:float">2.22</varFloat>
<varString xsi:type="xsd:string">duet</varString>
</item>
<item xsi:type="ns3:SOAPStruct">
<varInt xsi:type="xsd:int">1</varInt>
<varFloat xsi:type="xsd:float">1.1</varFloat>
<varString xsi:type="xsd:string">un</varString>
</item>
</inputStructArray>
</ns1:echoStructArray>
</SOAP-ENV:Body>
</SOAP-ENV:Envelope>
```

We will examine some of this output in more detail as we walk through the example. But first, here is the Apache SOAP 2.2 EchoTestClient in its entirety:

```
package samples.interop;

import java.util.Vector;
import org.apache.soap.*;
import org.apache.soap.encoding.SOAPMappingRegistry;
import org.apache.soap.encoding.soapenc.*;
import org.apache.soap.rpc.*;
import org.apache.soap.messaging.*;
import java.net.URL;
import org.apache.soap.util.xml.*;
import java.io.*;
import org.w3c.dom.*;
import org.apache.soap.util.*;
import java.lang.reflect.*;

/** A quick-and-dirty client for the Interop echo test services as defined
 * at http://www.xmethods.net/ilab.
 *
 * Defaults to the Apache endpoint, but you can point it somewhere else via
 * the command line:
 *
 *     EchoTestClient http://some.other.place/
 *
 * DOES NOT SUPPORT DIFFERENT SOAPACTION URIS YET.
 *
 * @author Glen Daniels (gdaniels@macromedia.com)
 */
public class EchoTestClient
{
  SOAPMappingRegistry smr =
    new SOAPMappingRegistry(Constants.NS_URI_CURRENT_SCHEMA_XSD);
```

```
//  public static final String DEFAULT_URL =
//     "http://nagoya.apache.org:5089/soap/servlet/rpcrouter";
   public static final String DEFAULT_URL =
     "http://localhost:8080/soap/servlet/rpcrouter";
// pick one!  First line works for round 1; second for round 2: base
public static final String ACTION_URI = "urn:soapinterop";
// public static final String ACTION_URI = "http://soapinterop.org/";

   public static final String OBJECT_URI = "http://soapinterop.org/xsd";
   public Header header = null;

   public static void main(String args[])
   {
     URL url = null;

     try {
       if (args.length > 0) {
         url = new URL(args[0]);
       } else {
         url = new URL(DEFAULT_URL);
       }
     } catch (Exception e) {
       e.printStackTrace();
     }

     EchoTestClient eTest = new EchoTestClient();
     eTest.doWork(url);
   }

   private static boolean equals(Object obj1, Object obj2) {
     if (obj1 == null) return (obj2 == null);
     if (obj1.equals(obj2)) return true;
     if (!obj2.getClass().isArray()) return false;
     if (!obj1.getClass().isArray()) return false;
     if (Array.getLength(obj1) != Array.getLength(obj2)) return false;
     for (int i=0; i<Array.getLength(obj1); i++)
       if (!equals(Array.get(obj1,i),Array.get(obj2,i))) return false;
     return true;
   }

   public void doWork(URL url)
   {
     IntDeserializer intDser = new IntDeserializer();
     FloatDeserializer floatDser = new FloatDeserializer();
     StringDeserializer stringDser = new StringDeserializer();
     ArraySerializer arraySer = new ArraySerializer();
     DataSerializer dataSer = new DataSerializer();
     smr.mapTypes(Constants.NS_URI_SOAP_ENC,
         new QName(OBJECT_URI, "SOAPStruct"), Data.class, dataSer, dataSer);

     Integer i = new Integer(5);
     Parameter p = new Parameter("inputInteger", Integer.class, i, null);
     smr.mapTypes(Constants.NS_URI_SOAP_ENC,
```

```
            new QName("", "Return"), null, null, intDser);
doCall(url, "echoInteger", p);

p = new Parameter("inputFloat", Float.class, new Float(55.5), null);
smr.mapTypes(Constants.NS_URI_SOAP_ENC,
    new QName("", "Return"), null, null, floatDser);
doCall(url, "echoFloat", p);

p = new Parameter("inputString", String.class, "Hi there!", null);
smr.mapTypes(Constants.NS_URI_SOAP_ENC,
    new QName("", "Return"), null, null, stringDser);
doCall(url, "echoString", p);

p = new Parameter("inputStruct", Data.class,
    new Data(5, "Hola, baby", (float)10.0), null);
smr.mapTypes(Constants.NS_URI_SOAP_ENC,
    new QName("", "Return"), null, null, dataSer);
doCall(url, "echoStruct", p);

p = new Parameter("inputIntegerArray", Integer[].class, new Integer[]{
                new Integer(5),
                new Integer(4),
                new Integer(3),
                new Integer(2),
                new Integer(1)}, null);
smr.mapTypes(Constants.NS_URI_SOAP_ENC,
    new QName("", "Return"), null, null, arraySer);
doCall(url, "echoIntegerArray", p);

p = new Parameter("inputFloatArray", Float[].class, new Float[]{
                new Float(5.5),
                new Float(4.4),
                new Float(3.3),
                new Float(2.2),
                new Float(1.1)}, null);
smr.mapTypes(Constants.NS_URI_SOAP_ENC,
    new QName("", "Return"), null, null, arraySer);
doCall(url, "echoFloatArray", p);

p = new Parameter("inputStringArray", String[].class, new String[]{
                "First",
                "Second",
                "Fifth (just kidding :))",
                "Fourth",
                "Last"}, null);
smr.mapTypes(Constants.NS_URI_SOAP_ENC,
    new QName("", "Return"), null, null, arraySer);
doCall(url, "echoStringArray", p);

p = new Parameter("inputStructArray", Data[].class, new Data[]{
                new Data(5, "cinqo", new Float("5.55555").floatValue()),
                new Data(4, "quattro", (float)4.4444),
                new Data(3, "tres", (float)3.333),
```

```
                    new Data(2, "duet", (float)2.22),
                    new Data(1, "un", (float)1.1)}, null);
    smr.mapTypes(Constants.NS_URI_SOAP_ENC,
        new QName("", "Return"), null, null, arraySer);
    doCall(url, "echoStructArray", p);
  }

  public void doCall(URL url, String methodName, Parameter param)
  {
    try {
      Call call = new Call( );
      Vector params = new Vector( );
      params.addElement(param);
      call.setSOAPMappingRegistry(smr);
      call.setTargetObjectURI(ACTION_URI);
      call.setEncodingStyleURI(Constants.NS_URI_SOAP_ENC);
      call.setMethodName(methodName);
      call.setParams(params);
      if (header != null)
        call.setHeader(header);

      String soapAction = ACTION_URI;
//      System.out.println("soapAction: " + soapAction);
/*      if (true) {
        soapAction = soapAction + methodName;
      }
*/
      Response resp = call.invoke(url, soapAction);

      // check response
      if (!resp.generatedFault( )) {
        Parameter ret = resp.getReturnValue( );
        Object output = ret.getValue( );
        Object input = param.getValue( );

        if (equals(input,output)) {
          System.out.println(methodName + "\t OK");
        } else {
          System.out.println(methodName + "\t FAIL: " + output);
        }
      }
      else {
        Fault fault = resp.getFault ( );
        System.err.println (methodName + " generated fault: ");
        System.out.println ("  Fault Code   = " + fault.getFaultCode( ));
        System.out.println ("  Fault String = " + fault.getFaultString( ));
      }

    } catch (Exception e) {
      e.printStackTrace( );
    }
  }
}
```

Getting it to work

Let's examine some of this code in detail. First, here is what we did to get around the mismatch of the schema namespace URIs. The value passed into the mapping registry is based on a default, which was initialized to use the older value:

```
public class EchoTestClient
{
  SOAPMappingRegistry smr =
    new SOAPMappingRegistry(Constants.NS_URI_CURRENT_SCHEMA_XSD);
```

Apache SOAP 2.2 supports the 2001 schema—it just does not default to it. We could have simply changed this line of code, but changing it doesn't fix the problem everywhere. Instead, we got the *Constants.java* file from the Apache SOAP distribution; updated Constants.NS_URI_CURRENT_SCHEMA_XSD to default to the desired value; and recompiled the Constants, SoapEncUtils, and ArraySerializer classes:

```
/*  Changed this:
public static final String NS_URI_CURRENT_SCHEMA_XSI =
    NS_URI_1999_SCHEMA_XSI;
  public static final String NS_URI_CURRENT_SCHEMA_XSD =
    NS_URI_1999_SCHEMA_XSD;
*/
// To this:
  public static final String NS_URI_CURRENT_SCHEMA_XSI =
    NS_URI_2001_SCHEMA_XSI;
  public static final String NS_URI_CURRENT_SCHEMA_XSD =
    NS_URI_2001_SCHEMA_XSD;
```

We also commented out the following lines in the doWork( ) method of the test:

```
        String soapAction = ACTION_URI;
/*      if (true) {
        soapAction = soapAction + methodName;
        }
*/
        Response resp = call.invoke(url, soapAction);
```

Almost every test we tried did not like having the method name appended to the soapAction header. It's good that the author of the code was aware of this problem and isolated it so it could be turned on and off easily. Also, depending on what round of tests we wanted to run, we had to change the action URI; the Round 1 tests expected the URI *urn:soapinterop*, while the current Round 2: base tests expect *http:/ /soapinterop.org/*:

```
// pick one!  First line works for round 1; second for round 2: base
public static final String ACTION_URI = "urn:soapinterop";
// public static final String ACTION_URI = "http://soapinterop.org/";
```

The Apache Axis version of the same test didn't need any modification because it is a new test that presumably works only against the Round 2 tests.

Default serialization of data

The mapping registry maintains the relationship between the XML datatypes and their corresponding Java types. It is also a utility that marshals and unmarshals the data between the Java representation and the SOAP envelope representation. It accomplishes this task by maintaining a list of serialization and deserialization classes for each datatype it knows about.

By default, the SOAPMappingRegistry is instantiated with the appropriate mappings and serializers/deserializers for each type that it supports.

The default serialization mapping for the String class creates the XML rendition. The SOAP envelope resulting from this call looks like:

```
<?xml version='1.0' encoding='UTF-8'?>
<SOAP-ENV:Envelope xmlns:SOAP-ENV="http://schemas.xmlsoap.org/soap/envelope/"
    xmlns:xsi="http://www.w3.org/2001/XMLSchema-instance"
    xmlns:xsd="http://www.w3.org/2001/XMLSchema">
  <SOAP-ENV:Body>
    <ns1:echoString
        xmlns:ns1="urn:soapinterop"
        SOAP-ENV:encodingStyle="http://schemas.xmlsoap.org/soap/encoding/">
      <inputString
          xmlns:ns2="http://www.w3.org/2001/XMLSchema"
          xsi:type="ns2:string">
        Hi there!
      </inputString>
    </ns1:echoString>
  </SOAP-ENV:Body>
</SOAP-ENV:Envelope>
```

Note the inclusion of the xsi:type attribute. Not all SOAP toolkits that participated in the Round 1 testing supported this attribute.

These default mappings may be overridden by calling the mapTypes( ) method. The mapTypes( ) method takes the following parameters:

- A namespace for the schema
- A QName for the element that represents the parameter/return value[*]
- An instance of a class that describes the data
- An instance of an object that performs the serialization of the Java object into the XML representation
- An instance of an object that deserializes the XML data back into the Java object

For example, the following objects are part of Apache SOAP's serialization framework and are included in the org.apache.soap.encoding.soapenc package:

```
IntDeserializer intDser = new IntDeserializer();
FloatDeserializer floatDser = new FloatDeserializer();
```

---

[*] A QName is a namespace-qualified element name, for which the namespace is optional.

```
StringDeserializer stringDser = new StringDeserializer();
ArraySerializer arraySer = new ArraySerializer();
```

In the EchoTestClient, the call to mapTypes( ) is necessary for the "Return" because the SOAP Toolkit that services the request may not support the placement of the xsi:type attribute in the response envelope. The type information for the parameter is specified along with its name and value when the parameter object is constructed:

```
p = new Parameter("inputString", String.class, "Hi there!", null);
smr.mapTypes(Constants.NS_URI_SOAP_ENC,
    new QName("", "Return"), null, null, stringDser);
doCall(url, "echoString", p);
```

Default mappings are available for more complicated objects, such as arrays. The following code constructs a method invocation with a parameter that is an array of 5 integers, with the values of 1 through 5:

```
p = new Parameter("inputIntegerArray", Integer[].class, new Integer[]{
                    new Integer(5),
                    new Integer(4),
                    new Integer(3),
                    new Integer(2),
                    new Integer(1)}, null);
smr.mapTypes(Constants.NS_URI_SOAP_ENC,
    new QName("", "Return"), null, null, arraySer);
doCall(url, "echoIntegerArray", p);
```

The serialization framework knows how to traverse the array, using the appropriate serialization classes for each member element (in this case, all of type Integer). The serialized output looks like:

```
<?xml version='1.0' encoding='UTF-8'?>
<SOAP-ENV:Envelope
  xmlns:SOAP-ENV="http://schemas.xmlsoap.org/soap/envelope/"
    xmlns:xsi="http://www.w3.org/2001/XMLSchema-instance"
    xmlns:xsd="http://www.w3.org/2001/XMLSchema">
  <SOAP-ENV:Body>
    <ns1:echoIntegerArray
        xmlns:ns1="urn:soapinterop"
        SOAP-ENV:encodingStyle="http://schemas.xmlsoap.org/soap/encoding/">
      <inputIntegerArray
          xmlns:ns2="http://schemas.xmlsoap.org/soap/encoding/"
          xsi:type="ns2:Array"
          xmlns:ns3="http://www.w3.org/2001/XMLSchema"
          ns2:arrayType="ns3:int[5]">
        <item xsi:type="ns3:int">5</item>
        <item xsi:type="ns3:int">4</item>
        <item xsi:type="ns3:int">3</item>
        <item xsi:type="ns3:int">2</item>
        <item xsi:type="ns3:int">1</item>
      </inputIntegerArray>
    </ns1:echoIntegerArray>
  </SOAP-ENV:Body>
</SOAP-ENV:Envelope>
```

Custom serialization

Part of the test involves sending a complex data structure represented as a SOAP struct.* The structure contains three data items: an integer, a string, and a float. Creating a custom data serialization requires the following steps:

1. Create a Java object to describe the data.
2. Create a custom class to perform the serialization/deserialization.
3. Plug them into the mapping registry.

In the following code, DataSerializer is a custom class that we will explain shortly. The custom object, the serializer, and the deserializer are plugged into the mapping registry with the call to mapTypes():

```
DataSerializer dataSer = new DataSerializer();
smr.mapTypes(Constants.NS_URI_SOAP_ENC,
    new QName(OBJECT_URI, "SOAPStruct"), Data.class, dataSer, dataSer);
```

As shown in the following listing, the setup for call() is similar to the setup that was used for the "built-in" types:

```
p = new Parameter("inputStruct", Data.class,
    new Data(5, "Hola, baby", (float)10.0), null);
doCall(url, "echoStruct", p);
```

Here's the SOAP envelope generated by the call:

```
<?xml version='1.0' encoding='UTF-8'?>
<SOAP-ENV:Envelope
    xmlns:SOAP-ENV="http://schemas.xmlsoap.org/soap/envelope/"
    xmlns:xsi="http://www.w3.org/2001/XMLSchema-instance"
    xmlns:xsd="http://www.w3.org/2001/XMLSchema">
  <SOAP-ENV:Body>
    <ns1:echoStruct xmlns:ns1="urn:soapinterop"
        SOAP-ENV:encodingStyle="http://schemas.xmlsoap.org/soap/encoding/">
      <inputStruct xmlns:ns2="http://soapinterop.org/xsd"
        xsi:type="ns2:SOAPStruct">
        <varInt xmlns:ns3="http://www.w3.org/2001/XMLSchema"
            xsi:type="ns3:int">
          5
        </varInt>
        <varFloat xmlns:ns4="http://www.w3.org/2001/XMLSchema"
            xsi:type="ns4:float">
          10.0
        </varFloat>
        <varString xmlns:ns5="http://www.w3.org/2001/XMLSchema"
            xsi:type="ns5:string">
          Hola, baby
        </varString>
      </inputStruct>
```

---

* A struct is a complex datatype defined by SOAP encoding.

```
      </ns1:echoStruct>
    </SOAP-ENV:Body>
  </SOAP-ENV:Envelope>
```

The next listing shows the Java class that represents the data structure. It holds the data and implements an equals( ) method that the EchoTestClient uses to compare results:

```java
class Data
{
  Integer myInt;
  String myString;
  Float myFloat;

  public Data( )
  {
  }

  public Data(int i, String s, float f)
  {
    myInt = new Integer(i);
    myString = s;
    myFloat = new Float(f);
  }

  public String toString( )
  {
    return "Data[MyInt=" + myInt + ", MyString='" +
      myString + "', myFloat=" + myFloat + "]";
  }

  /**
   * Equality comparison.
   */
  public boolean equals(Object object) {
    if (!(object instanceof Data)) return false;

    Data that= (Data) object;

    if (!this.myInt.equals(that.myInt)) return false;
    if (!this.myFloat.equals(that.myFloat)) return false;

    if (this.myString == null) {
      if (that.myString != null) return false;
    } else {
      if (!this.myString.equals(that.myString)) return false;
    }

    return true;
  };
}
```

The custom DataSerializer class implements both the Serializer and Deserializer interfaces; these interfaces define the marshall( ) and unmarshall( ) methods, respectively. Putting both methods in one class and using that class for both serialization and deserialization is a common design strategy. The marshall( ) method simply calls the individual marshall( ) method for each datatype in the Java class. Likewise, the unmarshall( ) method calls the individual unmarshall( ) method for each type in the SOAP struct and returns a JavaBean instance:

```
package samples.interop;

import java.util.Vector;
import org.apache.soap.*;
import org.apache.soap.encoding.SOAPMappingRegistry;
import org.apache.soap.encoding.soapenc.*;
import org.apache.soap.rpc.*;
import org.apache.soap.messaging.*;
import java.net.URL;
import org.apache.soap.util.xml.*;
import java.io.*;
import org.w3c.dom.*;
import org.apache.soap.util.*;
import java.lang.reflect.*;

public class DataSerializer implements Serializer, Deserializer
{
  public void marshall(String inScopeEncStyle, Class javaType, Object src,
                       Object context, Writer sink, NSStack nsStack,
                       XMLJavaMappingRegistry xjmr, SOAPContext ctx)
    throws IllegalArgumentException, IOException
  {
    if(!javaType.equals(Data.class))
    {
      throw new IllegalArgumentException("Can only serialize Data instances");
    }

    Data data = (Data)src;

    nsStack.pushScope( );
    if(src!=null)
    {
      SoapEncUtils.generateStructureHeader(inScopeEncStyle,
                                           javaType,
                                           context,
                                           sink,
                                           nsStack,xjmr);

      sink.write(StringUtils.lineSeparator);

      xjmr.marshall(inScopeEncStyle, Integer.class, data.myInt, "varInt",
                    sink, nsStack, ctx);
      sink.write(StringUtils.lineSeparator);
      xjmr.marshall(inScopeEncStyle, Float.class, data.myFloat, "varFloat",
                    sink, nsStack, ctx);
      sink.write(StringUtils.lineSeparator);
      xjmr.marshall(inScopeEncStyle, String.class, data.myString, "varString",
                    sink, nsStack, ctx);
      sink.write(StringUtils.lineSeparator);
```

```
      sink.write("</" + context + '>');
    }
    else
    {
      SoapEncUtils.generateNullStructure(inScopeEncStyle,
                                          javaType,
                                          context,
                                          sink,
                                          nsStack,xjmr);
    }
    nsStack.popScope( );
  }

  public Bean unmarshall(String inScopeEncStyle, QName elementType, Node src,
                         XMLJavaMappingRegistry xjmr, SOAPContext ctx)
    throws IllegalArgumentException
  {
    Element root = (Element)src;
    String name = root.getTagName( );

    if (SoapEncUtils.isNull(root))
    {
      return new Bean(Data.class, null);
    }

    Data ret = new Data( );
    NodeList list = root.getElementsByTagName("varInt");
    if (list == null || list.getLength( ) == 0) {
        throw new IllegalArgumentException(
        "No 'varInt' Element (deserializing Data struct)");
    }
    Element el = (Element)list.item(0);
    ret.myInt = new Integer(DOMUtils.getChildCharacterData(el));

    list = root.getElementsByTagName("varFloat");
    if (list == null || list.getLength( ) == 0) {
        throw new IllegalArgumentException(
        "No 'varFloat' Element (deserializing Data struct)");
    }
    el = (Element)list.item(0);
    ret.myFloat = new Float(DOMUtils.getChildCharacterData(el));

    list = root.getElementsByTagName("varString");
    if (list == null || list.getLength( ) == 0) {
      throw new IllegalArgumentException(
        "No 'varString' Element (deserializing Data struct)");
    }
    el = (Element)list.item(0);
    ret.myString = ((Text)el.getFirstChild()).getData( );

    return new Bean(Data.class, ret);
  }
}
```

Next, the custom structs are aggregated into an array:

```
p = new Parameter("inputStructArray", Data[].class, new Data[]{
                  new Data(5, "cinqo", new Float("5.55555").floatValue()),
                  new Data(4, "quattro", (float)4.4444),
                  new Data(3, "tres", (float)3.333),
                  new Data(2, "duet", (float)2.22),
                  new Data(1, "un", (float)1.1)}, null);
smr.mapTypes(Constants.NS_URI_SOAP_ENC,
    new QName("", "Return"), null, null, araySer);
doCall(url, "echoStructArray", p);
}
```

The output looks like...well, you get the idea. Because the Data type is already plugged into the serialization framework, the default array handling mechanism can just call Dataserializer to do its work.

The server

All this coding, marshalling, and unmarshalling is required because we are using a dynamic call interface. On the service side, we don't need any of this work; we just make an RPC call and Apache SOAP takes care of the rest. The server runtime needs only the information specified in a deployment descriptor. The EchoTest Java service from Apache SOAP 2.2 is comparatively uninteresting:

```java
package samples.interop;

/** An implementation of the interop echo service as defined at
 * http://www.xmethods.net/ilab.
 *
 * @author Glen Daniels (gdaniels@macromedia.com)
 */
public class EchoTestService
{
  public void nop()
  {
  }

  public int echoInteger(int i)
  {
    return i;
  }

  public float echoFloat(float f)
  {
    return f;
  }

  public String echoString(String str)
  {
    return str;
  }
```

```
    public Data echoStruct(Data data)
    {
      return data;
    }

    public int [] echoIntegerArray(int [] ii)
    {
      return ii;
    }

    public float [] echoFloatArray(float [] ff)
    {
      return ff;
    }

    public String [] echoStringArray(String [] ss)
    {
      return ss;
    }

    public Data [] echoStructArray(Data [] ds)
    {
      return ds;
    }
}
```

In an environment in which the client and service interfaces are automatically generated by a tool, such as one that implements JAX-RPC, this coding is moot because it is hidden from the developer. When you need to understand interoperability issues between clients and services, however, it is critical to understand the concepts behind them. In the future, we may reach a state in which interoperability "just works" between almost any client and server-side implementations; however, that future is still remote.

Fun with Testing

We ran a couple of other tests as well. We tried pointing the Apache SOAP client at the Round 2: Base tests for MS SOAP Toolkit Version 3.0 and got the following results. The first three invocations failed, and the other five succeeded:

```
java EchoTestClient http://mssoapinterop.org/stkV3/Interop.wsdl

[SOAPException: faultCode=SOAP-ENV:Client; msg=No Deserializer found to
deserialize a ':Result' using encoding style 'http://schemas.xmlsoap.org/soap/
encoding/'.; targetException=java.lang.IllegalArgumentException: No Deserializer
found to deserialize a ':Result' using encoding style 'http://schemas.xmlsoap.org/
soap/encoding/'.]
        at org.apache.soap.rpc.Call.invoke(Call.java:246)
        at EchoTestClient.doCall(EchoTestClient.java:222)
        at EchoTestClient.doWork(EchoTestClient.java:142)
        at EchoTestClient.main(EchoTestClient.java:114)
```

```
[SOAPException: faultCode=SOAP-ENV:Client; msg=No Deserializer found to
deserialize a ':Result' using encoding style 'http://schemas.xmlsoap.org/soap/
encoding/'.; targetException=java.lang.IllegalArgumentException: No Deserializer
found to deserialize a ':Result' using encoding style 'http://schemas.xmlsoap.org/
soap/encoding/'.]
        at org.apache.soap.rpc.Call.invoke(Call.java:246)
        at EchoTestClient.doCall(EchoTestClient.java:222)
        at EchoTestClient.doWork(EchoTestClient.java:147)
        at EchoTestClient.main(EchoTestClient.java:114)
[SOAPException: faultCode=SOAP-ENV:Client; msg=No Deserializer found to
deserialize a ':Result' using encoding style 'http://schemas.xmlsoap.org/soap/
encoding/'.; targetException=java.lang.IllegalArgumentException: No Deserializer
found to deserialize a ':Result' using encoding style 'http://schemas.xmlsoap.org/
soap/encoding/'.]
        at org.apache.soap.rpc.Call.invoke(Call.java:246)
        at EchoTestClient.doCall(EchoTestClient.java:222)
        at EchoTestClient.doWork(EchoTestClient.java:152)
        at EchoTestClient.main(EchoTestClient.java:114)
echoStruct       OK
echoIntegerArray OK
echoFloatArray   OK
echoStringArray  OK
echoStructArray  OK
```

The errors occurred for the following reasons:

- The generated response did not contain the xsi:type information for the return value.

- The test client we used looked for an element with the name <Return>. The generated response used the name <Result> instead.

- To compensate for this problem, we added the following code, which adds another entry in the SOAPMappingRegistry for the "Result" element. This addition is made for each datatype:

```
p = new Parameter("inputString", String.class, "Hi there!", null);
smr.mapTypes(Constants.NS_URI_SOAP_ENC,
    new QName("", "Return"), null, null, stringDser);
smr.mapTypes(Constants.NS_URI_SOAP_ENC,
    new QName("", "Result"), null, null, stringDser);
doCall(url, "echoString", p);
```

In recognition of this issue, the MS SOAP Toolkit Version 3.0 site supports two versions of the test: one that expects and returns xsi:type information and one that does not. The test we picked was the untyped version—hence the errors. The typed version of the test is located at *http://mssoapinterop.org/stkV3/InteropTyped.wsdl*.

We could have used that version to begin with and declared victory, but we wanted to go through the exercise with you because this issue can arise when communicating between two different kinds of toolkits.

We tried the same test with the Apache Axis version of the Echo Test client and got the following results:

```
java TestClient
URL: http://mssoapinterop.org/stkV3/Interop.wsdl
echoString               OK
echoStringArray          OK
echoInteger              OK
echoIntegerArray         OK
echoFloat                OK
echoFloatArray           OK
echoStruct               OK
echoStructArray          OK
echoVoid                 OK
echoBase64               OK
echoHexBinary            OK
echoDate                 OK
echoDecimal              OK
echoBoolean              OK
echoMap                  Fail: WSDLReader:None of the matching operations for
soapAction http://soapinterop.org/ could successfully load the incoming request.
Potential typemapper problem
echoMapArray             Fail: WSDLReader:None of the matching operations for
soapAction http://soapinterop.org/ could successfully load the incoming request.
Potential typemapper problem
```

Using other test clients through a browser interface

Many SB Interop participants have built a browser client that remotely executes a test client on your behalf. Figure 9-1 shows the interface to one such site for Iona XMLBus (*http://interop.xmlbus.com:7002/InteropTest/index.jsp*). You can type in any known WSDL endpoint that participates in the testing and learn how an XMLBus client fared against the remote service.

Figure 9-2 shows an example of the results.

Other Interoperability Resources

Given the importance of interoperability to the future of web services, it shouldn't be surprising that many other developers and corporations have created useful resources. In this section, we'll look at a few of them. Simon Fell has developed a web site where developers can post their servers and clients. If a server implementation is updated, the notification service is called automatically and runs a registered test suite to verify interoperability. Registering for notifications when server or client updates are posted is also possible.

Several vendors, such as Iona, Borland, and HP, offer interoperability test facilities on their web sites. These sites provide client- and server-side implementations of the interoperability labs for testing. Iona also offers a site that features its daily build for interoperability testing.

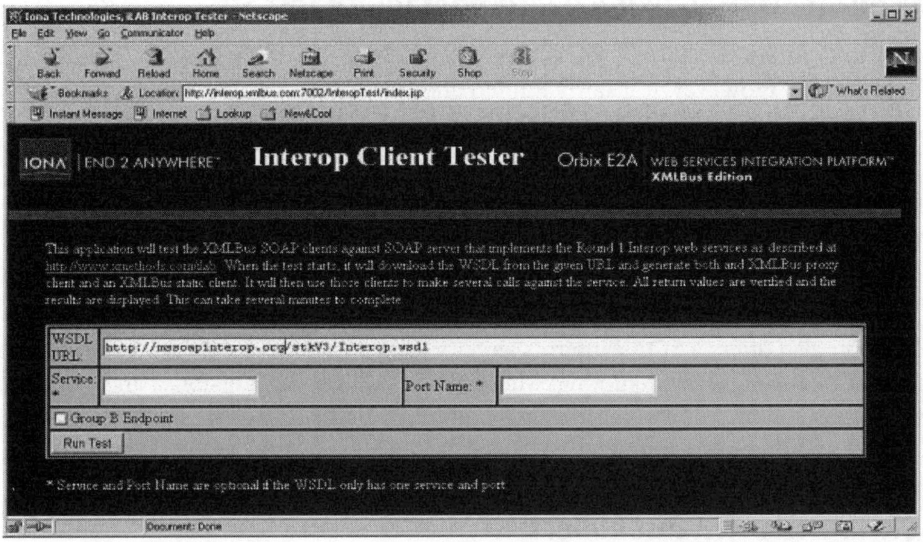

Figure 9-1. The browser interface used for running SB Interop clients remotely

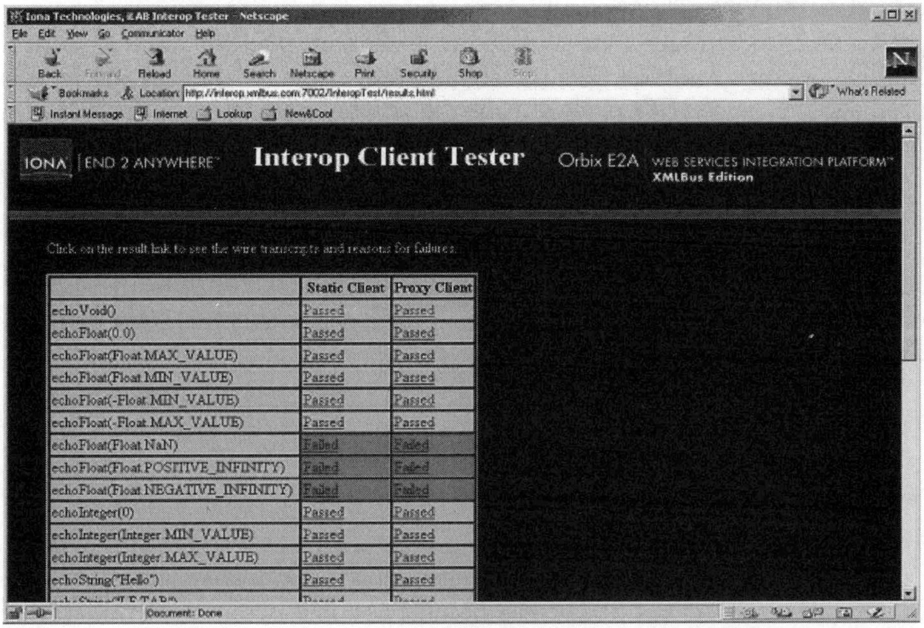

Figure 9-2. Test results from browser-based remote client testing

Microsoft SOAP Toolkit 3.0 Interoperability Test Site

Microsoft offers a SOAP 1.1 message validator to test interoperability (see "Resources"). However, it is fairly limited and does not support encoding (either Section 5 or user-defined), external schema validation, or service description support.

Microsoft differentiates between conformance and validation and offers this tool as a SOAP message validation tool. In contrast, a conformant SOAP message "does not violate any of the sections in its specification, and therefore ensures the highest degree of interoperability with vendor implementations that also conform to the same standard specification."

Microsoft also offers a SOAP Interop server site (see "Resources"). It provides test services for ASP.Net, .NET remoting, Microsoft SOAP Toolkit Version 2 and Version 3, and results for interoperability testing between Microsoft SOAP Toolkit Version 2, ASP.Net and other environments such as Apache 2.2 and Axis, SOAPLite, and IONA.

SOAP Version 1.2 Test Collection

The W3C XML Protocol Working Group is developing a test collection to verify implementation compliance to the SOAP 1.2 specification. The latest draft is dated November 16, 2001. The test collection summarizes "testable assertions" from the specification, and the tests are intended to determine whether a SOAP processor implemented each assertion. The test suite includes tests for the core specification, encoding, RPC, and HTTP binding. How the assertions are tested varies. For example, the first assertion (A1), which is part of the Core specification tests, is:

> A SOAP node receiving a SOAP message MUST perform processing according to the SOAP processing model and, if appropriate, generate SOAP Faults, SOAP responses and send additional SOAP messages, as provided by the remainder of this specification.

A specific test is not provided for this assertion because it is tested by the entire test suite.In other cases, specific tests are provided for the assertion. Assertion A2, also part of Core, states that:

> Each SOAP node MUST act in the role of the special SOAP actor named "http://www.w3.org/2001/09/soap-envelope/actor/next" and can additionally assume the roles of zero or more other SOAP actors.

Two tests are provided for this assertion.

The W3C has not determined which parts of the SOAP 1.2 specification are mandatory and must be supported for an implementation to claim compliance. For example, support for SOAP encoding could become optional, so an implementation not supporting it could still be considered compliant with the specification. Compliance, or performing successfully against the test suite, is not considered W3C certification for an implementation.

Xmethods

Xmethods maintains a list of web services and SOAP implementations. It provides a mechanism to register new services and manage services that are listed. It also offers a new service notification subscription, which notifies the subscriber whenever a new service is added to the site. Xmethods coordinated Round 1 of the SOAPBuilders Interoperability Test Lab.

SalCentral

SalCentral is a web services brokerage that advertises itself as "the Napster of web services" and "the world's largest brokerage for schemas, reviews and quality assurance information on web services." SalCentrals offer a free service called "Web Services Watch" that notifies the subscriber if a predefined event occurs. One example is a change to the schema or service details. Independent testing for web services is also provided through a Test Lab, which includes interoperability testing across several SOAP toolkits (including .NET).

Lucin Corporation, an Internet development company, maintains SalCentral. The site also coordinates a community mailing list for the exchange of information regarding XML Schema–defined web services.

Resources

- SOAPBuilders Interop Lab Round 1: *http://www.xmethods.net/ilab/*
- SOAPBuilders Interop Lab Round 2: *http://www.whitemesa.com/interop.htm*
- The SOAPBuilders discussion site: *http://groups.yahoo.com/group/soapbuilders/*
- The Web Services Interoperability Organization: *http://www.ws-i.org*
- SOAPWare.org, a directory for SOAP 1.1 developers, includes links to specifications, implementations, services, communities, developers, tutorials, articles and news. In particular, it includes:
  - Userland's SOAP 1.1 Validator Web App. It also maintains a list of validated servers: *http://validator.soapware.org/*
  - "A Busy Developer's Guide to SOAP 1.1" by Dave Winer and Jake Savin of UserLand Software (4/2/01): *http://www.soapware.org/bdg*
  - White Mesa, which offers a live endpoint for interoperability SOAP-RPC service requests and links to client applications that can test an interoperability base service: *http://www.whitemesa.com/*
- Simon Fell's site to register services and interoperability lab test results: *http://www.pocketsoap.com/registration/*

- Simon Fell's PocketSOAP, SOAP-related components, tools and source code (for Windows, originally developed for PocketPC): *http://www.pocketsoap.com*
- The SOAP newbies discussion group: *http://groups.yahoo.com/group/soap-newbies*
- The SalCentral web services brokerage: *http://www.salcentral.com/salnet/ webserviceswsdl.asp*
- Paul Kulchenko's Perl modules, which interface with SOAP and a SOAP Cookbook for Perl: *http://www.soaplite.com/*
- Apache SOAP: *http://xml.apache.org/soap/index.html*
- Apache's next generation SOAP implementation, Axis: *http://xml.apache.org/ axis/index.html*
- Borland Delphi Interop Round 2 test site: *http://soap-server.borland.com/ WebServices/Default.htm*
- IBM DeveloperWorks web services resources: *http://www-106.ibm.com/ developerworks/webservices/?loc=dwmain*
- IONA interoperability test client and servers: *http://www.xmlbus.com/work/ interoperability/*

Microsoft sites are also available:

- The MSDN web services site: *http://msdn.microsoft.com/library/*
- MSDN SOAP community links: *http://msdn.microsoft.com/library/default. asp?url=/library/en-us/dnsoap/html/soapcommunity.asp*
- MSDN global XML web services interoperability resources: *http://msdn. microsoft.com/library/default.asp?url=/library/en-us/dnsrvspec/html/ globalxmlwebsrvinterop.asp*
- The Microsoft SOAP 1.1 message validator: *http://msdn.microsoft.com/library/ default.asp?url=/library/en-us/dnsoap/html/soapvalidator.asp*
- The Microsoft SOAP Interop Server: *http://www.mssoapinterop.org/*
- Gotdotnet: *http://www.gotdotnet.com*

Several sites have information about SOAP and J2EE:

- Java Community Process: *http://www.jcp.org*
- A list of all Java Specification Requests (JSRs): *http://www.jcp.org/jsr/all/index.en.jsp*
- The Java Web Services Developer Pack Winter 01 bundle and tutorial: *http:// java.sun.com/xml/downloads/javaxmlpack.html*

Information on the XML Protocol Working Group:

- SOAP Version 1.2 drafts: *http://www.w3.org/2000/xp/Group/*
- SOAP Version 1.2 test collection: *http://www.w3.org/2000/xp/Group/1/09/ts.html*

Magazine articles and interviews:

- "SOAP InterOpera." Steve Gillmor. *XML Magazine*, June/July 2001: *http://www.devx.com/premier/mgznarch/xml/2001/soapinterview/soapinterview-1.asp*
- "Technologist Inteview: Dave Winer, A Challenge to Microsoft." *XML Magazine*, December 2001: *http://www.fawcette.com/xmlmag/2001_12/magazine/features/interview2/page6.asp*

CHAPTER 10

Web Services Security

The advent of web services reveals new issues that didn't exist in previous closed environments. New levels of openness and new characteristics of data exchange and interoperability also mean that we face new challenges for securing our data and identities:

- Corporate applications and their interfaces are publicly available for all to see. They are available via port 80, which is generally accepted as an open hole in the firewall through which all HTTP traffic flows. Don't assume that just because something is tunneled through port 80 that it is safe. Applications that provide frontends for your critical data will increasingly be exposed through HTTP and accessible to anyone in the outside world. If taken to the extreme, these applications can even be published in a public directory for anyone to discover.

- Data wrapped in SOAP envelopes provides a way to discern the structure and meaning of data being sent over the wire.

- Sending and receiving parties don't have to be implemented by using the same software platforms; i.e., they don't have to have the same security libraries from the same vendor. Therefore, we need a set of standardized, platform-independent security solutions.

- XML is extremely verbose. Encryption is expensive enough as it is. Wrapping data in XML can increase the size of the data that needs to be encrypted tremendously.

- The vision of web services includes enabling spontaneous supply-chain communities or trading communities via dynamic discovery. This vision requires complex interactions, in which a SOAP message traverses multiple intermediaries. You may not have a pre-existing business arrangement with some of these intermediaries, and these intermediaries may not be built on a common infrastructure. How are encryption keys managed in such an environment?

A new class of security techniques is being developed to address these issues. Many of the issues are still being identified or have solutions that are still in their early stages. However, existing security technologies with proven track records won't be abandoned anytime soon. In fact, these new techniques are intended to build upon or augment existing security technologies such as Public Key Infrastructures (PKI), Secure HTTP (HTTPS), and the Secure Sockets Layer (SSL). These technologies are better addressed by a book on general security issues, so we'll only discuss them minimally. Instead, this chapter focuses on new security issues and solutions that have come about as a result of web services and their related technologies.

Incorporating Security Within XML

The sort of HTTP-based web commerce we've seen so far achieves security by relying on the SSL, which ultimately places responsibility for security at the level of the transport protocol. While this approach has been adequate so far, we need a new set of capabilities that allow the use of digital certificates, digital signatures, and authentication within XML documents; we should not rely on the underlying transport to do everything. After all, SOAP and web services are supposed to be protocol-independent, and therefore can't rely on transport protocols for security. Additionally, incorporating security features within the XML documents themselves has many benefits for web services, which can now make judgments about the document payload and what restrictions can be placed on it.

Much of what we discuss here is based on the concepts of PKI and nonrepudiation. Here's a brief description of what these concepts entail.

Public Key Infrastructure (PKI)

Public key cryptography relies on a mathematical algorithm that generates encryption and decryption keys that are used in pairs. When a key from a key pair is used to encrypt the data, only the other key from the pair can be used to decrypt it. One key is public, and the other is kept private. In sender-receiver/encryption-decryption usage, the sender uses the recipient's public key to encrypt the data. Only the intended receiving party can decrypt the encrypted data because only this party has the appropriate private key.

It's also possible to encrypt a document with your private key; then anyone who has access to your public key (in theory, anyone—the purpose of a public key to be public) can decrypt it. While this technique doesn't sound useful, it ensures that a digitally signed document has not been tampered with. We will talk about this topic in more detail in the section "XML Encryption" later in this chapter.

The problematic part of public key cryptography is the generation, distribution, and verification of keys. If I want to do business with you, how do I get your key? How do I know that the key I receive is your key and not a forgery? The PKI is supposed to solve this problem. We will talk about how the PKI relates to the latest technology proposals in the section "Key retrieval."

Nonrepudiation

In the context of web services, nonrepudiation means that the recipient can verify that an XML document (anything from a purchase order to an RPC request) actually came from the sender it claims to have come from and hasn't been modified along the way. It's the electronic equivalent of saying, "You can't tell me that you didn't want your house painted blue; here's the work order, and here's your signature on it." More technically, nonrepudiation means that proper authentication is in place (sufficient to verify the identities of all participants in the transaction), and enough of a digital trail has been left to go back to any given event and verify that:

- This is you.
- You made a request.
- This is exactly what you requested and you presented the request in this form.

Much of nonrepudiation involves the use of a digital signature.

XML Digital Signatures

A digital signature (not to be confused with a digital certificate) is the electronic equivalent of a written signature. It is used by distributed applications to authenticate the identity of the sender of a message or document. It also ensures that the message or document is unchanged.

The XML digital signature specification defines an optional XML element that facilitates the inclusion of a digital signature within an XML document. It provides any web service with the ability to ensure data integrity, authentication, and nonrepudiation with any other web service.

In addition to specifying syntax, the specification makes recommendations about the types of data that require a digital signature. The most thought-provoking recommendation relates to the signing of visual items (such as Cascading Style Sheets and browser plug-ins) that are external to the XML data itself, but will eventually be used to render the XML data. As a rule, the specification recommends that if the representation of XML data is for visual display, then to preserve validity of the signed information over time, both the XML data and the items applied for visual representation should be signed. The specification suggests that this recommendation should be applied to nonvisual renderings, such is audio, as well.

Here is a digitally signed version of *PO.xml*. The purchase order information is unchanged, but the document is much larger; most of it now consists of a <Signature> element:

```
<PurchaseOrder xmlns="urn:oreilly-jaws-samples">
    <shipTo country="US">
        <name>Joe Smith</name>
        <street>14 Oak Park</street>
```

```xml
        <city>Bedford</city>
        <state>MA</state>
        <zip>01730</zip>
    </shipTo>
    <items>
        <item partNum="872-AA">
            <productName>Candy Canes</productName>
            <quantity>444</quantity>
            <price>1.68</price>
            <comment>I want candy!</comment>
        </item>
    </items>
    <Signature Id="EnvelopedSig" xmlns="http://www.w3.org/2000/09/xmldsig#">
      <SignedInfo Id="EnvelopedSig.SigInfo">
        <CanonicalizationMethod Algorithm=
            "http://www.w3.org/TR/2001/REC-xml-c14n-20010315"/>
        <SignatureMethod Algorithm=
            "http://www.w3.org/2000/09/xmldsig#rsa-sha1"/>
        <Reference Id="EnvelopedSig.Ref" URI="">
          <Transforms>
            <Transform Algorithm=
                "http://www.w3.org/2000/09/xmldsig#enveloped-signature"/>
          </Transforms>
          <DigestMethod Algorithm=
              "http://www.w3.org/2000/09/xmldsig#sha1"/>
          <DigestValue>
            yHIsORnxE3nAObbjMKVo1qEbToQ=
          </DigestValue>
        </Reference>
      </SignedInfo>
      <SignatureValue Id="EnvelopedSig.SigValue">
GqWAmNzBCXrognOBlC2VJYA8CS7gu9xH/XVWFaO8eY9HqVnrfU6Eh5Ig6wlcvj4RrpxnNklBnOuvv
JCKqllQy4e76Tduvq/N8kVdOSkYf2QZAC+j1IqUPFQe8CNAOCfUrHZdiS4TDDVv4sfOV1c6UBj7zT
7leCQxAdgpOg/2Cxc=
      </SignatureValue>
      <KeyInfo Id="EnvelopedSig.KeyInfo">
        <KeyValue>
          <RSAKeyValue>
          <Modulus>
AIvPY8i2eRs9C5FRc61PAOtQ5fM+g3R1Yr6mJVd5zFrRRrJzB/awFLXb73kSlWqHao+3nxuF38r
RkqiQOHmqgsoKgWChXmLuQ5RqKJi1qxOG+WoTvdYY/KB2q9mTDjOX8+OGlkSCZPRTkGIKjD7rw4
Vvml7nKlqWg/NhCLWCQFWZ
          </Modulus>
          <Exponent>AQAB</Exponent>
          </RSAKeyValue>
        </KeyValue>
      </KeyInfo>
    </Signature>
</PurchaseOrder>
```

The first step toward creating a digital signature is ensuring that it and the data being signed can't be tampered with. This step is accomplished by applying a mathematical algorithm called a secure hash to a portion of the message data. The result is called the "digest" of the message. The next step is to take that digest, plus all the additional information that will be signed (in our example, in the `<SignedInfo>` element), digest it again, encrypt it, and write it into the XML message itself as the digital signature. In *PO.xml*, the selected algorithm and the initial digest are contained in the `<DigestMethod>` and `<DigestValue>` elements. The final digested, encrypted digital signature is contained in the `<SignatureValue>` element, and the decryption key is stored in the `<KeyInfo>` element. The recipient can determine whether the signature is valid by decrypting the digest and recreating the whole process that was performed by the sender to create the digest. If the resulting digest matches the original, the signed content was probably not tampered with.

The `<Reference>` Element

The `<Reference>` element provides information used to generate the message digest. This information includes any data transformation or normalization used along the way, including canonicalization. For instance, you can associate a digital signature to an XML document in different ways:

Enveloped
> The signature is a child of the data being signed.

Enveloping
> The signature encloses the data being signed.

Detached
> The signature is a sibling of the element being signed and is referenced by a local link, or it can be located elsewhere on the network.

This information needs to be carried within the signature using the `<Transforms>` tag. In our example, we chose to use the enveloped method:

```
<Transforms>
  <Transform Algorithm=
      "http://www.w3.org/2000/09/xmldsig#enveloped-signature"/>
</Transforms>
```

Other examples of transforms are base64 encoding, XPATH filtering, XSLT transformation, and schema validation.

In our example, the selected algorithm and the digest are specified with these tags:

```
<DigestMethod Algorithm=
    "http://www.w3.org/2000/09/xmldsig#sha1"/>
<DigestValue>
  yHIsORnxE3nAObbjMKVo1qEbToQ=
</DigestValue>
```

It's worth taking a more detailed look at the `<Signature>` element. The `<SignedInfo>` element is required; it specifies the data that is actually signed and the algorithms used to sign it. `<SignedInfo>` has three elements: `<CanonicalizationMethod>`, `<SignatureMethod>`, and `<Reference>`.

Canonicalization

A secure hash is intolerant of minor changes in a document. Any change, even the introduction of a space, produces a completely different hash. This intolerance of change is essential to the nature of a secure hash; it must be next to impossible to modify the original document in such a way that it still produces the same hash or to predict how a change to a document will change the hash. However, this feature presents a problem for XML. XML documents are frequently parsed and reparsed as they are transferred from the sender to the recipient, and parsers can make insignificant modifications (such as the elimination of whitespace). Canonicalization puts the document into a standard format before computing the digest, so we can be confident that the sender and receiver will compute the same digest regardless of what processing occurred along the way.

This canonical format was standardized by the W3C in the XML-Canonicalization (xml-c14n) specification.* Here are the high-level rules that an xml-c14n-compliant canonical conversion covers in detail:

- The document is encoded in UTF-8.
- Line breaks are normalized to #xA (hexadecimal A, decimal 10, or ASCII newline) on input, before parsing.
- Attribute values are normalized, as if by a validating processor.
- Character and parsed entity references are replaced.
- CDATA sections are replaced by their character content.
- The XML declaration and document type declaration (DTD) are removed.
- Empty elements are converted to start-end tag pairs.
- Whitespace outside of the document element and within start and end tags is normalized.
- All whitespace in character content is retained (excluding characters removed during line feed normalization).
- Attribute value delimiters are set to quotation marks (double quotes).
- Special characters in attribute values and character content are replaced by character references.
- Superfluous namespace declarations are removed from each element.
- Default attributes are added to each element.
- Lexicographic order is imposed on the namespace declarations and attributes of each element.

---

* *http://www.w3.org/TR/2001/REC-xml-c14n-20010315.*

The Signature Method

The second step involved in creating the digest is tracking and specifying the actual method used to create the signature (denoted by the `<SignatureMethod>` element). Once the canonical version of the XML is derived, the data that is part of the `<SignedInfo>` element needs to be converted into the actual signature value (and placed in the `<SignatureValue>` element). The `<SignatureMethod>` element dictates the algorithm that will be used for this operation.

The algorithm used to create the signature and, finally, the signature itself, are specified by the `<SignatureMethod>` and `<SignatureValue>` tags:

```
<SignatureMethod Algorithm=
    "http://www.w3.org/2000/09/xmldsig#rsa-sha1"/>
<Reference Id="EnvelopedSig.Ref" URI="">
    ...
<SignatureValue Id="EnvelopedSig.SigValue">
GqWAmNzBCXrognOBlC2VJYA8CS7gu9xH/XVWFaO8eY9HqVnrfU6Eh5Ig6wlcvj4RrpxnNklBnOuvv
JCKqllQy4e76Tduvq/N8kVdOSkYf2QZAC+j1IqUPFQe8CNAOCfUrHZdiS4TDDVv4sfOV1c6UBj7zT
7leCQxAdgpOg/2Cxc=
</SignatureValue>
```

When the receiver gets the message, the signature is decrypted using the sender's public key, the verified digest, and by verifying the sender's signature. In the following listing, the `<KeyInfo>` element holds the decryption key:

```
<KeyInfo Id="EnvelopedSig.KeyInfo">
  <KeyValue>
    <RSAKeyValue>
      <Modulus>
AIvPY8i2eRs9C5FRc61PAOtQ5fM+g3R1Yr6mJVd5zFrRRrJzB/awFLXb73kSlWqHao+3nxuF38r
RkqiQOHmqgsoKgWChXmLuQ5RqKJi1qxOG+WoTvdYY/KB2q9mTDjOX8+OGlkSCZPRTkGIKjD7rw4
Vvml7nKlqWg/NhCLWCQFWZ
      </Modulus>
      <Exponent>AQAB</Exponent>
    </RSAKeyValue>
  </KeyValue>
</KeyInfo>
```

Note that the XML signature doesn't address trust of such key information. The application has to determine how trustworthy the key is. Unless there is another way to verify that the supplied decryption key does belong to the sender, there is little point to the process. Anyone could intercept the message, change its contents, regenerate a public/private key pair, and re-sign the document (asserting that the public key belongs to the sender). This is when digital certificates come into play. The certificate contains the binding between the identity of the public key's owner and the key itself. If `<KeyInfo>` is omitted, the recipient is expected to identify the key that will be used, based on the application context. This type of issue is addressed in the XKMS specification, which is discussed in the later section "Key Management." Using XKMS or another PKI infrastructure, the recipient of the message can obtain the digital certificate, extract the public key from it, and verify that this key does belong to the sender.

XML Encryption

The next step beyond incorporating a digital signature into an XML document is encrypting the document (or portions of the document). XML encryption extends the power of the XML digital signature system by enabling the encryption of the message that has been signed digitally. The specification outlines a standard way to encrypt any form of digital content and permits encryption of an entire XML message, a partial XML message, or an XML message that contains sections that were previously encrypted.[*]

Here is *PO.xml* with the contents of the <Items> tag encrypted:

```
<PurchaseOrder xmlns="urn:oreilly-jaws-samples">
    <shipTo country="US">
        <name>Joe Smith</name>
        <street>14 Oak Park</street>
        <city>Bedford</city>
        <state>MA</state>
        <zip>01730</zip>
    </shipTo>
    <items>
      <EncryptedData Id="ED" Nonce="16"
        Type=http://www.w3.org/2001/04/xmlenc#Content
        xmlns="http://www.w3.org/2001/04/xmlenc#"
        xmlns:ds="http://www.w3.org/2000/09/xmldsig#"
        <EncryptionMethod Algorithm
          ="http://www.w3.org/2001/04/xmlenc#aes128-cbc"/>
        <ds:KeyInfo>
          <ds:KeyName>jaws</ds:KeyName>
        </ds:KeyInfo>
        <CipherData>
          <CipherValue>
dRDdYjYs11jW5EDyOlucPkWsBB3NmKOAFNxvFjfeUKxP75cx7KPOPB3BjXPg14kJv74i7FOOXZ5Whq
OISswIkdN/pIVeqRZWqOVjFA8izR6wqOb7UCpH+weoGtOUFOEkIDGbemm23eu812Ob5eYVL8n/DtO8
1OhYeCXksSMGUZiUNj/tfBCAjvqG2jlslQM6n4jJ3QNaR4+B2RisOD6Ln+x2UtNu2J7wIYmlUe7mSg
ZiJ5eHym8EpkE4vjmr2oCWwTUu91xcayZtbEpOFVFs6A==
          </CipherValue>
        </CipherData>
      </EncryptedData>
    </items>
    <Signature Id="EnvelopedSig" xmlns="http://www.w3.org/2000/09/xmldsig#">
        ...
    </Signature>
</PurchaseOrder>
```

The encrypted part of the document has two new tags: <EncryptedData> and <CipherData>. The <EncryptedData> element defines the encryption scheme to be applied. Here, convenience schemes on the W3C web site perform the encryption.

---

[*] *http://www.w3.org/TR/xmlenc-core/.*

The <CipherData> element is created to contain the encrypted serialization of the <Items> element. In this example, the result is contained within the <CipherValue> element, although as an alternative, you can use a URI to point to another location where the cipher resides by using the <CipherReference> element. The <EncryptionMethod> and <KeyInfo> tags are optional. As shown earlier, it is possible to obtain information about the sender's public key through XKMS or other means, such as PKI.

This ability to encrypt data on an as-needed basis is an incredibly powerful tool that allows web services to provide their own security features. It neatly avoids the limitations encountered when applying external encryption—in particular, the "all or nothing" nature of external encryption.

Java Toolkits

When creating the examples used here, we examined a couple of Java toolkits for XML security: IBM XML Security Suite and the Phaos XML Toolkit. Both were fairly new at the time, but were sufficient enough to produce these examples. The toolkits both use Xerces and Xalan to parse the XML data and use their own APIs to assemble the signatures and encrypt the data. Each has a decent set of sample programs or utilities for generating a certificate containing a public/private key pair. Each has examples for creating signed documents using the enveloped, enveloping, or detached method. Each has good samples for encrypting and decrypting portions of a document based on specifying an element tag. The IBM toolkit uses its own custom parser extensions so you can use an Xpath expression, such as /PurchaseOrder/ShipTo, to identify the element to be encrypted. The Phaos sample simply used parser APIs such as doc.getElementsByTagName(tagName) to access the element to be encrypted, as shown in the following listing:

```
// Copyright © Phaos Technologies
public class XEncryptTest
{
    public static void main (String[] args) throws Exception
    {
        ...     // usage, command line args...

        // get the XML file and retrieve the XML Element to be encrypted
        File xmlFile = new File(inputFileName);
        DocumentBuilderFactory dbf = DocumentBuilderFactory.newInstance();
        dbf.setNamespaceAware(true);
        DocumentBuilder db = dbf.newDocumentBuilder();
        Document doc = db.parse(xmlFile);
        Element inputElement = null;
        NodeList list = doc.getElementsByTagName(tagName);
        if (list.getLength() != 0)
            inputElement = (Element) list.item(0);
        else
```

```
{
    System.err.println("XML element with tagName "
        + tagName + " unidentified.");
    System.exit(1);
}

// Create a new XEEncryptedData instance with the owner
// Document of the input xml file,the data type URI and
// the Id "ED" for this EncryptedData element.
XEEncryptedData encData
    = XEEncryptedData.newInstance(doc, "ED", dataType);

... // determine encryption algorithm

// set up the EncryptionMethod child element
XEEncryptionMethod encMethod = encData.createEncryptionMethod(algURI);
encData.setEncryptionMethod(encMethod);

// set up the symmetric key to be used in encryption
SymmetricKey key = null;
File keyFile = new File(keyFileName);

... // File stuff

// set up the ds:KeyInfo child element with the keyName
XSKeyInfo keyInfo = encData.createKeyInfo();
keyInfo.addKeyInfoData(encData.createKeyName(keyName));
encData.setKeyInfo(keyInfo);

// set a nonce value to be prepended to the plain text
byte[] nonce = new byte[16];
encData.setNonce(RandomBitsSource.getDefault().randomBytes(nonce));

// encrypt the XML element and replace it with the
// newly generated EncryptedData element
System.out.print("Encrypting the XML data ... ");
XEEncryptedData newEncData
    = XEEncryptedData.encryptAndReplace(inputElement, key, encData);
System.out.println("done");

// output the XML Document with the new EncryptedData element to a file
...
    }
}
```

The critical piece of this code is the call to encryptAndReplace( ). This method does just what its name implies: it takes the element that we've given it (which we found earlier by calling getElementsByTagName( )), encrypts it by using the given key, and replaces the original element with the appropriately tagged, encrypted element.

The Phaos toolkit was much easier to set up and run than the IBM toolkit. All the necessary *.jar* files were bundled into a single download; the IBM toolkit required downloading a beta version of Xerces, a beta version of Xalan, and a Java Cryptology

Extensions (JCE) toolkit from IBM, Sun, Cryptix, or IAIK. Both toolkits had the sorts of problems that you would expect from a 1.0 or pre-1.0 product, but that situation will probably get better over time. Web services security is a pretty big hole that needs to be filled, and many vendors will have offerings in this area.

Single-sign-on

Single-sign-on authentication is the ability for an end user or application to access other applications within a secure environment without needing to be validated by each application. The most common example of single-sign-on technology is in web-based corporate intranet applications. In this setting, users want to use various applications that allow access to timesheets, expense reports, 401K plan information, and health benefits. Requiring each application to authenticate each user individually is inconvenient, slow, and limits the value of the intranet site. The best approach is to allow access to all applications without additional intervention after the initial signon, using a profile that defines what the user is allowed to do.

Many companies provide products for web-based, single-sign-on authentication and authorization, including companies such as Netegrity, Securant (now a part of RSA), Oblix, and Verisign. In general, these products use an intermediary process that controls and manages the passing of user credentials from one application to another. Users are assigned a ticket that carries their rights information and simultaneously allows them to access many applications without the need to authenticate each one. This ticket allows applications within the secure environment to shift the burden of authentication and authorization to a trusted third party, leaving the application free to focus on implementation of business logic.

The single-sign-on concept is easily extended to web services. Web services can be given a ticket (placed in an XML/SOAP message) that can be used to validate the service with other web services. However, the secure use of web services will depend on the ability to exchange user credentials on a scale never seen before. Individual services will reside in a variety of protected environments, each using various security products and technologies. Providing a way to integrate these environments and enable their interoperability is critical for the secure and effective use of these services.

Recognizing the need to provide an interoperable, single-sign-on specification for web services, the industry leaders in this market have come together to create the adoption of a standard. Based on XML, the Security Assertion Markup Language (SAML) is an almost complete specification proposed by the Organization for the Advancement of Structured Information Standards (OASIS). The primary goal of SAML is to enable interoperability between different systems that provide security services. The SAML specification does not define new technology or approaches for authentication or authorization. Rather, it defines a common XML language that describes the information or outputs generated by these systems. A completed SAML draft is expected by early 2002. OASIS will accept specifications for approval during the second quarter of 2002. In the meantime, Microsoft and Sun Microsystems are both working on competing systems that will offer the same capabilities, but are platform-specific.

Many single-sign-on vendors have already released toolkits based on early versions of SAML, with promises for free upgrades once the specification is complete. The first to market was Netegrity, with the release of the JSAML Toolkit to build Java-based applications that use SAML. This toolkit allows Java-based web services to incorporate single-sign-on solutions that work with other SAML-based security environments. It is available for free from their web site.

Key Management

One of the biggest challenges for deploying all these new encryption, digital signature, and authentication technologies will be to keep all public and private keys, digital signatures, and digital certificates organized and secure. Several PKI products currently on the market are designed to simplify the management of these security components. However, there is still no standard way to access these systems in a SOAP-based web services environment.

The XML Key Management Specification (XKMS) is an emerging effort under the auspices of the W3C. It aims to provide standardized XML-based transaction definitions for the management of authentication, encryption, and digital signature services. XKMS is designed to complement and enhance the XML Digital Signature and XML Encryption standards already emerging at the W3C, not compete with them. As discussed in a previous section, the XML Encryption and XML Digital Signature specifications describe how to use and incorporate encryption keys and digital certificates. However, these specifications assume that the web service responsible for processing the XML exists in an environment where keys and certificates are kept safe and secure. It also assumes that the web service programmer knows which certificates and keys to use.

XKMS will provide a standardized set of XML definitions that allow developers to have a trusted third party locate and provide the appropriate keys and certificates. This trusted third party will act as an intermediary that frees the web service programmer from having to track the availability of keys or certificates and ensure their validity.

In short, XKMS will provide a standardized set of XML definitions that allow developers to use remote trusted third-party services that provide encryption and decryption services, and the creation, management, and authentication of keys and digital signatures. The specification maps a set of tags that can be used to query external key management and signature validation services and a set of tags for these services to use when sending responses. For example, a client might ask a remote service to answer questions such as, "Is this certificate valid?" or, "I have a reference to a key that you are allegedly managing…what is its value?" The next section provides an overview of some of these requests and responses.

Key retrieval

XKMS provides a simple retrieval method for obtaining a decryption key from a remote source. This retrieval method relies on the use of the <RetrievalMethod> tag within the <KeyInfo> element, as defined by XML-SIG. The following document assumes that a service exists that can provide information about a given key:[*]

```
<ds:KeyInfo>
   <ds:RetrievalMethod
      URI="http://www.PKeyDir.test/CheckKey"
      Type="http://www.w3.org/2000/09/xmldsig#X509Certificate"/>
</ds:KeyInfo>
```

This lookup is very simple and does not require the service to enforce the validity of the key it returns.

Location service

The location service defines a set of tags that an application client uses to query a remote service for information about a public key. For example, if a web service client wants to encrypt something based on the value of the recipient's public key, it first needs to contact the key location service to obtain that key. The following listing shows the <Locate>, <Query>, and <Respond> tags used in the request:

```
<Locate>
  <Query>
    <ds:KeyInfo>
      <ds:KeyName>Alice Cryptographer</ds:KeyName>
    </ds:KeyInfo>
  </Query>
  <Respond>
    <string>KeyName</string>
    <string>KeyValue</string>
  </Respond>
</Locate>
```

The <Query> tag provides the name of the requested key, and the <Respond> element lists the items that the client would like to know about. The response looks like this:

```
<LocateResult>
  <Result>Success</Result>
  <Answer>
    <ds:KeyInfo>
      <ds:KeyName>Alice Cryptographer</ds:KeyName>
      <ds:KeyValue>Some key value</ds:KeyValue>
    </ds:KeyInfo>
  </Answer>
</LocateResult>
```

---

[*] Example from *http://www.w3.org/TR/xkms/*.

Validate Service

The Validate Service is a trusted third party that validates a binding between a key and an attribute such as a name. For instance, given the following query:

```
<Validate>
  <Query>
    <Status>Valid</Status>
    <ds:KeyInfo>
      <ds:KeyName>...</ds:KeyName>
      <ds:KeyValue>...</ds:KeyValue>
    </ds:KeyInfo>
  </Query>
  <Respond>
    <string>KeyName</string>
    <string>KeyValue</string>
  </Respond>
</Validate>
```

the Validate Service would produce the following results:

```
<ValidateResult>
  <Result>Success</Result>
  <Answer>
    <KeyBinding>
      <Status>Valid</Status>
      <KeyID>http://www.xmltrustcenter.org/assert/20010120-39</KeyID>
      <ds:KeyInfo>
        <ds:KeyName>...</ds:KeyName>
        <ds:KeyValue>...</ds:KeyValue>
      </ds:KeyInfo>
      <ValidityInterval>
        <NotBefore>2000-09-20T12:00:00</NotBefore>
        <NotAfter>2000-10-20T12:00:00</NotAfter>
      </ValidityInterval>
    </KeyBinding>
  </Answer>
</ValidateResult>
```

In the previous listing, the <Result> and <Status> elements have different meanings. The Success indicated by the <Result> element simply indicates that the request was processed successfully by the service. The <Status> indicates the results of the processing—in this case, the result is Valid. The optional <ValidityInterval> information shows the timespan for which the Validate Service's results are considered valid. Digital certificates and keys are not unconditionally valid; they can be (and frequently are) assigned a specific time limit, after which they expire and are no longer valid. In addition, XKMS also defines requests and responses for the following areas:

Key registration
> How to register your key information with a third-party KMS.

Key revocation
> How to send a request to the third-party KMS to tell it that you no longer want it to manage the key on your behalf.

Key recovery

> You forgot your private key. How to send a request to obtain it and what the response looks like. The specification does not dictate the rules under which the private key should be returned. For instance, it may be the policy of the service to revoke the old key and issue a new one. However, that decision is up to the policy of the individual provider.

Verisign is one of the primary drivers of XKMS. They have already released a Java toolkit that supports XKMS development. To download the product, visit *http://www.xmltrustcenter.org/xkms/download.htm*.

SOAP Security Extensions

As a container for XML-based messages, SOAP 1.1 has responsibilities to support the use of XML-based security technologies.

Digital Credentials Extensions to SOAP

As we mentioned in previous sections, to achieve end-to-end application security (encryption, authorization, and authentication), an exchange of digital credentials is required. Digital credentials come in different forms. The most commonly used credential is a digital certificate that conforms to a standard called X.509. Microsoft has recently announced plans to base its efforts on another type of credential called Kerberos tickets. In either case, these credentials hold information about the Holder, including information about the encryption methods being used and the Holder's digital signature.

Microsoft and IBM have proposed extending the SOAP 1.1 specification to include a security-specific credentials header, which would standardize the use of multiple types of credentials within a SOAP message. The motivation for the extensions is to give SOAP-based services the ability to sign portions of the SOAP envelope.

Digital Signature Extensions to SOAP

To use XML Digital Signatures (or any digital signature) effectively in SOAP messages, you need a standardized way to incorporate them into the message.

To address this need, IBM and Microsoft have proposed a set of SOAP 1.1 header extensions that standardize the use of digital signatures. The goal is to enable SOAP envelopes to contain a digital signature that can be used to sign one or more elements contained within the envelope.

Here is an example of the use of the Digital Signature extensions for SOAP:[*]

```
<SOAP-ENV:Envelope
  xmlns:SOAP-ENV="http://schemas.xmlsoap.org/soap/envelope/">
  <SOAP-ENV:Header>
    <SOAP-SEC:Signature
      xmlns:SOAP-SEC="http://schemas.xmlsoap.org/soap/security/2000-12"
      SOAP-ENV:actor="some-URI"
      SOAP-ENV:mustUnderstand="1">
      <ds:Signature xmlns:ds="http://www.w3.org/2000/09/xmldsig#">
        <ds:SignedInfo>
          <ds:CanonicalizationMethod
              Algorithm="http://www.w3.org/TR/2000/CR-xml-c14n-20001026">
          </ds:CanonicalizationMethod>
          <ds:SignatureMethod
              Algorithm="http://www.w3.org/2000/09/xmldsig#dsa-sha1"/>
          <ds:Reference URI="#Body">
            <ds:Transforms>
              <ds:Transform
                  Algorithm="http://www.w3.org/TR/2000/CR-xml-c14n-20001026"/>
            </ds:Transforms>
            <ds:DigestMethod Algorithm="http://www.w3.org/2000/09/xmldsig#sha1"/>
            <ds:DigestValue>j6lwx3rvEPOOvKtMup4NbeVu8nk=</ds:DigestValue>
          </ds:Reference>
        </ds:SignedInfo>
        <ds:SignatureValue>MCOCFFrVLtRlk=...</ds:SignatureValue>
      </ds:Signature>
    </SOAP-SEC:Signature>
  </SOAP-ENV:Header>
  <SOAP-ENV:Body
    xmlns:SOAP-SEC="http://schemas.xmlsoap.org/soap/security/2000-12"
    SOAP-SEC:id="Body">
    <m:GetLastTradePrice xmlns:m="some-URI">
      <m:symbol>IBM</m:symbol>
    </m:GetLastTradePrice>
  </SOAP-ENV:Body>
</SOAP-ENV:Envelope>
```

The XML Digital Signature is in its own namespace and is contained within the <ds:Signature> element. The wrapper for the signature is <SOAP-SEC:Signature>, which specifies the namespace for the signature and the intended reader of the signature (denoted by the <actor> element). The <actor> can be a SOAP intermediary or the final recipient of the message. The SOAP-ENV:mustUnderstand attribute tells intermediaries that they must know how to understand this header attribute or leave it unprocessed. The members of the XML Digital Signature are described in the previous section "XML Digital Signatures."

These extensions provide a standardized way to add digital signatures to SOAP messages. By extending the SOAP header to use the <SOAP-SEC:Signature> extension, any web service can add any type of digital signature to a SOAP message.

---

[*] From the W3C web site at *http://www.w3.org/TR/SOAP-dsig*.

The proposal also allows enough flexibility to allow the use of XML Encryption to secure portions of the SOAP messages. The addition of a `<SOAP-SEC:Encryption>` tag is still in the works.

Further Reading

Finally, we promised to suggest some reading. Here are a few suggestions:

Knudsen, Jonathan. *Java Cryptography*. O'Reilly & Associates, 1998.

Norberg, Stefan. *Securing Windows NT/2000 Servers for the Internet*. O'Reilly & Associates, 2000.

Oaks, Scott. *Java Security*. O'Reilly & Associates, 2001.

Schneier, Bruce. *Applied Cryptography*. John Wiley & Sons, 1995.

Spafford, Gene and Simson Garfinkel, *Practical UNIX and Internet Security*. O'Reilly & Associates, 1996.

XKMS resources:

> *http://www.w3.org/TR/xkms/*
> *http://www.xmltrustcenter.org/xkms*

SOAP-DSIG specification:

> *http://www.w3c.org/TR/SOAP-dsig* (Java Community Process JSRs—currently in nonpublic stage)

JSR 104 - XML Trust Service APIs:

> *http://www.jcp.org/jsr/detail/104.jsp*

JSR 105 - XML Digital Signature APIs:

> *http://www.jcp.org/jsr/detail/105.jsp*

JSR 106 - XML Digital Encryption APIs:

> *http://www.jcp.org/jsr/detail/105.jsp*

Credits

Many examples in this book are taken from the Apache SOAP distribution. We thank the Apache Software Foundation for their permission. They have requested that we print their license:

```
/*
 * The Apache Software License, Version 1.1
 *
 *
 * Copyright (c) 2001 The Apache Software Foundation.  All rights
 * reserved.
 *
 * Redistribution and use in source and binary forms, with or without
 * modification, are permitted provided that the following conditions
 * are met:
 *
 * 1. Redistributions of source code must retain the above copyright
 *    notice, this list of conditions and the following disclaimer.
 *
 * 2. Redistributions in binary form must reproduce the above copyright
 *    notice, this list of conditions and the following disclaimer in
 *    the documentation and/or other materials provided with the
 *    distribution.
 *
 * 3. The end-user documentation included with the redistribution,
 *    if any, must include the following acknowledgment:
 *       "This product includes software developed by the
 *        Apache Software Foundation (http://www.apache.org/)."
 *    Alternately, this acknowledgment may appear in the software itself,
 *    if and wherever such third-party acknowledgments normally appear.
 *
 * 4. The names "SOAP" and "Apache Software Foundation" must
 *    not be used to endorse or promote products derived from this
 *    software without prior written permission. For written
 *    permission, please contact apache@apache.org.
 *
 * 5. Products derived from this software may not be called "Apache",
 *    nor may "Apache" appear in their name, without prior written
```

```
*    permission of the Apache Software Foundation.
*
* THIS SOFTWARE IS PROVIDED ''AS IS'' AND ANY EXPRESSED OR IMPLIED
* WARRANTIES, INCLUDING, BUT NOT LIMITED TO, THE IMPLIED WARRANTIES
* OF MERCHANTABILITY AND FITNESS FOR A PARTICULAR PURPOSE ARE
* DISCLAIMED.  IN NO EVENT SHALL THE APACHE SOFTWARE FOUNDATION OR
* ITS CONTRIBUTORS BE LIABLE FOR ANY DIRECT, INDIRECT, INCIDENTAL,
* SPECIAL, EXEMPLARY, OR CONSEQUENTIAL DAMAGES (INCLUDING, BUT NOT
* LIMITED TO, PROCUREMENT OF SUBSTITUTE GOODS OR SERVICES; LOSS OF
* USE, DATA, OR PROFITS; OR BUSINESS INTERRUPTION) HOWEVER CAUSED AND
* ON ANY THEORY OF LIABILITY, WHETHER IN CONTRACT, STRICT LIABILITY,
* OR TORT (INCLUDING NEGLIGENCE OR OTHERWISE) ARISING IN ANY WAY OUT
* OF THE USE OF THIS SOFTWARE, EVEN IF ADVISED OF THE POSSIBILITY OF
* SUCH DAMAGE.
* ======================================================================
*
* This software consists of voluntary contributions made by many
* individuals on behalf of the Apache Software Foundation.  For more
* information on the Apache Software Foundation, please see
* <http://www.apache.org/>.
*/
```

In Chapter 10, we borrowed an example from the documentation for the Phaos XML Toolkit. We want to thank them for permission. For more information about their products, see *http://www.phaos.com* (or call 1-888-997-4267).

We've also used, with permission, some pieces of sample code from our employers, Sonic Software and BEA. For more information about their products, see *http://www. sonicsoftware.com* (1-866-438-7664) and *http://www.bea.com* (1-800-812-4232).

Index

We'd like to hear your suggestions for improving our indexes. Send email to *index@oreilly.com*.

About the Authors

David A. Chappell is vice president and chief technology evangelist for Sonic Software. David has over 18 years of industry experience building software tools and infrastructure for application developers. As Director of Engineering for SonicMQ, Progress Software's award-winning Java Message Service (JMS) Internet Commerce Messaging System, David oversaw the design and development of the first commercial implementation of JMS in the marketplace. David has a cross-platform background in designing and developing Internet-based middleware and distributed object systems across a broad range of technologies, including DCOM, CORBA, and EJB. David's experience also includes development of client/server infrastructure, graphical user interfaces, and language interpreters. David is coauthor of *Java Message Service* (O'Reilly) and *Professional ebXML Foundations* (Wrox). His articles have been published in *Network World*, *XML Journal*, *Java Developers Journal*, and *Web Service Journal*.

Tyler Jewell is director of technical evangelism at BEA Systems, Inc. Tyler is an expert educator, mentor, and lecturer on enterprise technologies. He is a frequent speaker at industry events and has presented at Software Developer's Expo, the O'Reilly Conference on Enterprise Java, and the International Java Developers conference. Tyler is coauthor of *Mastering Enterprise JavaBeans 2.0* (Wiley) and *Professional Java Server Programming* (Wrox) and is a member of O'Reilly's Editorial Masthead. He is also on the editorial boards of Sys-Con's *WebLogic Developer's Journal* and *Web Services Journal*. Tyler maintains a monthly J2EE column at *http://www.onjava.com* and is the technology advisor to *http://www.theserverside.com*.

Colophon

Our look is the result of reader comments, our own experimentation, and feedback from distribution channels. Distinctive covers complement our distinctive approach to technical topics, breathing personality and life into potentially dry subjects.

The animal on the cover of *Java™ Web Services* is a European ibex. The European ibex, also called the Alpine ibex, is a wild goat that lives in the central and southern European Alps. The mammal used to be common in high altitudes of the Alps, but is now a rare and protected species. Male ibexes are distinguished by their long, semicircular horns, which can grow as long as 30 inches. When threatened, ibexes fight with their horns or hide in rocky areas.

The ibex has played a prominent role in Alpine life for thousands of years. Archeologists document 13,000-year-old paintings of ibexes in French caves that depict the animal as a hunting target. Alpine folklore, in which ibex body parts were considered powerful, also popularized hunting of the animal. Until the 18th century, the European ibex lived throughout the Austrian, French, Italian, and Swiss Alps and was hunted extensively. Within the next 200 years, the ibex's habitat shrunk considerably, and herds were found only in northern Italy. Government protection and reintroduction efforts have expanded its habitat in recent decades. Ironically, hunting has also contributed to the recovery of the ibex population in Europe; the animal was reintroduced specifically as a trophy game animal in several Alpine regions, and international hunting expeditions (which feature the ibex and other local wildlife) are now an important source of income for many local populations.

Ann Schirmer was the production editor and copyeditor for *Java™ Web Services*. Matt Hutchinson proofread the book. Claire Cloutier, Jeff Holcomb, and Matt Hutchinson provided quality control. David Chu, Phil Dangler, Julie Flanagan, Sue Willing, and Leanne Soylemez provided production assistance. John Bickelhaupt wrote the index.

Emma Colby designed the cover of this book, based on a series design by Edie Freedman. The cover image is a 19th-century engraving from the Dover Pictorial Archive. Emma Colby produced the cover layout with QuarkXPress 4.1 using Adobe's ITC Garamond font.

Melanie Wang designed the interior layout, based on a series design by David Futato. Neil Walls converted the files from Microsoft Word to FrameMaker 5.5.6 using tools created by Mike Sierra. The text font is Linotype Birka; the heading font is Adobe Myriad Condensed; and the code font is LucasFont's TheSans Mono Condensed. The illustrations that appear in the book were produced by Robert Romano and Jessamyn Read using Macromedia FreeHand 9 and Adobe Photoshop 6. The tip and warning icons were drawn by Christopher Bing. This colophon was written by Ann Schirmer.

Other Titles Available from O'Reilly

Java

Java Performance Tuning, 2nd Edition

By Jack Shirazi
2nd Edition January 2003
588 pages, ISBN 0-596-00377-3

Significantly revised and expanded, this second edition not only covers Java 1.4, but adds new coverage of JDBC, NIO, Servlets, EJB and JavaServer Pages. The book remains a valuable resource for teaching developers how to create a tuning strategy, how to use profiling tools to understand a program's behavior, and how to avoid performance penalties from inefficient code, making them more efficient and effective. The result is code that's robust, maintainable and fast!

Java Security, 2nd Edition

By Scott Oaks
2nd Edition May 2001
618 pages, ISBN 0-596-00157-6

The second edition focuses on the platform features of Java that provide security—the class loader, bytecode verifier, and security manager—and recent additions to Java that enhance this security model: digital signatures, security providers, and the access controller. The book covers in depth the security model of Java 2, version 1.3, including the two new security APIs: JAAS and JSSE.

Java Database Best Practices

By George Reese
1st Edition June 2003
304 pages, ISBN 0-596-00522-9

Java Database Best Practices rescues developers from having to slog through books on each of the various APIs before they figure out which method to use! This guide introduces each of the dominant APIs, explores the methodology and design components that use those APIs, and then offers practices most appropriate for different types and makes of databases, and different types of applications.

Java RMI

By William Grosso
1st Edition November 2001
576 pages, ISBN 1-56592-452-5

Enterprise Java developers, especially those working with Enterprise JavaBeans, and Jini, need to understand RMI technology in order to write today's complex, distributed applications. O'Reilly's *Java RMI* thoroughly explores and explains this powerful but often overlooked technology. Included is a wealth of real-world examples that developers can implement and customize.

Java Data Objects

By David Jordan & Craig Russell
1st Edition April 2003
384 pages, ISBN 0-596-00276-9

This book, written by the JDO Specification Lead and one of the key contributors to the JDO Specification, is the definitive work on the JDO API. It gives you a thorough introduction to JDO, starting with a simple application that demonstrates many of JDO's capabilities. It shows you how to make classes persistent, how JDO maps persistent classes to the database, how to configure JDO at runtime, how to perform transactions, and how to make queries.

Java Swing, 2nd Edition

By Marc Loy, Robert Eckstein, David Wood, James Elliott & Brian Cole
2nd Edition November 2002
1278 pages, ISBN 0-596-00408-7

This second edition of *Java Swing* thoroughly covers all the features available in Java 2 SDK 1.3 and 1.4. More than simply a reference, this new edition takes a practical approach. It is a book by developers for developers, with hundreds of useful examples, from beginning level to advanced, covering every component available in Swing. Whether you're a seasoned Java developer or just trying to find out what Java can do, you'll find *Java Swing*, 2nd edition an indispensable guide.

O'REILLY®

To order: 800-998-9938 • order@oreilly.com • www.oreilly.com
Online editions of most O'Reilly titles are available by subscription at safari.oreilly.com
Also available at most retail and online bookstores.

Java

Java Extreme Programming Cookbook

By Eric M. Burke & Brian M. Coyner
1st Edition March 2003
288 pages, ISBN0-596-00387-0

Brimming with over 100 "recipes" for getting down to business and actually doing XP, the *Java Extreme Programming Cookbook* doesn't try to "sell" you on XP; it succinctly documents the most important features of popular open source tools for XP in Java—including Ant, Junit, HttpUnit, Cactus, Tomcat, XDoclet—and then digs right in, providing recipes for implementing the tools in real-world environments.

Java Enterprise Best Practices

By The O'Reilly Java Authors,
edited by Robert Eckstein
1st Edition December 2002
288 pages, ISBN 0-596-00384-6

This book is for intermediate and advanced Java developers, the ones who have been around the block enough times to understand just how complex—and unruly—an enterprise system can get. Each chapter in this collection contains several rules that provide insight into the "best practices" for creating and maintaining projects using the Java Enterprise APIs. Written by the world's leading Java experts, this book covers JDBC, RMI/CORBA, Servlets, JavaServer Pages and custom tag libraries, XML, Internationalization, JavaMail, Enterprise JavaBeans, and performance tuning.

Java Cookbook

By Ian Darwin
1st Edition June 2001
882 pages, ISBN 0-59600-170-3

This book offers Java developers short, focused pieces of code that are easy to incorporate into other programs. The idea is to focus on things that are useful, tricky, or both. The book's code segments cover all of the dominant APIs and many specialized APIs and should serve as a great "jumping-off place" for Java developers who want to get started in areas outside their specialization.

Learning Java, 2nd Edition

By Pat Niemeyer &
Jonathan Knudsen
2nd Edition June 2002
832 pages, ISBN 0-596-00285-8

This new edition of *Learning Java* comprehensively addresses important topics such as web applications, servlets, and XML. It provides full coverage of all Java 1.4 language features including assertions and exception chaining as well as new APIs such as regular expressions and NIO, the new I/O package. New Swing features and components are described along with updated coverage of the JavaBeans component architecture using the open source NetBeans IDE the latest information about Applets and the Java Plug-in for all major browsers.

Mac OS X for Java Geeks

By Will Iverson
1st Edition April 2003
304 pages, ISBN 0-596-00400-1

Mac OS X for Java Geeks delivers a complete and detailed look at the OS X platform for Java development. Based on the new 1.4 JDK and the 10.2 release of Mac OS X from Apple Computer, this is the most thorough guide available for both new and experienced Java developers who want to create cross-platform applications that take advantage of Mac OS X's unique functionality.

Java Management Extensions

By J. Steven Perry
1st Edition June 2002
312 pages, ISBN 0-596-00245-9

Java Management Extensions is a practical, hands-on guide to using the JMX APIs. This one-of-a kind book is a complete treatment of the JMX architecture (both the instrumentation level and the agent level), and it's loaded with real-world examples for implementing Management Extensions. It also contains useful information at the higher level about JMX (the "big picture") to help technical managers and architects who are evaluating various application management approaches and are considering JMX.

O'REILLY®

To order: *800-998-9938* • *order@oreilly.com* • *www.oreilly.com*
Online editions of most O'Reilly titles are available by subscription at *safari.oreilly.com*
Also available at most retail and online bookstores.

Java

Java Servlet Programming, 2nd Edition

By Jason Hunter with William Crawford
2nd Edition April 2001
780 pages, ISBN 0-596-00040-5

The second edition of this popular book has been completely updated to add the new features of the Java Servlet API Version 2.2, and new chapters on servlet security and advanced communication. In addition to complete coverage of the 2.2 specification, we have included bonus material on the new 2.3 version of the specification.

Java & XML, 2nd Edition

By Brett McLaughlin
2nd Edition September 2001
528 pages, ISBN 0-596-000197-5

New chapters on Advanced SAX, Advanced DOM, SOAP, and data binding, as well as new examples throughout, bring the second edition of *Java & XML* thoroughly up to date. Except for a concise introduction to XML basics, the book focuses entirely on using XML from Java applications. It's a worthy companion for Java developers working with XML or involved in messaging, web services, or the new peer-to-peer movement.

JavaServer Pages, 2nd Edition

By Hans Bergsten
2nd Edition August 2002
712 pages, ISBN 0-596-00317-X

Filled with useful examples and the depth, clarity, and attention to detail that made the first edition so popular with web developers, *JavaServer Pages*, 2nd Edition is completely revised and updated to cover the substantial changes in the 1.2 version of the JSP specifications, and includes coverage of the new JSTL Tag libraries—an eagerly anticipated standard set of JSP elements for the tasks needed in most JSP applications, as well as thorough coverage of Custom Tag Libraries.

J2EE Design Patterns

By William C.R. Crawford
& Jonathan Kaplan
1st Edition July 2003 (est.)
352 pages (est.), ISBN 0-596-00427-3

Crawford and Kaplan's *J2EE Design Patterns* takes a different approach than just simply presenting another catalog of design patterns. The authors broaden the scope by discussing ways to choose design patterns when building an enterprise application from scratch, looking closely at the real world tradeoffs that Java developers must weigh when architecting their applications. They also extend design patterns into areas not covered in other books, presenting original patterns for data modeling, transaction/process modeling, and interoperability. This design pattern book breaks the mold.

Enterprise JavaBeans, 3rd Edition

By Richard Monson-Haefel
3rd Edition September 2001
592 pages, ISBN 0-596-00226-2

Enterprise JavaBeans has been thoroughly updated for the new EJB Specification. Important changes in Version 2.0 include a completely new CMP (container-managed persistence) model that allows for much more complex business function modeling; local interfaces that will significantly improve performance of EJB applications; and the "message driven bean," an entirely new kind of Java bean based on asynchronous messaging and the Java Message Service.

Java Message Service

By Richard Monson-Haefel &
David Chappell
1st Edition December 2000
238 pages, ISBN 0-596-00068-5

This book is a thorough introduction to Java Message Service (JMS) from Sun Microsystems. It shows how to build applications using the point-to-point and publish-and-subscribe models; use features like transactions and durable subscriptions to make applications reliable; and use messaging within Enterprise JavaBeans. It also introduces a new EJB type, the MessageDrivenBean, that is part of EJB 2.0, and discusses integration of messaging into J2EE.

O'REILLY®

To order: 800-998-9938 • order@oreilly.com • www.oreilly.com
Online editions of most O'Reilly titles are available by subscription at safari.oreilly.com
Also available at most retail and online bookstores.

How to stay in touch with O'Reilly

1. Visit our award-winning web site

http://www.oreilly.com/

★ "Top 100 Sites on the Web"—PC Magazine
★ CIO Magazine's Web Business 50 Awards

Our web site contains a library of comprehensive product information (including book excerpts and tables of contents), downloadable software, background articles, interviews with technology leaders, links to relevant sites, book cover art, and more. File us in your bookmarks or favorites!

2. Join our email mailing lists

Sign up to get email announcements of new books and conferences, special offers, and O'Reilly Network technology newsletters at:

http://elists.oreilly.com

It's easy to customize your free elists subscription so you'll get exactly the O'Reilly news you want.

3. Get examples from our books

To find example files for a book, go to:

http://www.oreilly.com/catalog

select the book, and follow the "Examples" link.

4. Work with us

Check out our web site for current employment opportunities:

http://jobs.oreilly.com/

5. Register your book

Register your book at:

http://register.oreilly.com

6. Contact us

O'Reilly & Associates, Inc.
1005 Gravenstein Hwy North
Sebastopol, CA 95472 USA
TEL: 707-827-7000 or 800-998-9938
      (6am to 5pm PST)
FAX: 707-829-0104

order@oreilly.com
For answers to problems regarding your order or our products. To place a book order online visit:

http://www.oreilly.com/order_new/

catalog@oreilly.com
To request a copy of our latest catalog.

booktech@oreilly.com
For book content technical questions or corrections.

corporate@oreilly.com
For educational, library, government, and corporate sales.

proposals@oreilly.com
To submit new book proposals to our editors and product managers.

international@oreilly.com
For information about our international distributors or translation queries. For a list of our distributors outside of North America check out:

http://international.oreilly.com/distributors.html

adoption@oreilly.com
For information about academic use of O'Reilly books, visit:

http://academic.oreilly.com

O'REILLY®

To order: *800-998-9938* • *order@oreilly.com* • *www.oreilly.com*
Online editions of most O'Reilly titles are available by subscription at *safari.oreilly.com*
Also available at most retail and online bookstores.